THE COMPLETE BOOK OF BIBLE TRIVIA:
BAD GUYS EDITION

D1491359

THE COMPLETE **BOOK** OF

BIBLE TRIVIA

BAD GUYS EDITION

J. STEPHEN LANG

Tyndale House Publishers, Inc.
WHEATON, ILLINOIS

Visit Tyndale's exciting Web site at www.tyndale.com

TYNDALE is a registered trademark of Tyndale House Publishers, Inc.

Tyndale's quill logo is a trademark of Tyndale House Publishers, Inc.

The Complete Book of Bible Trivia: Bad Guys Edition

Designed by Ron Kaufmann

Unless otherwise indicated, Scripture quotations are taken from the *Holy Bible,* King James Version. In many
instances, the author has chosen to modernize an archaic word or phrase.

Library of Congress Cataloging-in-Publication Data

Lang, J. Stephen.
   The complete book of Bible trivia : bad guys ed. / J. Stephen Lang.—Bad guys ed.
     p. cm. — (Complete book)
   ISBN-13: 978-1-4143-0379-6 (pbk.)
   ISBN-10: 1-4143-0379-3 (pbk.)
   1. Bible—Examinations, questions, etc. I. Title. II. Complete book (Wheaton, Ill.)
   BS612.L26 2005
220—dc22   2005000429

Printed in the United States of America

10   09   08   07   06   05
6   5   4   3   2   1

CONTENTS

WHY TOUR THE BIBLE'S ROGUES' GALLERY?

Back in 1988, I published *The Complete Book of Bible Trivia*. Several years later, after more than 700,000 copies have been sold, I'm happily aware that readers love that book's hodgepodge of questions and answers about the Bible. So here, for both your improvement and entertainment, is a new collection of questions and answers about the Bible, all related to the general theme of "bad guys." Why bad guys? Well, let's face it: Evil fascinates us, and so do evil people. That can be a bad thing or a good thing. Seeing evil people doing their dirty deeds can make us want to be like them—or it can stiffen our resolve to be better than they are. We can learn a lot from the stories of saints, but we can learn a lot from the sinners as well.

Back in the 1700s, a French author wrote the scandalous novel *Dangerous Liaisons,* which has been made into a movie several times. This tale of upper-class seducers corrupting the innocent is fascinating, even though the main characters are rotten to the core. Some church leaders of the day scolded the author for writing such a book, but other church leaders took the opposite view: that readers (especially young ones) would do well to read the spicy book if only to learn the crafty ways of the wicked—and thus learn to avoid them. (Worth noting: At the end of *Dangerous Liaisons,* the bad characters get the punishment they deserve.)

The Bible has an even richer store of bad characters, some of them so rotten that their names have passed into the language—a jezebel is a wicked, scheming, immoral woman; a Judas is a conniving traitor; simony (from the name of Simon Magus) is the crime of buying and selling religious offices, and so on. Some of these are as bad as or worse than anyone you will meet in *Dangerous Liaisons.* And consider some of the others: Cain, the Pharaoh of the Exodus, King Ahab of Israel, that mysterious 666 person (or force?) of the book of Revelation . . . well, the Bible is a veritable rogues' gallery. We can, and should, read about these characters—and learn lessons from them as well as from the more saintly folk.

And speaking of saints, not all the saints were saintly all the time. The Bible presents people, "warts and all," so we see the God-loving, brave, poetic David—and also the adulterous, violent, scheming David. We see Solomon the wise and Solomon the idolater. Paul, the great apostle of Christianity, went through an early phase as the great persecutor of Christians. Peter, the loving and loyal disciple of Jesus, at a critical point in time denied he even knew Jesus. And Jacob, the father of the 12 tribes of Israel—well, we see a lot of warts in the Bible's warts-and-all portrait of him.

In the book you are now holding, we will look at some of the Bible's most notorious villains—and also at some of its noble characters who had their bad moments. Considering that the Bible tells us that "all have sinned, and come short of the glory of God" (Romans 3:23), all of us fall into the general category of "bad boys" (and "bad girls"). As you may have heard, that is the central message of the New Testament: The one person who had no evil in him at all (Jesus) offered himself up as a sacrifice for the rest of us. Evil doesn't have the last word, for good is stronger than evil, which is why it's appropriate that the Bible ends with that very dramatic book about good versus evil—Revelation.

So, just as the Bible ends on a positive note, so does this introduction. I hope you enjoy these questions and answers about the Bible's bad guys and their many crimes. I think you will learn something positive along the way.

PART 1

THE ROGUES' GALLERY

THE DEVIL, YOU SAY

He goes by many names in the Bible—Satan, the devil, the evil one, etc. The Old Testament doesn't say that much about him, but the New Testament does, for Jesus made it clear that the devil and a horde of demons had dedicated themselves to making human life unpleasant (not to mention keeping mankind out of heaven). As nasty as Satan is, however, the Bible makes it clear that human beings are responsible for their own sins. Comedian Flip Wilson's old line, "The devil made me do it," doesn't square with the Bible. The devil does tempt people, but people themselves choose to do wrong.

1. Which two Gospels tell the story of Jesus being tempted by Satan?
2. What ferocious animal does 1 Peter compare Satan to?
3. In which Epistle did Paul refer to Satan as "the god of this world"?
4. What, according to the New Testament, is the final place for Satan?
5. In which Gospel did Jesus refer to Satan as "the prince of this world"?
6. What is Satan the father of?
7. Which prophet spoke of the fallen Lucifer, usually taken to refer to Satan as a fallen angel?
8. According to the parable of the sower, what happens when someone hears the word of the Kingdom and does not understand it?
9. According to John's Gospel, Satan was from the very beginning both a liar and a _____.
10. In which Epistle did Paul call Satan the "spirit that now worketh in the children of disobedience"?
11. Which Gospel uses the name Beelzebub?
12. What book of the Bible speaks of the demonic Abaddon and Apollyon, both names for Satan?
13. Which apostle spoke of the contrast between Christ and Belial (presumably another name for the devil)?
14. Which prophet spoke of "weeping for the king of Tyrus" in a passage that has traditionally been interpreted as referring to Satan instead of a human king?
15. In Luke's Gospel, Jesus referred to seeing the fall of Satan. What did he compare the fall to?
16. Whom did Satan provoke to do a census in Israel?
17. Which disciple did Satan enter into?

18. Which disciple was told by Jesus that Satan wanted to sift him "like wheat"?
19. What New Testament man did Satan provoke to lie to the Holy Spirit?
20. In the story of Satan's tempting of Jesus, what did he suggest Jesus turn into bread?
21. What does Satan masquerade as in the present world?
22. According to Jude's epistle, who disputed with Satan over the body of Moses?
23. What book of the Bible describes Satan's appearance?
24. What book of the Bible identifies Satan as being the serpent who tempted Adam and Eve?
25. Which Old Testament book depicts Satan as a kind of prosecutor in the heavenly court?
26. In the book of Zechariah, where did the prophet see Satan standing?
27. Satan offered to give Jesus power over all the world's kingdoms if he would do what?
28. What often-used prayer mentions Satan?
29. In which Epistle does Paul tell Christians, "Do not give place to the devil"?
30. What common word in our language is rooted in the Greek word translated "devil"?
31. Who promised Christians that "the God of peace will soon crush Satan under your feet"?
32. What affliction did Paul attribute to the power of Satan?
33. Where were Jesus and Satan when Satan suggested that Jesus test God and the angels?
34. In Ephesians 2, Paul referred to Satan as the "prince of the power of the _____."
35. Which disciple was Jesus speaking to when he said, "Get thee behind me, Satan!"?
36. Which apostle described the "whole armor of God" that would protect Christians against the wiles of the devil?
37. What book of the Bible refers to an earthly city "where Satan's throne is"?
38. Which Epistle divides the human race into "the children of God" and "the children of the devil"?
39. In Revelation, what angel leads the fight against Satan?
40. Which Epistle says that the devil has the power of death?

41. Complete this verse from the Epistle of James: "Resist the devil, and he will _____ from you."
42. Which Epistle warns people against being "puffed up" with pride as Satan is?
43. In 1 John, we are told that the Son of God was manifested so that he might destroy the _____ of the devil.
44. The book of Revelation refers to a "synagogue of Satan" existing in what two cities?
45. When Satan is in the form of a great red dragon, how many heads does he have?

THE DEVIL, YOU SAY (ANSWERS)

1. *Matthew (4:1-11) and Luke (4:1-13)*
2. *A roaring lion (1 Peter 5:8)*
3. *2 Corinthians (4:4)*
4. *The lake of fire and brimstone (Revelation 20:10)*
5. *John (14:30; 16:11)*
6. *Lies (John 8:44)*
7. *Isaiah (Isaiah 14:12)*
8. *The wicked one (Satan) snatches from the heart what was sown (Matthew 13:19).*
9. *A murderer (John 8:44)*
10. *Ephesians (2:2)*
11. *Matthew (Matthew 12:24)*
12. *Revelation (9:11)*
13. *Paul (2 Corinthians 6:15)*
14. *Ezekiel (Ezekiel 28:11-19)*
15. *Lightning falling from heaven (Luke 10:18)*
16. *David (1 Chronicles 21:1)*
17. *Judas Iscariot (Luke 22:3-4)*
18. *Peter (Luke 22:31)*
19. *Ananias (Acts 5:3)*
20. *Stones (Matthew 4:3-4)*
21. *An angel of light (2 Corinthians 11:14)*
22. *The archangel Michael (Jude 1:9)*

23. None. Because Satan is evil, artists naturally portray him as ugly. But Revelation does describe a "dragon" that is clearly referring to Satan. See question 45.

24. None. The Bible doesn't name the serpent.

25. Job. In chapters 1 and 2, Satan plays the role of one who likes to test righteous people (like Job) to find out if they're really as virtuous as God believes they are.

26. At the right side of Israel's high priest (Zechariah 3:1)

27. Fall down and worship Satan (Matthew 4:8-10). Jesus refused, of course.

28. The Lord's Prayer. Though most Bible versions have "deliver us from evil," the original Greek words can also mean "the evil one," which would obviously be referring to Satan (Matthew 6:13).

29. Ephesians (4:26-27)

30. Diabolical, from the Greek word diabolos, which literally means "slanderer" or "accuser" or even "opponent"

31. Paul (Romans 16:20)

32. A "thorn in the flesh" (2 Corinthians 12:7-9). We don't know exactly what this "thorn" was.

33. On the highest point of the Temple. Satan suggested that if Jesus threw himself down, God's angels would protect him (Matthew 4:5-7).

34. Air (Ephesians 2:2)

35. Peter (Matthew 16:23). Jesus didn't mean that Peter was literally Satan, but that Peter was (at that moment) acting as an adversary, which is what the word Satan literally means.

36. Paul (Ephesians 6:11-18)

37. Revelation (2:12-13). This is a reference to the city of Pergamos. It may mean that persecution of Christians was taking place there.

38. 1 John (3:10)

39. Michael (Revelation 12)

40. Hebrews (2:14). It is probably referring to the fact that death was brought into the world by the serpent's tempting of Adam and Eve.

41. Flee (James 4:7)

42. 1 Timothy (3:6)

43. Works (1 John 3:8)

44. Smyrna and Philadelphia (Revelation 2:8-9; 3:7-9). We aren't sure just what a "synagogue of Satan" was.

45. Seven heads (Revelation 12:3). This is an interesting case of the "good" number seven being connected with a very evil person.

IT STARTED WITH ADAM . . .

Adam, the bad boy? Yes, definitely—the very first one, in fact. Think back to Genesis: God created man and gave him a lovely world to live in, free from sorrow and pain. But man stupidly and selfishly messed things up by disobeying God. Theology teaches that all of us are "Adams"—going our own way instead of obeying God's, and suffering the consequences. You might say that Adam and Eve were all of us. In a sense (sorry to have to tell you this!), that makes us all bad boys and girls, for we all give in to our selfish impulses just as the First Couple did.

1. What was the one rule God imposed on Adam in the Garden?
2. What was the penalty if that rule was broken?
3. What lie did the serpent tell Eve about the rule God had laid down?
4. What was the immediate result of eating the forbidden fruit?
5. What was Adam's excuse when God asked him if he had eaten the forbidden fruit?
6. What excuse did Eve offer?
7. How did God punish the serpent for what it had done?
8. What was Eve's punishment for disobeying?
9. What laborious penalty was imposed on Adam?
10. According to God's curse, what grew in the soil that was not there before?
11. God banished the two from Eden because of the chance they might do what?
12. What barred them from going back to Eden?
13. Although Adam was sentenced to die, how long did God allow him to live?
14. Which Old Testament book begins with the word *Adam*?
15. Which Gospel traces Jesus' family tree all the way back to Adam?
16. Theologians refer to Adam's disobedience and its results as "the _____ of man."
17. What Old Testament man asked the question, "Have I concealed my sins like Adam"?
18. Which prophet wrote that the sinful Israelites "like Adam have broken the covenant?"
19. Which New Testament letter says that Adam was a "type" or "pattern" of Christ?

20. What did Paul mean when he wrote that "in Adam all die"?
21. In which Epistle does Paul worry that Christians may be led astray just as Eve was deceived by the serpent?
22. In which Epistle does Paul state that Eve was deceived by the serpent although Adam was not?
23. What classic of world literature, written by John Milton, tells the story of Adam and Eve and their disobedience in great detail?
24. Author Roark Bradford retold the Garden of Eden story in what popular book?
25. What American humor author wrote *The Diary of Adam and Eve*?
26. Various Christian sects over the centuries have called themselves Adamites. What practice are they noted for?
27. The doctrine that all human beings inherit the sinful nature of Adam is known as the doctrine of _____ sin.
28. What human body part is connected with the story of Adam's disobedience?
29. In the popular 1966 movie *The Bible . . . In the Beginning,* what future TV star played Adam?
30. What movie has the Adam story and other Bible stories acted out by a cast of plantation slaves?

IT STARTED WITH ADAM . . . (ANSWERS)

1. *Adam and Eve were not to eat from the tree of the knowledge of good and evil (Genesis 2:17).*

2. *"You shall surely die" (Genesis 2:17).*

3. *That if she and Adam ate the fruit, they would not die, but they would be "like God" (Genesis 3:4-5)*

4. *Adam and Eve realized they were naked, and suddenly they were ashamed enough to cover themselves (Genesis 3:7).*

5. *He blamed Eve for giving him the fruit (Genesis 3:12).*

6. *She blamed the serpent for deceiving her (Genesis 3:13).*

7. *It would forever crawl on its belly (Genesis 3:14).*

8. *She would suffer the pain of childbirth, and her husband would dominate her (Genesis 3:16).*

9. *He would have to work hard to get his food, and he would eventually die and return to the dust (Genesis 3:17-19).*

10. *Thorns and thistles—in other words, plants that scratch and that hinder agriculture (Genesis 3:18)*

11. *Eat from the tree of life and live forever (Genesis 3:22)*

12. *The Cherubim (type of angel) and a flaming sword (Genesis 3:24)*

13. *930 years (Genesis 5:5)*

14. *1 Chronicles, which opens with a "family tree" of the human race*

15. *Luke (3:23-38). Matthew's genealogy of Jesus only traces the line back to Abraham.*

16. *Fall—as in "Adam fell from grace"*

17. *Job (Job 31:33). This is one of several passages in the Bible where translators aren't sure if the Hebrew word* adam *refers to Adam the individual or to humanity in general. The word has both meanings.*

18. *Hosea (Hosea 6:7). As in question 17, translators aren't sure whether to use the word* Adam *or* man.

19. *Romans (5:14). Paul meant that Christ, like Adam, was a "new beginning" for the human race.*

20. *All humans, being Adam's descendants, must die physical death as Adam did, but the "second Adam," Christ, allows people to be raised again (1 Corinthians 15:22).*

21. *2 Corinthians (11:3-4)*

22. *1 Timothy (2:14). But because both disobeyed God, both were still guilty.*

23. Paradise Lost

24. *Ol' Man Adam and His Chillun, published in 1928*

25. *Samuel Clemens, also known as Mark Twain*

26. *Going naked, because Adam and Eve originally went naked in Eden*

27. *Original—as in, "from the origin," because Adam was the original human being*

28. *The Adam's apple, the protrusion of the voice box seen in the neck, more so in men than in women. Tradition says that the lump is the bite of the forbidden fruit that is forever stuck in Adam's throat.*

29. *Michael Parks, famous (briefly) for the series Then Came Bronson*

30. The Green Pastures

WICKED, WICKED AHAB

As noted elsewhere, most of the kings in the Bible (and throughout history) are pretty rotten characters, but wicked Ahab of Israel has a claim to the title Baddest of the Bad. The books of Kings devote a lot of space to this nasty fellow, and the chronicle of his reign could be called Dirty Deeds Done Royally.

1. What foreign-born princess became Ahab's wife and partner in crime?
2. What false god did Ahab's wife lead him to worship?
3. What saintly and outspoken prophet was a continual thorn in Ahab's side, so much so that he called the prophet the "troubler of Israel"?
4. What punishment for Ahab's wickedness was foretold by the prophet in 1 Kings 17?
5. What other punishment came upon the land as a result of the first?
6. On what site did Ahab's 450 Baal prophets have a famous show-down with the lone prophet Elijah?
7. What man was Elijah told to anoint as king to replace Ahab and his dynasty?
8. What piece of land did Ahab want so badly that he was willing to execute the owner in order to get it?
9. What tragedy did Elijah prophesy for Ahab as the result of the dirty deed in question 8?
10. What did Ahab do as a result of Elijah's prophecy?
11. What good king of Judah did Ahab ally himself with in order to boot out the Syrians?
12. Who was the one faithful prophet who predicted that Ahab would die in battle, despite what the false prophets had said?
13. What punishment did Ahab prescribe for the prophet for predicting disaster?
14. What sneaky trick did Ahab pull when he and King Jehoshaphat went into battle against the Syrians?
15. How was Ahab killed in the battle?
16. Where did the dogs lick up the blood of Ahab?
17. What two wicked sons of Ahab reigned after his death?
18. What evil, idol-worshipping daughter of Ahab married the king of Judah?
19. How many sons—all exterminated by Jehu—did Ahab have?

20. In what gruesome way were these sons slaughtered as punishment for their father's sins?
21. Centuries after Ahab's death, which prophet lamented that the evil practices of Ahab's house were still being committed?
22. In what classic American novel is the main character a ship captain named Ahab?
23. What 1946 play by Norman Nicholson concerns the conflict between Ahab and Elijah?

WICKED, WICKED AHAB (ANSWERS)

1. Jezebel, who was so vile that there is a separate set of questions devoted to her (1 Kings 16:31)

2. Baal (1 Kings 16:31)

3. Elijah (1 Kings 18:17)

4. A long, long drought—"there shall not be dew nor rain" (1 Kings 17:1)

5. A famine (1 Kings 18:2). Naturally a long drought would affect the crops.

6. Mount Carmel (1 Kings 18:20-40)

7. Jehu (1 Kings 19:16)

8. Naboth's vineyard, which Naboth refused to sell, so Ahab had him executed on false charges (1 Kings 21:1-16)

9. Dogs would lick up Ahab's blood in the very spot where Naboth was killed, and his entire dynasty would be wiped out (1 Kings 21:19-24).

10. He repented—temporarily, anyway (1 Kings 21:27-29).

11. Jehoshaphat (1 Kings 22)

12. Micaiah (1 Kings 22:8-28)

13. Prison, with nothing but bread and water (1 Kings 22:27)

14. He disguised himself, while insisting that Jehoshaphat wear his royal garb (1 Kings 22:30).

15. Someone drew his bow and the arrow hit him between the sections of his armor, fatally wounding him (1 Kings 22:34).

16. The pool of Samaria, where the harlots bathed (1 Kings 22:37-38)

17. Ahaziah, then Jehoram (2 Kings 1)

18. Athaliah (2 Kings 8:18), who helped spread the Baal cult from Israel into Judah

19. Seventy (2 Kings 10)

20. *They were beheaded, and their heads were sent in baskets to Jehu, who ordered that they be piled up in two heaps by the town gates (2 Kings 10:7-8).*

21. *Micah (Micah 6:1, 16), who was referring to the worship of idols*

22. *Moby Dick, by Herman Melville. There are several characters with biblical names in the book, including an Elisha.*

23. The Old Man of the Mountains

END TIME BADDY: THE BEAST, ANTICHRIST, 666, ETC.

Who—or what—is the "Beast" mentioned in Revelation? People have been guessing for 2,000 years. Pick some powerful historical figure—Nero, Hitler, Stalin, Napoleon, even a good person like Martin Luther or Abraham Lincoln—and chances are that some group of people thought he was the Beast, the Antichrist, or the evil figure symbolized by the number 666. Of course, we aren't sure if the Beast is a single person or a nation or even an ideology. We know only that he/it is opposed to God and his saints and will cause great suffering before the end comes. We won't ask you here to speculate about who (or what) you think the Beast is (or was), but to merely think about what you know about the Bible's predictions about the Beast, the Antichrist(s), and the "666" person.

1. Who predicted that there would be "false christs" who would deceive people by performing miracles?
2. What book of the Bible states that many antichrists have already come into the world?
3. According to John, what teaching identifies an antichrist?
4. Where, according to Revelation 11, does the Beast come from?
5. According to Revelation 13, where does the Beast come from?
6. From what wicked creature does the Beast derive his power?
7. What three fearsome animals does the Beast resemble?
8. What happens to the Beast to make the world follow him?
9. What people do not worship the Beast?
10. Where does the second beast come from?
11. What awesome miracle does the second beast perform?
12. On what parts of the body are people required to get the "mark of the Beast"?
13. Why do people have to get the mark of the Beast?

14. What, exactly, is 666?
15. What fate awaits those who worship the Beast or receive his mark?
16. Those who resist the Beast are depicted holding what musical instruments?
17. What physical affliction is poured out on those who worship the Beast?
18. The three evil spirits that come out of the mouth of the Beast, the dragon, and the false prophet looked like what?
19. Which aide of the Beast is destroyed with him in a lake of burning brimstone?
20. How long are those who do not worship the Beast entitled to reign with Christ?
21. Who is thrown into the eternal fire along with the Beast and the false prophet?
22. What brief Epistle of Paul foretold a "man of sin" who would do horrible things before Christ's return?
23. Which Old Testament prophet foretold a 10-horned beast that would persecute the saints before the end of time?
24. In Ezekiel, what evil prince seems to fit the description of the Beast or the Antichrist?

END TIME BADDY: THE BEAST, ANTICHRIST, 666, ETC. (ANSWERS)

1. Jesus (Matthew 24:24)

2. 1 John (2:18)

3. Denying that Jesus is the Christ, God's son (1 John 2:22). By the way, anti doesn't necessarily mean "against" but can also mean "in place of."

4. The abyss—meaning, the lower depths (Revelation 11:7)

5. The sea (Revelation 13:2)

6. The dragon (Revelation 13:2). Mysterious as Revelation is, we can be pretty certain that the dragon means Satan, the devil.

7. A leopard, bear, and lion (Revelation 13:2). Obviously this isn't literal, but is meant to symbolize fear and terror by using images of three wild animals that humans greatly fear.

8. He recovers from a fatal wound—or, more precisely, one of his seven heads recovers from a fatal wound (Revelation 13:3).

9. Those whose names are in the Book of Life—referring, obviously, to Christians (Revelation 13:8)

10. Out of the earth (Revelation 13:11)

11. Making fire come down from heaven (Revelation 13:13)

12. The forehead or the right hand (Revelation 13:16)

13. In order to either buy or sell (Revelation 13:17)

14. The "number of the Beast"—whatever that may mean (Revelation 13:18). Christians have spilled a lot of ink trying to connect 666 with some specific person's name. But 666 may be merely symbolic—six being the "imperfect" number as opposed to the "perfect" number seven.

15. Eternal torment (Revelation 14:9-11)

16. Harps (Revelation 15:2)

17. Painful sores (Revelation 16:2)

18. Frogs (Revelation 16:13)

19. The false prophet (Revelation 19:20)

20. A thousand years—that is, a millennium (Revelation 20:4)

21. The devil (Revelation 20:10)

22. 2 Thessalonians (2:3-4). Some translations have "man of lawlessness." Obviously Paul is referring to someone like the Beast of Revelation.

23. Daniel (Daniel 7:23-27). The books of Daniel and Revelation depict the Beast as having 10 horns, and both books explain that the 10 horns represent 10 kings.

24. Gog, the prince of Magog (Ezekiel 38–39). Revelation uses the names Gog and Magog to refer to two powers hostile to the saints (Revelation 20:8).

 ## RAISING—AND HISSING—CAIN

The human race's firstborn child has a bad reputation, and rightly so. Cain, son of Adam and Eve, was also the first human being to shed human blood—and his choices of victim were pretty limited! See how much you actually know about the original murderer.

1. What was Cain's occupation?
2. What caused Cain to hate his brother Abel?
3. What was God referring to when he told Cain, "You must rule over it"?
4. Where did the world's first murder take place?
5. What was Cain's evasive answer when God asked him, "Where is your brother Abel?"
6. What curse did God put on Cain for his evil deed?

7. What son was given to Adam and Eve in place of the murdered Abel?
8. One of the greatest mysteries of the Bible is where Cain got his
   _____.
9. Which New Testament book notes that "by faith, Abel offered unto God a more excellent sacrifice than Cain"?
10. According to 1 John, Cain killed Abel for what reason?
11. What short New Testament letter pronounces a "woe" on those who have "taken the way of Cain"?
12. *The Wanderings of Cain* is by an English poet, famous for *Kubla Khan* and *The Rime of the Ancient Mariner*—and also famous for being an opium addict. Who was he?
13. What English poet, famous for his unconventional morals, wrote *Cain: A Mystery*?
14. What famous novel by John Steinbeck takes its name from the land where Cain dwelt?
15. What does *Cain-colored* refer to in paintings of the Bible?
16. What was the mark of Cain?
17. The Cainites, a sect that broke off from Christianity in the second century, claimed to honor Cain and to read a "Gospel" by which disciple?
18. What religion refers to Cain and Abel as Kabil and Habil?
19. What does the expression "curse of Cain" mean?

RAISING—AND HISSING—CAIN (ANSWERS)

1. Farmer, or "worker of the soil," as the old versions have it (Genesis 4:2)

2. For some reason (we aren't told what), the Lord accepted Abel's sacrifice but not Cain's (Genesis 4:5).

3. Sin. God was referring to Cain's getting control of his anger (Genesis 4:7).

4. Out in the field (Genesis 4:8). Presumably Cain thought no one, including God, would see what happened.

5. "I do not know. Am I my brother's keeper?" (Genesis 4:9).

6. He was made to be a wanderer on the earth (Genesis 4:12).

7. Seth (Genesis 4:25)

8. Wife, who is mentioned in Genesis 4:17. Was she his sister? Why didn't Genesis mention her before? Cain's wife still puzzles people.

9. Hebrews (11:4)

10. Because he was evil and Abel was good (1 John 3:12)

11. *Jude (1:11)*

12. *Samuel Taylor Coleridge*

13. *Lord Byron, who apparently found Cain an appealing character*

14. *East of Eden. The novel is based—loosely—on the story of Adam, Cain, and Abel.*

15. *Straw-colored hair. In paintings, Cain was often shown with yellowish hair and beard, for whatever reason.*

16. *A brand put on Cain by God (Genesis 4:15). The expression "mark of Cain" is still used to refer to the stigma on any social outlaw.*

17. *Judas Iscariot. Actually, there have been several groups calling themselves Cainites, all claiming to honor rebels such as Cain, Judas, and Satan.*

18. *Islam*

19. *Continuous wandering, based on God's decree that Cain would be a fugitive on the earth*

 ## THOSE HELLISH HERODS

Talk about dysfunctional families—and not only mean to each other (sometimes to the point of murder), but mean in general. Whenever you see the name *Herod* in the Bible, you know you're dealing with a pretty loathsome character. And, interestingly enough, the Bible authors weren't very helpful in using the name, so the Herod at the time of Jesus' birth was neither the Herod of the later Gospels nor the Herod of the book of Acts. Thankfully, world historians have filled in a lot of the details about these guys. Whichever Herod you're reading about, believe that he was "bad to the bone."

1. What horrible deed done by Herod the Great is recorded in Matthew 2?
2. Who told Joseph to take Mary and the baby Jesus to Egypt to flee from Herod?
3. What lie did Herod tell the wise men who were seeking the baby Jesus?
4. After Herod's death, why did Joseph and the family still avoid settling in Herod's kingdom?
5. Despite Herod's cruel life, what one project of his was something that all Jews valued highly?
6. The Herod that ruled in the later Gospels had what official title?

7. What saintly man suffered beheading by the order of Herod?
8. Why had the man in question 7 displeased Herod so much?
9. What name has tradition assigned to Herod's dancing step-daughter?
10. What Jewish party did the Herodians, Herod's supporters, ally with in order to trap Jesus?
11. What famous question did those two groups pose to Jesus in order to try to trap him?
12. When Herod first heard of Jesus' fame, who did Herod think Jesus was?
13. What one decent member of the Herod family is mentioned (in passing) in the Gospels?
14. What Jewish group informed Jesus that Herod wanted to kill him?
15. What kind of animal did Jesus call Herod?
16. At what famous miracle did Jesus warn people to beware "the leaven of the Pharisees and the leaven of Herod"?
17. Which Gospel mentions that Jesus' supporters included Joanna, the wife of Herod's steward?
18. Why did Pilate send the captured Jesus to Herod?
19. What did Herod hope to see Jesus do?
20. What did Herod and his men do to Jesus before sending him back to Pilate?
21. What effect did the Jesus incident have on Pilate and Herod?
22. Which of the four Gospels makes no mention of any of the Herods?
23. In Acts, which of the twelve apostles was executed by order of Herod the king?
24. What method of execution did he use?
25. Which apostle did Herod imprison in order to please the Jews?
26. What miraculous event thwarted Herod's persecution of this apostle?
27. What was the guards' punishment for letting the apostle escape?
28. What led a crowd of people to call out, "The voice of a god and not of a man"?
29. What two things are given credit for the dramatic death of Herod?
30. What famous prisoner was detained in the judgment hall Herod had built?
31. Which member of the family was the captured Paul brought before?
32. What popular musical features Herod asking Jesus to "walk across my swimming pool"?

33. The phrase "It out-Herods Herod" occurs in which famous play by Shakespeare?
34. Which holiday, observed by Catholic and Eastern Orthodox churches, recalls one of the cruel acts of Herod?
35. What much-visited site in Jerusalem was built by order of Herod?

THOSE HELLISH HERODS (ANSWERS)

1. He ordered the slaughter of the infants of Bethlehem, hoping to destroy the new "king of the Jews" (Matthew 2:16). This was the man history calls "Herod the Great."

2. An angel (Matthew 2:13)

3. That he, too, wanted to worship the new "king" (Matthew 2:8)

4. Herod's wicked son Archelaus reigned in his place, and he was hardly better than his father (Matthew 2:22). He was so despised that the Romans eventually replaced him with one of their own men as governor.

5. The Temple, which he had rebuilt lavishly. This was the Temple that Jesus and the apostles would have known and visited.

6. Tetrarch, meaning a ruler of a fourth of an area. Historians know him as Herod Antipas.

7. John the Baptist (Matthew 14:1-12)

8. John spoke out against Herod's stealing his brother's wife, Herodias, which was against Jewish law (Matthew 14:3-4).

9. Salome, whose dancing pleased her stepdad so much that he rewarded her with John's head on a platter, as she requested

10. The Pharisees (Matthew 22:15-17)

11. They asked whether it was lawful to pay taxes to Rome (Matthew 22:17-22).

12. John the Baptist, come back from the dead (Mark 6:14)

13. Philip, who happened to be the first husband of Herodias, who left him for Herod Antipas (Mark 6:17; Luke 3:1)

14. The Pharisees, again (Luke 13:31). They weren't trying to save Jesus but to frighten him.

15. "That fox," probably referring to his craftiness (Luke 13:32)

16. The miracle of the loaves and fishes, where four thousand were fed (Mark 8:1-15)

17. Luke (8:3)

18. Jesus was a Galilean, and Herod was ruler of Galilee, even though both men were in Jerusalem at the time (Luke 23:6-7).

19. Perform a miracle (Luke 23:8)

20. *Mocked him and put him in a gorgeous robe (Luke 23:11)*

21. *According to Luke's Gospel, it made them friends (Luke 23:12).*

22. *John's, for some unknown reason*

23. *James, brother of John (Acts 12:2). By the way, this is the New Testament's third Herod. History knows him as Herod Agrippa I, grandson of the first Herod, nephew of the second.*

24. *Beheading by the sword (Acts 12:2)*

25. *Peter (Acts 12:3-4)*

26. *Peter was delivered from prison by an angel (Acts 12:3-19) on the very night he would have been executed.*

27. *Herod ordered their execution (Acts 12:19).*

28. *Herod had made a speech (apparently a very impressive one) while dressed in his royal robes (Acts 12:20-22).*

29. *He was struck down by an angel but also "eaten by worms" (Acts 12:23).*

30. *The apostle Paul (Acts 23:35). Some Bible versions have "pretorium" instead of "judgment hall."*

31. *The man called simply Agrippa in Acts 25–26. He was of the Herod family, and history knows him as Herod Agrippa II, the son of the man struck down in Acts 12.*

32. *Jesus Christ Superstar. The irreverent number known as "Herod's Song" conveys the mockery Luke described.*

33. *Hamlet. The phrase meant "to outdo in cruelty and ranting." In old plays, Herod was always portrayed as extremely loud and violent.*

34. *The Feast of the Holy Innocents, referring to the slaughter of the Bethlehem babies ordered by Herod (Matthew 2). Catholics observe it on December 28, Orthodox on December 29.*

35. *The Wailing Wall, also called the Western Wall. It is all that remains of the huge Temple complex that Herod built.*

THE PAINTED WOMAN: JEZEBEL

Refer to a woman as a jezebel, and chances are that people will know you are talking about a really bad woman. The original Jezebel really was very, very bad, probably one of the nastiest characters in the Bible. She was also one of the most interesting, and her story has a very colorful (and satisfying) end. See how much you know about the Bible's baddest bad girl.

1. What idol-worshipping king of Israel was Jezebel's husband?
2. What foreign (and idol-worshipping) land did Jezebel hail from?
3. What palace servant hid the Lord's prophets in a cave to save them from Jezebel's mass executions?
4. How many pagan prophets dined at Jezebel's table?
5. What had the prophet Elijah done that caused Jezebel to swear to kill him within a day?
6. What did Jezebel promise Ahab she could obtain for his pleasure?
7. How did Jezebel go about getting Naboth's property?
8. What horrid fate did the prophet Elijah foretell for Jezebel?
9. Which prophet anointed Jehu to take vengeance on Jezebel and the whole royal family?
10. What was foretold as the final fate of Jezebel?
11. Jehu accused Jezebel of what two serious sins?
12. What caused Jezebel to "paint her face"?
13. What slur did Jezebel cast at Jehu?
14. What did the palace eunuchs do to bring about Jezebel's death?
15. What indignity was inflicted on the fallen Jezebel?
16. What was left of Jezebel when Jehu's men went to bury her?
17. Which New Testament book refers to an evil prophetess named Jezebel?
18. What noted English poet wrote *A King's Daughter*, a drama about Jezebel?

THE PAINTED WOMAN: JEZEBEL (ANSWERS)

1. Ahab

2. Sidon. Her father was Ethbaal, king of the Sidonians (1 Kings 16:31).

3. Obadiah (1 Kings 18:4)

4. Four hundred (1 Kings 18:19)

5. He executed hundreds of her Baal priests (1 Kings 19:1-2).

6. The vineyard of Naboth, who had refused to sell it to him (1 Kings 21:7)

7. She had two false witnesses accuse him of treason and blasphemy. After he was stoned to death, Ahab took possession of his vineyard (1 Kings 21:9-16).

8. Dogs would eat her body (1 Kings 21:23).

9. Elisha (2 Kings 9:1-7)

10. No one would bury her (2 Kings 9:10).

11. *Whoredoms and witchcraft (2 Kings 9:22). This reference to "whoredoms" explains why we use jezebel to refer to a loose woman.*

12. *She knew Jehu was coming to execute her, so she fixed her face and hair, apparently wanting to "die pretty" (2 Kings 9:30). The reference to "painting her face" is the source of our phrase "painted woman."*

13. *She called him Zimri as a reminder that not long before, Zimri had murdered the king—and very quickly died himself (2 Kings 9:31).*

14. *Threw her out a window (2 Kings 9:32-33)*

15. *Horses trampled on her (2 Kings 9:33).*

16. *Her skull, feet, and hands (2 Kings 9:35)*

17. *Revelation (2:20)*

18. *John Masefield*

THE KISS-OF-DEATH MAN: JUDAS ISCARIOT

Not counting Satan, Judas is the ultimate bad boy of the New Testament—maybe of the whole Bible. It's still jarring to read that one of Jesus' own handpicked disciples betrayed him. His character fascinates people, and there have been many efforts (such as in *Jesus Christ Superstar*) to make this bad boy look less bad. Frankly, the efforts have failed, and people will continue to refer to any treacherous person as a Judas.

1. In what location did Judas greet Jesus with a kiss?
2. How much money did the Jewish priests give Judas to betray Jesus?
3. What two Gospels say that Satan "entered into" Judas?
4. What is the meaning of Judas's last name, Iscariot?
5. What book of the Bible states that Judas died when he fell headlong into a field, bursting his insides?
6. On what occasion did Jesus identify Judas as the one who would betray him?
7. What position of trust did Judas have among the twelve disciples?
8. Which Gospel says that Judas changed his mind and returned his blood money to the priests?
9. What other disciple referred to Judas as the "guide" for those who arrested Jesus?

10. In what famous poem is Judas shown in the lowest circle of hell, being gnawed on eternally by Satan?
11. According to Matthew's Gospel, how did Judas die?
12. What author of several popular novels based on the Bible wrote *I, Judas*?
13. What burial ground for paupers is named for the place purchased by Judas's betrayal money?
14. What did Judas do with the thirty pieces of silver he received for betraying Jesus?
15. An old legend says that Judas is released from hell one day per year to cool himself off in what location?
16. Several kinds of plants are called "Judas trees." For what reason?
17. In paintings, what color hair does Judas usually have?
18. In paintings of the Last Supper, what is Judas usually holding with one of his hands?
19. What is the connection between Judas and the unlucky number 13?
20. *Judas* is the New Testament form of what common Old Testament name?

THE KISS-OF-DEATH MAN: JUDAS ISCARIOT (ANSWERS)

1. *The garden of Gethsemane, where Judas had led the armed mob to capture Jesus (Matthew 26:47-50)*

2. *Thirty pieces of silver (Matthew 26:15). By the way, this amount was the price of a slave, according to the Old Testament.*

3. *Luke (22:3) and John (13:27)*

4. *We aren't sure, but it most likely means "from Kerioth," which was a town in Judea.*

5. *Acts (1:18)*

6. *The Last Supper (Matthew 26:19-25)*

7. *He was in charge of the group's money, according to John 13:29.*

8. *Matthew (27:3-5)*

9. *Peter (Acts 1:16)*

10. *The Divine Comedy by Dante*

11. *He hung himself (Matthew 27:5).*

12. *Taylor Caldwell*

13. It's called a potter's field (Matthew 27:7), at that time intended to be a place for burying foreigners, but later the term was extended to include burial for paupers and criminals and anyone else outside mainstream society.

14. Returned it to the priests and threw it down in the Temple (Matthew 27:3-5)

15. On an ice floe

16. Their red (or pink) flowers are supposedly the drops of blood of the dead Judas.

17. Red, probably as a way of distinguishing him from the other disciples

18. The bag containing the 30 pieces of silver he had gotten for agreeing to betray Jesus

19. Jesus had twelve disciples—11 good ones, and one bad one (Judas). So, counting Jesus, there were 12 good men in the group, but the 13th (Judas) was bad.

20. Judah, of course

TEN VILLAINS, PURELY AT RANDOM

1. Who plotted to have the entire Hebrew nation completely exterminated?
2. Who committed the first murder?
3. Who acknowledged the innocence of Jesus but allowed him to be crucified anyway?
4. Who made numerous attempts to swindle Jacob, who ultimately prospered?
5. Which king made oaths of love and loyalty to David while frequently trying to kill him?
6. What evil king of Israel was led into even more wickedness by his beautiful and scheming wife?
7. Who ordered the killing of infant boys in Bethlehem?
8. What treacherous son led a revolt against his father, the king of Israel?
9. Which ruler, who had already had John the Baptist beheaded, was Jesus made to appear before?
10. What two traitorous army captains murdered their king as a favor to David and were then executed by David for treachery?

TEN VILLAINS, PURELY AT RANDOM (ANSWERS)

1. Haman, minister of Persia (Esther)

2. Cain, who murdered his brother (Genesis 4:8)

3. *Pontius Pilate (John 18:29–19:22)*

4. *Laban, his father-in-law (Genesis 29–31)*

5. *Saul (1 Samuel 17–19)*

6. *Ahab, husband of Jezebel (1 Kings 16:31-33)*

7. *Herod, known to history as Herod the Great (Matthew 2:16)*

8. *Absalom, son of David (2 Samuel 15–18)*

9. *Herod Antipas (Matthew 14:10; Luke 23:7)*

10. *Recab and Baanah, captains of Ish-bosheth (2 Samuel 4)*

PART 2

POWER CORRUPTS

MEN WITH CROWNS: KINGS AND OTHER RULERS

You might say the Bible has a limited government attitude toward kings. In ancient times, as today, wise people were aware that if you gave one man a lot of power, he would probably abuse it. Though there are a few noble kings in the pages of the Bible, most of the kings, pharaohs, and other rulers were a pretty sorry bunch—like many kings throughout history. The sad truth about kings is that they have the power to do a lot of good, but they seldom do so. They prefer the pursuit of wealth, power, and sex more than the public good. (Has anything changed?) No wonder people of faith were (and are) constantly reminded that the only king who deserves their devotion is God himself.

1. What Babylonian king hosted a banquet where a phantom hand left a message on the palace wall?
2. Which king of Israel was murdered while he was drunk?
3. Which king of Salem was also a priest of the Most High God?
4. Which king of Gerar took Sarah away from Abraham?
5. What Hebrew captive interpreted the dreams of the Egyptian pharaoh?
6. What three kings listened to the prophet Elisha as he prophesied to the accompaniment of a harp?
7. Which king attacked the Israelites on their way into Canaan, only to be completely destroyed later?
8. Which king of Sidon gave his daughter Jezebel as a wife to Ahab?
9. Which king of Bashan was famous for having an enormous iron bed?
10. Who was the last king of Judah?
11. Which king of Hazor organized an alliance against Joshua?
12. What military man captured 31 kings?
13. Which king of Moab sent the prophet Balaam to curse Israel?
14. Which king of Mesopotamia was sent by God to conquer the faithless Israelites?
15. What Canaanite king during the time of the judges was noted for having 900 iron chariots?
16. What son of Gideon (Jerubbaal) was proclaimed king in Shechem?
17. Which king of the Amalekites was captured by Saul and cut into pieces by Samuel?

18. What much-married king is considered the author of the Song of Solomon?
19. With what Philistine king did David seek refuge when he fled from Saul?
20. What shepherd boy, the youngest of eight sons, was anointed by Samuel in front of his brothers?
21. Which king wanted to see miracles when the arrested Jesus was sent to him?
22. Which king of Tyre sent cedar logs and craftsmen to King David?
23. Which prophet had a vision of a time when the Lord would gather the kings of the earth together and put them all in a pit?
24. What man (David's oldest son) tried to make himself king of Israel?
25. What wise king foolishly made an alliance with Egypt when he married the pharaoh's daughter?
26. What Egyptian king gave refuge to Jeroboam when he fled from Solomon?
27. Which king had a strange dream about an enormous, fruitful tree that was suddenly chopped down, leaving only a dry stump?
28. What man (one of Solomon's officials) had his reign over Israel foretold by the prophet Ahijah?
29. Which king of Judah was constantly at war with King Jeroboam of Israel?
30. Which king was confronted by the prophet Nathan because of his adulterous affair?
31. Which king of Israel reigned only two years and was murdered while he was fighting against the Philistines?
32. What man violently protested having a king in Israel, though he himself anointed the first two kings?
33. Which city did King Jeroboam use as his capital when the northern tribes split from the southern tribes?
34. Which king of Israel reigned only seven days and killed himself by burning down his palace around him?
35. Which king of Ethiopia was supposed to aid Hezekiah in breaking the power of the Assyrians?
36. Which king led Israel into sin by allowing his evil wife to introduce Baal worship into the country?
37. Who was the last king of Israel?
38. Which king of the Amorites refused to let the Israelites pass through his kingdom on their way to Canaan?
39. Which king called Elijah the worst troublemaker in Israel?

40. What evil king of Judah was humbled and repentant after being taken to Babylon in chains?
41. Which king was told by the prophet Micaiah that his troops would fall in battle?
42. What saintly king had a fleet built to sail for gold, though the ships never sailed?
43. Which king of Israel consulted the god Baalzebub after falling off his palace balcony?
44. Which king of Moab was famous as a sheep farmer?
45. Who became king of Syria after he smothered King Ben-hadad with a wet cloth?
46. Which king of Judah led the country into sin by marrying the daughter of the wicked Ahab?
47. Who is the only king in the Bible referred to as "the Mede"?

MEN WITH CROWNS: KINGS AND OTHER RULERS (ANSWERS)

1. *Belshazzar (Daniel 5:1-30)*
2. *Elah (1 Kings 16:8-10)*
3. *Melchizedek (Genesis 14:18)*
4. *Abimelech (Genesis 20:2)*
5. *Joseph (Genesis 41:1-36)*
6. *The king of Israel, Jehoshaphat of Judah, and the king of Edom (2 Kings 3:11-19)*
7. *King Arad (Numbers 21:1-3)*
8. *Ethbaal (1 Kings 16:31)*
9. *Og (Deuteronomy 3:11)*
10. *Zedekiah (2 Kings 25:1-7)*
11. *Jabin (Joshua 11:1-5)*
12. *Joshua (Joshua12:7-24)*
13. *Balak (Numbers 22:2-6)*
14. *Chushan-rishathaim (Judges 3:8)*
15. *Jabin (Judges 4:2-3)*
16. *Abimelech (Judges 9:6)*
17. *Agag (1 Samuel 15:8, 32-33)*
18. *Solomon (Song of Solomon 1:1)*
19. *Achish of Gath (1 Samuel 21:10)*

20. *David (1 Samuel 16:6-13)*
21. *Herod (Luke 23:8)*
22. *Hiram (2 Samuel 5:11)*
23. *Isaiah (Isaiah 24:21-22)*
24. *Adonijah (1 Kings 1:5-53)*
25. *Solomon (1 Kings 3:1)*
26. *Shishak (1 Kings 11:40)*
27. *Nebuchadnezzar (Daniel 4:10-18)*
28. *Jeroboam (1 Kings 11:26-40)*
29. *Abijam, or Abijah (1 Kings 15:6)*
30. *David (2 Samuel 12:1-15)*
31. *Nadab (1 Kings 15:26-27)*
32. *Samuel (1 Samuel 8–10)*
33. *Tirzah*
34. *Zimri (1 Kings 16:15-18)*
35. *Tirhakah (2 Kings 19:9)*
36. *Ahab (1 Kings 16:29-33)*
37. *Hoshea (2 Kings 17:4)*
38. *Sihon (Numbers 21:21-26)*
39. *Ahab (1 Kings 18:17)*
40. *Manasseh (2 Chronicles 33:10-13)*
41. *Ahab (1 Kings 22:15-20)*
42. *Jehoshaphat (1 Kings 22:48)*
43. *Ahaziah (2 Kings 1:2)*
44. *Mesha (2 Kings 3:4)*
45. *Hazael (2 Kings 8:7-15)*
46. *Jehoram (2 Kings 8:16-18)*
47. *Darius (Daniel 5:31)*

PROPHETS FOR PROFIT

The Hebrew word for prophet was *nabi,* meaning something like "mouthpiece" or "spokesman." The true prophets preached because they felt compelled to speak out on God's behalf. By contrast, the false prophets (and there were more of them than the true sort) spoke whatever they thought the people—or the king they served—wanted to hear. These "hired tongues" were notorious for leading people astray, and making money from their lies.

1. What wilderness prophet of the Lord confronted 450 prophets of Baal in a famous showdown on Mount Carmel to pray for rain?
2. Who warned that false prophets would appear as wolves in "sheep's clothing"?
3. What false prophet wore a yoke that Jeremiah broke?
4. What false prophet put on some iron horns and told King Ahab he would be victorious in battle?
5. What false prophet was a sorcerer and an attendant of the proconsul, Sergius Paulus?
6. Which prophetess is mentioned as an intimidator of Nehemiah?
7. What evil prophetess is referred to in Revelation by the name of an Old Testament queen?
8. What false prophet of Moab had a confrontation with his talking donkey?
9. Who claimed that in the end times, false prophets would appear and "perform great signs and miracles"?
10. What book of the Bible speaks of the wonders of a false prophet who is in cahoots with the Beast?
11. Which apostle wrote that believers must "test the spirits to see if they are from God " because of so many false prophets around?
12. When wicked King Ahab assembled 400 false prophets to determine whether to go to war, who was one faithful prophet who insisted on telling the truth?
13. Why did Jesus say, "Woe to you when all men speak well of you"?
14. In Revelation, what is the ultimate fate of the false prophet?
15. Which Epistle warns that the false prophets are "bringing swift destruction on themselves"?
16. To what faithful prophet did God say, "The prophets are prophesying lies in my name"?

17. What sad book of the Old Testament says that "the visions of your prophets were vain and foolish"?
18. In Deuteronomy, what punishment was prescribed for any Israelite who prophesied in the name of false gods?
19. Which prophet said that God "foils the signs of false prophets and makes fools of diviners"?
20. When Elijah faced the 450 prophets of Baal on Mount Carmel, there were also 400 prophets of what other god?

PROPHETS FOR PROFIT (ANSWERS)

1. Elijah (1 Kings 18)
2. Jesus (Matthew 7:15)
3. Hananiah (Jeremiah 28)
4. Zedekiah (1 Kings 22:1-12)
5. Barjesus (Acts 13:6-11)
6. Noadiah (Nehemiah 6:14)
7. Jezebel (Revelation 2:20)
8. Balaam (Numbers 22–24)
9. Jesus (Matthew 24:24)
10. Revelation (19:20)
11. John (1 John 4:1)
12. Micaiah, whom Ahab then put in prison (1 Kings 22:6-27)
13. Because that was how the false prophets were always treated (Luke 6:26)
14. He burns forever in the lake of brimstone (Revelation 19:20).
15. 2 Peter (2:1)
16. Jeremiah (Jeremiah 14:14-16)
17. Lamentations (2:14)
18. Death (Deuteronomy 18:20)
19. Isaiah (Isaiah 44:24-25)
20. Asherah, who was—strictly speaking—a goddess, not a god (1 Kings 18:19)

PLAYING AT THE PALACE

Say *palace* and people think of "lifestyles of the rich and famous." It would be just as fair to connect palaces with evil empires, because those mighty people who dwelled in luxury got their palaces through oppressive taxation and conquest. Small wonder that a few bad boys came to a bitter end in their palaces. Small wonder that the prophets condemned the idle and immoral rich who dwelled in palaces while mocking the poor.

1. In whose palace was there a feast where a hand wrote on the wall?
2. Who burned the royal palace of Israel with himself inside?
3. What mighty Babylonian ruler went insane while walking on the roof of his palace?
4. Which king took 13 years to build his palace?
5. Which nation's ambassadors were taken on a tour of the palace by King Hezekiah?
6. Who owned a coveted vineyard close to Israel's royal palace?
7. Which king of Israel was assassinated in his palace by Pekah?
8. Which king was told by the prophet Isaiah that his descendants would be eunuchs in the palace of Babylon?
9. In the Gospels, which enemy of Jesus is mentioned as living in a palace?
10. Who prophesied that wild beasts would frolic in the ruined palaces of Babylon?
11. Which prophet spoke of the Lord's fire falling as judgment on the palaces of wicked kingdoms?

PLAYING AT THE PALACE (ANSWERS)

1. Belshazzar's (Daniel 5:1-5). The next day, his kingdom was conquered.

2. Zimri (1 Kings 16:15-18), after his reign of seven days

3. Nebuchadnezzar (Daniel 4:28-33)

4. Solomon (1 Kings 7:1). The taxation and forced labor connected with his building projects led to the split of the kingdom after his death.

5. Babylon's (2 Kings 20:13-18). Years later the Babylonians would capture and burn that palace.

6. Naboth (1 Kings 21:1-19), who ended up murdered so wicked King Ahab could possess the vineyard

7. *Pekahiah (2 Kings 15:23-25)*
8. *Hezekiah (2 Kings 20:18)*
9. *Caiaphas, the high priest (Matthew 26:3)*
10. *Isaiah (Isaiah 13:19-22)*
11. *Amos (Amos 1–2)*

SAINTS ON SINNERS' PAYROLLS

The Lord moves in mysterious ways, which is obvious in the Bible's many stories of good people employed by bad governments. Somehow these folks, through their own talent and wisdom—but mostly through the grace of God—found themselves in positions of power and influence, shining the light of faith in a world that sorely needed it.

1. Which Hebrew—formerly a slave and a prisoner—governed Egypt?
2. What upright young man was made ruler over the whole province of Babylon?
3. Sergius Paulus, who became a Christian, was the deputy of what island?
4. What Persian king did Nehemiah serve under?
5. What church in Greece received greetings from believers that were workers in Caesar's household?
6. From what country was the eunuch who was baptized by Philip?
7. What Jewish man served as an honored official under Ahasuerus of Persia?
8. What Roman centurion of Caesarea was a godly man?
9. What three Hebrew men were appointed Babylonian administrators by Daniel?
10. What was the occupation of the Roman who had his beloved servant healed by Jesus?
11. What Jewish girl became queen of Persia?
12. The saintly Obadiah, a friend of the prophet Elijah, was the palace steward of what very wicked king?

SAINTS ON SINNERS' PAYROLLS (ANSWERS)

1. *Joseph (Genesis 42:3-6)*

2. *Daniel (Daniel 2:48)*

3. *Cyprus (Acts 13:4-7)*

4. *Artaxerxes (Nehemiah 2:1)*

5. *Philippi (Philippians 1:1; 4:22)*

6. *Ethiopia (Acts 8:27)*

7. *Mordecai (Esther 10:3)*

8. *Cornelius (Acts 10:1-2)*

9. *Shadrach, Meshach, and Abednego (Daniel 2:49)*

10. *A centurion (Luke 7:2-10)*

11. *Esther (Esther 2:17)*

12. *Ahab (1 Kings 18:1-16)*

 MORE MEN WITH CROWNS

Yep, the world's human rulers are often a pretty sorry lot. When you feel like complaining about your own government officials, dip into the pages of the Bible for a while. You may find that your own government doesn't look so bad by comparison.

1. Which king was criticized by the prophet Isaiah for showing Judah's treasure to Babylonian ambassadors?
2. What bad king of Judah was blinded and taken away in chains to Babylon?
3. What Syrian king besieged Samaria, causing great famine that led to cannibalism?
4. What Egyptian king fought against Judah and murdered King Josiah?
5. What future king of Judah had to be hidden as a boy to protect him from the wrath of wicked Queen Athaliah?
6. Who set up golden bulls at Dan and Bethel so his people would not go to Jerusalem to worship?
7. What good king of Judah was murdered by two of his court officials?

8. Which king of Israel made Elisha angry by not striking the ground enough with his arrows?
9. Which king of Judah showed mercy when he executed his father's murderers but spared their families?
10. Which king ran a beauty contest to pick a bride and wound up marrying a Jewish girl?
11. Which king of Judah was stricken with leprosy?
12. Which king of Israel was assassinated by Shallum after a six-month reign?
13. What cruel king of Israel assassinated King Shallum and ripped open the pregnant women of Tiphsah?
14. Which king of Egypt received an appeal for help from Hoshea of Israel, who wanted to throw off the Assyrian yoke?
15. Which king of Israel had much of his territory taken away by the Assyrian king?
16. What evil king of Judah sacrificed his son as a burnt offering and built a Syrian-style altar in Jerusalem?
17. Which king of Israel experienced a long famine and drought during his reign?
18. What Assyrian king brought about the fall of Samaria and the deportation of the Israelites to other countries?
19. What godly king of Judah tore down the idols in the country and broke the power of the Philistines?
20. Which king of Gezer opposed Joshua's army and was totally defeated, with no soldiers left alive?
21. What Assyrian king was killed by his sons while worshipping in the temple of the god, Nisroch?
22. Which king of Israel had a reputation as a fast and furious chariot driver?
23. Which king of Syria joined the king of Israel in attacking Judah?
24. What Assyrian king was given 38 tons of silver and gold from the house of the Lord as tribute money from Menahem of Israel?
25. Which king of Assyria had his army of 185,000 soldiers destroyed by the angel of the Lord?
26. What cruel king lied to the wise men about his desire to worship the infant Jesus?
27. Which king of Judah had the worst reputation for killing innocent people?
28. Which king of Judah reigned for only two years and was murdered by his court officials?

29. What godly king began his reign at age eight and led a major reform movement in Judah?
30. Who had a dream about a statue composed of different metals?
31. Which king reinstituted the celebration of Passover in Judah and invited the people of Israel to participate?
32. Which king of Judah was killed at the battle of Megiddo by the forces of Egypt?
33. Which king repented because of the preaching of the prophet Jonah?
34. Which king of Israel tricked the worshippers of Baal by gathering them together in a temple and slaughtering all of them?
35. Which king of Israel built the city of Samaria and made it his capital?
36. What Babylonian king sent his ambassadors to the court of Hezekiah, where they were shown all of Hezekiah's treasures?
37. Which son of Josiah was taken prisoner by Pharaohnechoh and never left Egypt?
38. Who reigned in Jerusalem when the Babylonian king's forces first attacked Judah?
39. Who was reigning in Judah when the Babylonians besieged Jerusalem and carried the nobles of the city away to Babylon?
40. Which king of Judah saw the country threatened by the Assyrian army of Sennacherib?
41. What Babylonian official burned down the Temple and palace and broke down the city walls of Jerusalem?
42. What foreign king did Esther marry?
43. Who was taken prisoner in Babylon, though he came to enjoy the favor of the Babylonian king?
44. What Babylonian king gave the deposed king of Judah a place of great honor in Babylon?
45. Which king burned the letter sent to him by the prophet Jeremiah?
46. Which king ordered Jezebel's servants to toss her out of a window?
47. Which king of Persia issued the decree that the people of Judah could rebuild their Temple?
48. Which king of Assur sent foreigners to settle in Israel after the Israelites had been taken away?
49. What Persian king received a letter complaining about the Jews rebuilding their Temple in Jerusalem?
50. What army officer was anointed king of Israel by one of Elisha's followers?

MORE MEN WITH CROWNS (ANSWERS)

1. Hezekiah (2 Kings 20:12-18). All things considered, Hezekiah was a good king, but the future would prove that showing his treasure to the Babylonians was a very foolish thing to have done.

2. Zedekiah (2 Kings 25:7). God often used bad kings to get rid of bad kings.

3. Ben-hadad (2 Kings 6:24-30)

4. Pharaohnechoh (2 Kings 23:29)

5. Joash (2 Kings 11:2)

6. Jeroboam (1 Kings 12:26-31)

7. Joash (2 Kings 12:20-21)

8. Joash (2 Kings 13:18-19)

9. Amaziah (2 Kings 14:1, 5-6)

10. Ahasuerus, or Xerxes (Esther 2:1-18)

11. Uzziah, also called Azariah (2 Kings 15:1, 5)

12. Zechariah (2 Kings 15:8-10)

13. Menahem (2 Kings 15:14-16)

14. So (2 Kings 17:4)

15. Pekah (2 Kings 15:29)

16. Ahaz (2 Kings 16:2-3, 10-11)

17. Ahab (1 Kings 18:1-2)

18. Shalmaneser (2 Kings 17:3-6)

19. Hezekiah (2 Kings 18:1-8)

20. Horam (Joshua 10:33)

21. Sennacherib (2 Kings 19:36-37)

22. Jehu (2 Kings 9:20)

23. Rezin (2 Kings 16:5)

24. Tiglath-pileser (2 Kings 16:7-8)

25. Sennacherib (2 Kings 19:35)

26. Herod (Matthew 2:7-8, 13)

27. Manasseh (2 Kings 21:16)

28. Amon (2 Kings 21:19-23)

29. Josiah (2 Kings 22:1–23:28)

30. Nebuchadnezzar (Daniel 2)

31. *Hezekiah (2 Chronicles 30:1-12)*
32. *Josiah (2 Kings 23:29-30)*
33. *The king of Nineveh (Jonah 3:6)*
34. *Jehu (2 Kings 10:18-28)*
35. *Omri (1 Kings 16:23-24)*
36. *Berodach-baladan (2 Kings 20:12-13)*
37. *Jehoahaz (2 Kings 23:33-34)*
38. *Jehoiakim (2 Kings 24:1)*
39. *Jehoiachin (2 Kings 24:15-16)*
40. *Hezekiah (2 Kings 18:13)*
41. *Nebuzaradan, captain of the guard for Nebuchadnezzar (2 Kings 25:8-11)*
42. *Ahasuerus, also known as Xerxes (Esther 2:16-17)*
43. *Jehoiachin (2 Kings 25:27-30)*
44. *Evil-merodach (2 Kings 25:27-30)*
45. *Jehoiakim (Jeremiah 36:23)*
46. *Jehu (2 Kings 9:2-3, 31-33)*
47. *Cyrus (Ezra 1:1-4)*
48. *Esarhaddon (Ezra 4:2)*
49. *Artaxerxes (Ezra 4:6-7)*
50. *Jehu (2 Kings 9:1-10)*

 BEASTLY PRIESTS

Priests in ancient times were responsible for offering up sacrifices to God (or some god), so the priests were often thought of as very special people, somehow "close" to the divine. Some priests were good and saintly folks, whereas others were downright scandalous in their behavior. The questions below deal with the more despicable ones.

1. What righteous king fired all the priests who had been appointed to serve pagan gods?
2. Which priests—two of Aaron's sons—were killed because they offered "strange fire" to the Lord?
3. Which king of Israel pretended to be loyal to the god Baal so he could arrange a mass execution all the Baal priests?

4. What reform priest was ordered to be killed by King Joash, a pupil of his father?
5. Which king ordered the execution of Ahimelech and other priests because they had conspired with David?
6. Who was the only priest to escape when Saul slaughtered the 85 priests of Nob?
7. What high priest had John and Peter arrested after the two disciples healed a lame man?
8. Which priest was told by Jeremiah that he would be taken to Babylon as a prisoner?
9. Which king of Israel sinned by appointing priests who had not been chosen by God?
10. In the time of the judges, what man was brassy enough to set up one of his sons as his priest without the authority to do so?
11. Which priest of Baal was killed in Jerusalem when a reform movement threw out all the idols?
12. Which king ordered the priest Urijah to make a copy of a pagan altar the king had seen in Damascus?
13. Which king reversed the reform policies of Jehoiada the priest immediately after Jehoiada died?
14. What evil priest had Jeremiah beaten and placed in chains?
15. Which priest was banished by Solomon, fulfilling a prophecy that Eli's descendants would be stripped of the priesthood?
16. Which priest received a letter criticizing him for not putting an iron collar on Jeremiah's neck?
17. What is the only parable of Jesus to have a priest as a character?
18. Which prophet locked horns with the wicked priest Amaziah at Bethel?
19. Which miracle of Jesus led the priests to conspire to have him executed?
20. When Adonijah tried to grab the throne of Israel, which priest took his side?
21. In which priest's home did the enemies of Jesus meet to plot against him?
22. What two apostles were met by a priest of Zeus, who tried to offer sacrifices to them?
23. What crime did the high priest charge Jesus with?
24. Which priest was made mute because he did not believe the prophecy given by an angel?
25. Which priest announced that Jesus should die because it was appropriate for one man to die for the people?

26. Which priest was told by the prophet Amos that his wife would become a prostitute?
27. According to John's Gospel, which priest was the first to examine the arrested Jesus?
28. What man asked the high priest for letters of commendation so he could work in the synagogues of Damascus?
29. What high priest ordered his men to slap Paul, which caused Paul to call him a whitewashed wall?
30. What two gluttonous priests were notorious for taking more than their share of sacrificial meat?
31. Which prophet predicted the Lord would cut out all the names of the pagan priests?
32. What was the penalty in Israel for disobeying a priest?
33. Which god's priests are mentioned in connection with the capture of the Ark of the Covenant by the Philistines?

BEASTLY PRIESTS (ANSWERS)

1. Josiah (2 Kings 23:5)

2. Nadab and Abihu (Numbers 3:4). We still aren't sure just what "strange fire" was, but it definitely angered God.

3. Jehu (2 Kings 10)

4. Zechariah (2 Chronicles 24:1, 20-21)

5. Saul (1 Samuel 22:13-18)

6. Abiathar (1 Samuel 22:20)

7. Annas (Acts 4:6)

8. Pashur (Jeremiah 20:6)

9. Jeroboam (1 Kings 13:33)

10. Micah (Judges 17:5)

11. Mattan (2 Kings 11:18)

12. Ahaz (2 Kings 16:11)

13. Joash (2 Chronicles 24:17-18)

14. Pashhur (Jeremiah 20:1-2)

15. Abiathar (1 Samuel 2:27-36; 1 Kings 2:26-27)

16. Zephaniah (Jeremiah 29:26)

17. *The Good Samaritan (Luke 10:30-36), in which the priest is definitely not an admirable figure*

18. *Amos (Amos 7:10-17)*

19. *The raising of Lazarus (John 11:43-53)*

20. *Abiathar (1 Kings 1:7)*

21. *Caiaphas's (Matthew 26:3)*

22. *Paul and Barnabas (Acts 14:13)*

23. *Blasphemy (Matthew 26:65)*

24. *Zechariah (Luke 1:20)*

25. *Caiaphas (John 11:49-50)*

26. *Amaziah (Amos 7:17)*

27. *Annas (John 18:13)*

28. *Saul (Acts 9:2)*

29. *Ananias (Acts 23:2-3)*

30. *Hophni and Phinehas (1 Samuel 2:12-17; 4:11)*

31. *Zephaniah (Zephaniah 1:1, 4)*

32. *Death (Deuteronomy 17:12)*

33. *Dagon's (1 Samuel 5:5)*

 THE EXILE FILES

You might define *exile* as "a vacation someplace you don't want to go." In the ancient world, it was a common punishment for many criminals. It was also the fate of people who found themselves booted out of their homeland for various reasons. In a time when home was something people yearned for, exile could be the cruelest of punishments. Sad to say, a lot of good folks suffered exile at the hands of bad folks in authority.

1. Which apostle (and New Testament author) was exiled to the bleak island of Patmos?
2. What often-quoted psalm is a lament of the exiles in Babylon?
3. Which prophet was exiled in Egypt with other people from Judah?
4. What was the first instance of exile in the Bible?
5. Who was brought down to Egypt and sold to a man named Potiphar?

6. Who chose to go into exile rather than risk being killed by his brother?
7. Who was exiled from the rest of the world?
8. Whom did Abraham banish to the desert?
9. Who stayed in Egypt until Herod died?
10. Who carried the people of Jerusalem off to Babylon?
11. What future king of Israel fled from Solomon and hid in Egypt?
12. What nation carried Israel into exile?
13. Who was in exile three years after killing his brother Amnon?
14. What land did Moses flee to when he left Egypt?
15. Who was exiled to the land of Nod? (Hint: murderer)
16. Which judge fled from his kin and lived in the land of Tob?
17. Christians were scattered throughout Judea and Samaria because of a persecution that began after whose death?
18. What exiled king of Judah became a friend of the king of Babylon?
19. Who predicted the Babylonian exile to Hezekiah?
20. Who was king in Israel when the Assyrians deported the people?
21. Which king of Judah was temporarily exiled in Assyria, where he repented of his evil ways?
22. Who was king when Jerusalem fell to the Babylonians?
23. Which prophet went into exile in the land of the Chaldeans?
24. Who was appointed governor of Judah after the people went into exile?
25. When the Assyrians deported the people of Israel, how many of the 12 original tribes were left?
26. What blind king died in exile in Babylon?
27. Which king issued an edict ending the exile of the Jews?
28. What Assyrian king carried the people of Israel into exile?
29. Which interpreter of dreams was in exile in Babylon?
30. Which prophet warned the wicked priest Amaziah that Israel would go into exile?
31. Which Epistles are addressed to God's people in exile?
32. How many years were the Israelites in Egypt?

THE EXILE FILES (ANSWERS)

1. John (Revelation 1:9)

2. Psalm 137, which begins with "By the rivers of Babylon."

3. Jeremiah (Jeremiah 43:5-7)

4. *God drove Adam and Eve out of the Garden (Genesis 3:24).*

5. *Joseph (Genesis 39:1)*

6. *Jacob (Genesis 27:41-45)*

7. *Noah and his family, because everyone else died (Genesis 7:23)*

8. *Hagar and her son, Ishmael (Genesis 21:14)*

9. *Joseph, Mary, and Jesus (Matthew 2:13-15)*

10. *Nebuchadnezzar (2 Kings 24:15)*

11. *Jeroboam (1 Kings 11:40)*

12. *Assyria (2 Kings 17:6)*

13. *Absalom (2 Samuel 13:28-29, 37-38)*

14. *Midian (Exodus 2:15)*

15. *Cain (Genesis 4:13-16)*

16. *Jephthah (Judges 11:3)*

17. *Stephen's (Acts 7:59-60; 8:1)*

18. *Jehoiachin (2 Kings 25:27-30)*

19. *Isaiah (2 Kings 20:12-19)*

20. *Pekah (2 Kings 15:29)*

21. *Manasseh (2 Chronicles 33:11-13)*

22. *Zedekiah (2 Chronicles 36:11-20)*

23. *Ezekiel (Ezekiel 1:1-3)*

24. *Gedaliah (2 Kings 25:22)*

25. *One—Judah (2 Kings 17:18)*

26. *Zedekiah (Jeremiah 52:11)*

27. *Cyrus of Persia (2 Chronicles 36:22-23)*

28. *Tiglath-pileser (2 Kings 15:29)*

29. *Daniel (Daniel 1:1-6)*

30. *Amos (Amos 7:17)*

31. *James and 1 Peter*

32. *Four hundred and thirty years (Exodus 12:40)*

VISITING DAY AT THE PRISON

Lawyers, police, and prison workers will readily tell you a basic truth about prisons: Most of the people there really *are* guilty of crimes. That was no doubt true in Bible times too, yet the Bible is full of stories of good people being thrown into prison without cause. So in this set of questions, it isn't the prisoners who were the bad boys but, more often, the authorities who imprisoned them. (In other words, the wrong ones were walking around free.)

1. What famous dreamer was imprisoned after being accused of trying to seduce Potiphar's wife?
2. Which kinsman of Jesus was imprisoned for criticizing King Herod's marriage to Herodias?
3. What two apostles were imprisoned in Jerusalem for preaching the gospel?
4. Who was imprisoned as a political enemy of the Philistines?
5. Whose brothers were imprisoned after being falsely accused of spying in Egypt?
6. Who was imprisoned for prophesying the destruction of the kingdom of Judah?
7. Which apostles remained in the prison at Philippi even after an earthquake opened the prison doors?
8. Who prophesied doom for King Asa and was imprisoned?
9. Which king of Judah was sent into exile in Babylon and put in prison but was later released and treated as a friend of the king of Babylon?
10. Who prophesied doom and defeat for King Ahab and was imprisoned for his harsh words?
11. Which king of Israel was imprisoned for defying Assyrian authority?
12. Which king of Judah was blinded and imprisoned because he defied Babylonian authority?
13. In which Epistle does Paul refer to Andronicus and Junias, his relatives and fellow prisoners?
14. According to Psalms, who "bringeth out those which are bound with chains"?
15. In Acts 5, who released the apostles from prison?
16. Who gloated that David had made himself a prisoner by entering a gated city?

17. What book of the Bible states that the Lord sets prisoners free?
18. In the time of King Ahaz, what neighboring nation had invaded Judah and carried away prisoners?
19. Which persecutor of Christians had them dragged off to prison but later became a Christian himself?
20. What book of the Bible says that Christians will have their faith tested by being put in prison by the devil?
21. Who referred to himself as an old man and a prisoner of Jesus Christ?
22. Which disciple told Jesus that he was ready to face prison—and even death—for him?
23. Which Epistle tells Christians to remember those in prison as if you were their fellow prisoners?
24. In Acts 12, who released the apostle Peter from prison?
25. In Acts 27, what near-fatal disaster occurred to Paul and other prisoners?

VISITING DAY AT THE PRISON (ANSWERS)

1. Joseph (Genesis 39:7-20). This is the first mention of prison in the Bible, by the way.

2. John the Baptist (Matthew 14:3-5)

3. Peter and John (Acts 3:1; 4:3)

4. Samson (Judges 16:20-21)

5. Joseph's (Genesis 42:1-35)

6. Jeremiah (Jeremiah 32:2)

7. Paul and Silas (Acts 16:16-34)

8. Hanani (2 Chronicles 16:7-10)

9. Jehoiachin (2 Kings 24:12; 25:27-30)

10. Micaiah (1 Kings 22:26-28)

11. Hoshea (2 Kings 17:4)

12. Zedekiah (2 Kings 25:6-7)

13. Romans (16:7)

14. The Lord (Psalm 68:6)

15. The angel of the Lord (Acts 5:19)

16. King Saul (1 Samuel 23:7)

17. Psalms (Psalm 146:7)

18. *Edom (2 Chronicles 28:17)*

19. *Saul, later known as the apostle Paul (Acts 8:3; 13:9)*

20. *Revelation (2:10)*

21. *Paul (Philemon 1:9)*

22. *Peter (Luke 22:33). Years later, as told in Acts, Peter did indeed go to prison.*

23. *Hebrews (13:3)*

24. *The angel of the Lord (Acts 12:7)*

25. *A shipwreck (Acts 27:27-44)*

ORDER IN THE COURT!

Trials fascinate us, as evidenced by the many court shows on television. They have fascinated humans throughout history; and no wonder, because we hope that justice will be done (though so often it isn't). Judges and juries are human and can be bribed—ditto for witnesses. Sometimes courts can simply be misguided. Sadly, the Bible is full of stories of innocent people being dragged before courts and councils where the real bad guys were the ones doing the judging. People of faith must set their hope on the ultimate Judge who will render a true verdict.

1. When Jesus was brought before the Jews' council, how many false witnesses were brought in to accuse him?
2. Who suggested to Moses that he appoint judges so that he would not have to judge all cases himself?
3. According to the Law, how many witnesses were necessary before a man could be tried and put to death?
4. What cynical king asked Jesus questions and then allowed him to be mocked?
5. According to Jesus, when his followers were dragged into court, they would not need to worry about their defense because someone else would speak through them. Who?
6. What stinging accusation of the Jews finally convinced Pilate to allow Jesus to be executed?
7. What person's presence at the trial of Peter and John kept the rulers and priests from punishing the two apostles?
8. When Stephen was brought to trial, what was the charge laid against him?

9. In what city were Paul and Silas tried, flogged, and jailed after they cast a demon out of a fortune-teller?
10. When Paul was mobbed in the Temple, who rescued him?
11. What Roman official gave Paul a centurion as a guard and told the centurion to allow Paul freedom to see whomever he wished?
12. What three rulers, hearing Paul defend himself in Caesarea, agreed that he deserved no punishment?

ORDER IN THE COURT! (ANSWERS)

1. *Two (Matthew 26:57-66)*
2. *His father-in-law, Jethro (Exodus 18)*
3. *At least two (Deuteronomy 17:6)*
4. *Herod (Luke 23:8-11)*
5. *The Spirit (Matthew 10:16-20)*
6. *They claimed that Pilate was no friend of Caesar (John 19:12).*
7. *The lame man whom Peter and John had healed (Acts 4:13-14)*
8. *That he taught that Jesus had aimed to change the customs taught by Moses (Acts 6:11-14)*
9. *Philippi (Acts 16:12, 16-24)*
10. *The chief Roman captain (Acts 22:27-30; 23:1-10)*
11. *Felix (Acts 24:22-23)*
12. *Festus, Agrippa, and Bernice (Acts 25:23–26:32)*

STILL MORE MEN WITH CROWNS

And once more, we take a look at those bad boys with power, the Bible's kings (most of whom should have been wearing prison garb instead of crowns). We can take some consolation in knowing that there is an afterlife.

1. Which king of Israel built pagan temples to please all his foreign wives?
2. What Persian king was publicly embarrassed by his disobedient wife?

3. Which son of Solomon caused the kingdom to split when he threatened the people of Israel?
4. Which king of Judah was murdered after he fled to Lachish?
5. Which king had a sinister prime minister named Haman?
6. Which king is believed to have written Ecclesiastes?
7. What two kings are mentioned as the authors of Proverbs?
8. What future king of Israel was out hunting his donkeys when Samuel came to anoint him?
9. What much-loved and much-quoted prophet was active during the reigns of Uzziah, Jotham, Ahaz, and Hezekiah and, according to tradition, was executed by Manasseh?
10. Which king had the apostle James executed with a sword and had Peter arrested?
11. What fat king of Moab was murdered by the judge Ehud?
12. Which king of Babylon went insane and lived in the fields, where he ate grass and let his hair and fingernails grow long?
13. Which king made a famous judgment about a baby that two women claimed was theirs?
14. Which king ordered Daniel thrown into the lions' den?
15. Which king of Judah tore down the pagan shrines and stamped out child sacrifice in Judah?
16. Which king of Judah sacrificed his sons in the fire but later became repentant?
17. What cruel king had the infant boys of Bethlehem slaughtered?
18. Which king broke his own law when he called on a medium to bring up the ghost of Samuel?
19. Who was the only king of Israel to kill both a king of Judah and a king of Israel?
20. Which king was referred to by Jesus as "that fox"?
21. What son of Saul was made king of Israel by Abner?
22. Which king executed John the Baptist after his wife's daughter asked for the head of John on a platter?
23. What Assyrian king attacked Ashdod, leading Isaiah to walk around naked for three years?
24. Which king, dressed in royal finery, was hailed as a god but then struck down by the angel of the Lord?
25. To which king did Paul tell the story of his conversion?
26. Which king gave his daughter as a wife for David?
27. Which Hebrew was given the daughter of the pharaoh as a wife?
28. According to Luke's Gospel, what Roman ruler ordered a census in the empire?

29. Who was the first king to reign at Jerusalem?
30. What saintly king of Judah was crippled with a foot disease in his old age?
31. Which king was reprimanded by his military commander for weeping too long over his dead son?
32. Which son of David tried to make himself king after David's death?
33. Who was king of Judah when the long-lost Book of the Law was found in the Temple?
34. Who received a visit from the queen of Sheba, whom he impressed with his wisdom?
35. Who is the only king who is said to have neither a mother nor a father?
36. Which king of Judah became king at age seven and was aided in his reign by the saintly priest Jehoiada?
37. Which king had the misfortune of his worst enemy being his son-in-law and his son's best friend?
38. Which king is considered by many scholars to be the author of 73 of the Psalms?
39. Which king built the first Temple in Jerusalem?
40. What army commander made Saul's son Ish-bosheth king over Israel?
41. What evil king of Israel pouted when he couldn't get a man to sell his plot of land?
42. Which psalm is supposed to be David's expression of guilt after his affair with Bathsheba?
43. Which king suffered from a fatal illness but was promised by Isaiah that God would give him 15 more years of life?
44. Which of the 10 plagues finally convinced the Egyptian pharaoh to let the Israelites leave?
45. Who reigned in Persia when Nehemiah heard the sad news about the walls of Jerusalem?
46. Which king of Judah purified the Temple and rededicated it to God?
47. Which apostle fled the soldiers of King Aretas in Damascus?
48. Which king of Israel was told by the prophet Jehu that the royal family would be wiped out because of its destruction of Jeroboam's dynasty?

STILL MORE MEN WITH CROWNS (ANSWERS)

1. Solomon (1 Kings 11:1-13), who, as 1 Kings makes clear, was both a good king and a bad king

2. Ahasuerus, or Xerxes (Esther 1:10-12)

3. Rehoboam (1 Kings 12:1-17)

4. Amaziah (2 Kings 14:18-19)

5. Ahasuerus, or Xerxes (Esther 3:1-10)

6. Solomon (Ecclesiastes 1:1)

7. Solomon and Lemuel (Proverbs 1:1; 31:1)

8. Saul (1 Samuel 9:15–10:1)

9. Isaiah (Isaiah 1:1)

10. Herod (Acts 12:1-3)

11. Eglon (Judges 3:14-26)

12. Nebuchadnezzar (Daniel 4:33)

13. Solomon (1 Kings 3:16-28)

14. Darius (Daniel 6)

15. Josiah (2 Kings 22:1; 23:3-15)

16. Manasseh (2 Chronicles 33:1-17)

17. Herod (Matthew 2:16)

18. Saul (1 Samuel 28:3-19)

19. Jehu, who killed Jehoram and Ahaziah (2 Kings 9:21-27)

20. Herod (Luke 13:1-32)

21. Ish-bosheth (2 Samuel 2:8-10)

22. Herod (Mark 6:14-28)

23. Sargon (Isaiah 20)

24. Herod (Acts 12:21-23)

25. Agrippa (Acts 26)

26. Saul (1 Samuel 18:27)

27. Joseph (Genesis 41:45)

28. Caesar Augustus (Luke 2:1)

29. David (2 Samuel 5:5-9)

30. Asa (1 Kings 15:23)

31. David (2 Samuel 19:1-8)

32. *Adonijah (1 Kings 1:5-53)*
33. *Josiah (2 Kings 22:3-10)*
34. *Solomon (1 Kings 10:1-13)*
35. *Melchizedek, king of Salem (Hebrews 7:1-3)*
36. *Jehoash (2 Kings 11:21–12:2)*
37. *Saul (1 Samuel 18:1-29)*
38. *David*
39. *Solomon (2 Chronicles 2:1–6:2)*
40. *Abner (2 Samuel 2:8-10)*
41. *Ahab (1 Kings 21:1-7)*
42. *Psalm 51*
43. *Hezekiah (2 Kings 20:1-6)*
44. *The deaths of the firstborn (Exodus 12:29-32)*
45. *Artaxerxes (Nehemiah 1:1; 2:1)*
46. *Hezekiah (2 Chronicles 29)*
47. *Paul (2 Corinthians 11:32-33)*
48. *Baasha (1 Kings 16:1-4)*

PART 3

MATERIAL GIRLS AND BOYS

THE ROOT OF ALL EVIL?

Does the Bible really say that money is the root of all evil? Not quite (see question 40, below), but almost. In fact, money can do a great deal of good in the world. But more often, money is a source of trouble because people tend to love it (and what it can buy) more than they love God or their fellow human beings.

1. What treacherous man do we associate with 30 pieces of silver?
2. What treacherous prostitute received a hefty amount of silver for betraying a Hebrew strongman?
3. What did the chief priests buy with the silver Judas returned to them?
4. Which priest of Judah placed a money collection box near the Temple's altar?
5. What New Testament prophet told Roman soldiers to be content with their pay and to avoid taking money by force?
6. Whom did Jesus send fishing in order to get money for taxes?
7. In the parable of Lazarus and the rich man, what did Abraham say to the rich man who wanted to keep his relatives out of hell?
8. Which bird does Jeremiah compare to a man who gains riches by unjust means?
9. Which prophet condemned the idle rich on their beds of ivory?
10. What character in a parable wasted his money on prostitutes?
11. In the time of the judges, what man stole 1,100 pieces of silver from his own mother?
12. What people were so affluent that they put gold chains around their camels' necks?
13. What saintly king had a fleet built to sail for gold, though the ships never sailed?
14. Which of Jesus' parables mentions a rich man dressed in purple robes?
15. What (formerly) rich man sat in a pile of ashes?
16. What figure is portrayed in these words by Isaiah: "He made his grave with the wicked, and with the rich in his death"?
17. What woman in the time of the judges had dedicated 1,100 shekels of silver to the making of idols?
18. Where was the first piggy bank?
19. What wealthy Christian woman made her living selling purple dye?

20. What wealthy woman had a son that died of sunstroke?
21. What wealthy man had 14,000 sheep?
22. What wealthy man buried Jesus in his own tomb?
23. Which apostle proclaimed, "I have coveted no man's silver, or gold, or apparel"?
24. Who healed a crippled beggar who was asking for money?
25. Who tried to buy the gift of the Holy Spirit with money?
26. Who told his followers not to bother carrying money with them?
27. What did Jesus use to drive the money changers out of the Temple?
28. What wicked king of Israel tried to buy a man's family estate by offering him money?
29. Who sold their brother into slavery for 20 pieces of silver?
30. What financial practice (the foundation of capitalism) was forbidden in the Old Testament Law?
31. Who is the first rich man mentioned in the Bible?
32. According to Psalm 19, what is much more desirable than fine gold?
33. According to Proverbs, what is more valuable than either gold or silver?
34. Which prophet invited people who had no money to come and dine at the Lord's feast?
35. Which prophet lamented that Israel's prophets and priests did their work strictly for money?
36. Which New Testament Epistle warns against Christian congregations showing favoritism to the rich?
37. Who sat and watched rich people casting large amounts of money into the Temple treasury?
38. What husband-and-wife pair was struck dead for lying to the apostles about a church contribution?
39. What corrupt Roman official detained Paul in jail, hoping for a bribe of money?
40. What book of the Bible says that money is the root of all evil?
41. What people burned their occult books and calculated their price at 50,000 silver coins?
42. What agitator made a killing selling silver statues of a pagan goddess?
43. Which servant of a prophet was stricken with leprosy as a punishment for his greed?

THE ROOT OF ALL EVIL? (ANSWERS)

1. Judas Iscariot, the disciple who betrayed Jesus for that amount (Matthew 26:14-15)

2. Delilah, who betrayed Samson and received 1,100 pieces of silver from each of the Philistine nobles (Judges 16:4-5)

3. A field to bury strangers in (Matthew 27:6-7)

4. Jehoiada (2 Kings 12:9)

5. John the Baptist (Luke 3:2, 14)

6. Peter (Matthew 17:24-27)

7. He tells him that the people have Moses and the prophets (Luke 16:25-31).

8. A partridge (Jeremiah 17:11)

9. Amos (Amos 6:1-4)

10. The Prodigal Son (Luke 15:11-30)

11. Micah (Judges 17:1-4). He is not the same as the prophet Micah, by the way.

12. The Midianites (Judges 8:26). Considering that the outlaw Midianites gained most of their wealth by riding their camels into robberies, this was probably appropriate.

13. Jehoshaphat (1 Kings 22:48)

14. The parable of the rich man and Lazarus (Luke 16:19-31)

15. Job (Job 2:7-8)

16. The Suffering Servant (Isaiah 53:9). This was, of course, a prophecy of Christ.

17. Micah's mother (Judges 17:1-4)

18. In the Temple at Jerusalem. It was a chest ordered by King Jehoash, that had a hole bored in the lid to keep priests from stealing funds from it (2 Kings 12:9).

19. Lydia (Acts 16:14)

20. The woman of Shunam (2 Kings 4:8-37), the hostess for the prophet Elisha

21. Job (Job 42:12)

22. Joseph of Arimathea (Matthew 27:57-60)

23. Paul (Acts 20:16, 33)

24. Peter (Acts 3:2-6)

25. Simon the sorcerer (Acts 8:9, 18-20)

26. Jesus (Matthew 10:5, 9)

27. A whip made out of cords (John 2:15)

28. Ahab, who tried to buy the vineyard of Naboth (1 Kings 21:2)

29. Jacob's sons, who sold Joseph to the Ishmaelites (Genesis 37:23-28)

30. *Lending money at interest to one's brother (Deuteronomy 23:19)*

31. *Abraham (Genesis 13:2), who "was very rich in cattle, in silver, and in gold"*

32. *The judgments of the Lord (Psalm 19:9-10)*

33. *Wisdom (Proverbs 16:16)*

34. *Isaiah (Isaiah 55:1)*

35. *Micah (Micah 3:11)*

36. *James (2:1-4)*

37. *Jesus (Mark 12:41)*

38. *Ananias and Sapphira, who sold some property, gave the money to the apostles, but lied about the amount they received (Acts 5:1-11)*

39. *Felix (Acts 24:4-26)*

40. *The Bible doesn't say that. What Paul said was, "The love of money is the root of all evil" (1 Timothy 6:10).*

41. *The people of Ephesus (Acts 19:17-19), who apparently had been rather caught up in the New Age movement*

42. *Demetrius, the silversmith of Ephesus, who made images of the temple of the goddess Artemis (Acts 19:24)*

43. *Gehazi, servant of Elisha (2 Kings 5:9-27)*

 ## RICH FOLKS V. POOR FOLKS

Though the Bible does mention some rich people who were both noble and faithful—Abraham and Solomon, for example—the rich generally don't come off looking very good. And though the poor aren't always saintly, they certainly do less harm than the rich, whose greed and materialism lead them to oppress and exploit others. It won't surprise you that the Old Testament prophets—and the greatest prophet of all, Jesus of Nazareth—had a pretty low opinion of the rich in general.

1. What wealthy man, deeply moved by meeting Jesus, gave half his goods to the poor?
2. What pagan conqueror carried off all the people of Jerusalem except the poorest?
3. Which Old Testament book forbids charging interest on loans to the poor?

4. What was a poor man's Bible?
5. Who told King David a parable of a poor man who had his one pet lamb taken away from him by a rich man?
6. Which New Testament Epistle warns churches against treating rich folks better than poor folks?
7. What festival of the Jews featured giving gifts to the poor?
8. What wise king said, "Better is a poor and a wise child than an old and foolish king"?
9. To whom did Jesus say, "If thou wilt be perfect, go and sell that thou hast, and give to the poor"?
10. Who protested Jesus' anointing with oil, saying that the money spent on the oil could have been given to the poor?
11. The Christians in Greece took up a love offering for the poor Christians in what city?
12. Who said, "Though I bestow all my goods to feed the poor, and though I give my body to be burned, and have not charity, it profiteth me nothing"?
13. Who had a dream of seven lean cattle coming out of the Nile River?
14. Who stated that, being a poor man, he couldn't possibly marry Saul's daughter?
15. Which judge of Israel protested that he wasn't fit to lead because he came from a poor family?
16. What commendable deed was done by a poor widow Jesus saw in the Temple?
17. Who accused the people of Israel of selling the poor for a pair of shoes?
18. What Christian woman was noted for helping the poor in the early church?
19. Matthew quotes Jesus as saying, "Blessed are the poor in spirit" (5:3). What does he say in Luke 6:20?
20. What did Elisha miraculously supply a poor widow with?

RICH FOLKS V. POOR FOLKS (ANSWERS)

1. The tax collector Zacchaeus (Luke 19:8)

2. Nebuchadnezzar (2 Kings 25:1-12)

3. Exodus (22:25)

4. A picture book widely used in the Middle Ages in place of the Bible. Used by the illiterate, it was probably the earliest book to be printed.

5. Nathan the prophet, who was condemning David's adultery with Bathsheba (2 Samuel 12:1-10)

6. James (2:1-4)

7. Purim, which is told of in the book of Esther

8. Solomon, who (according to tradition) is the author of Ecclesiastes (4:13)

9. The rich young ruler (Matthew 19:21)

10. The disciples (Matthew 26:9)

11. Jerusalem (Romans 15:26)

12. Paul (1 Corinthians 13:3)

13. The pharaoh in Joseph's time (Genesis 41)

14. David, who did indeed marry Saul's daughter (1 Samuel 18:23)

15. Gideon (Jerubbaal) (Judges 6)

16. She put two mites (coins) in the Temple treasury, even though this was almost all she owned (Mark 12:42).

17. The Lord (Amos 2:6)

18. Dorcas (Acts 9:36, 39)

19. "Blessed are the poor."

20. Large quantities of oil (2 Kings 4:1-7)

 ## MEAN MONEY: TAXES, BRIBES, ETC.

A very wise man observed that "the power to tax is the power to destroy." Every April 15, millions of people are groaning in agreement. Perhaps we wouldn't mind taxes if we thought they supported only worthy projects. But we are all-too-aware—as were the people of the Bible—that taxes are often used to fund oppression, corruption, and wasteful government. They are "mean money," and so are extortion and bribes. It won't surprise you that the Bible does not have a high opinion of "mean money" or the people who collect it.

1. Who warned the people of Israel that having a king would mean having heavy taxation?
2. Which tax collector climbed a tree to see Jesus?
3. Who kept Paul in prison, hoping Paul would bribe him for release?

4. Who advised that the Egyptians be taxed 20 percent of their produce in order to prepare for famine?
5. Who taxed the Israelites in order to pay off Pul, the king of Assyria?
6. Whom did Jesus send fishing in order to get money for taxes?
7. What noble prophet's sons were notorious for taking bribes?
8. What figure did Jesus use as a contrast to the humble tax collector?
9. What did the hungry Esau give up to Jacob in exchange for food?
10. What was Judas given to betray Jesus?
11. By what other name was the tax collector Matthew known?
12. What did John the Baptist tell the tax collectors who came to him for baptism?
13. Who offered Delilah silver if she could find out the secret of Samson's strength?
14. Who bribed the guards at Jesus' tomb to say that the disciples had stolen the body?
15. According to the Law, how much tax did all adult Israelites have to pay when the census was taken?
16. Which ruler imposed tax in Jesus' day?
17. Who taxed his subjects in order to pay tribute to Pharaohnechoh of Egypt?
18. Which king is remembered as placing a "heavy yoke" of taxation on Israel?
19. Which king of Israel paid tribute money to King Shalmaneser of Assyria?
20. Who laid a tax on the land?
21. To which king of Judah did the Philistines bring tribute?
22. What Persian king exempted the priests and Levites from paying taxes?
23. Which ruler's taxation led to Jesus being born in Bethlehem?
24. Whose wife was threatened with having her family's house burned down unless she found the answer to Samson's riddle?
25. Who made a feast for Jesus that was attended by many tax collectors?

MEAN MONEY: TAXES, BRIBES, ETC. (ANSWERS)

1. *Samuel (1 Samuel 8). Time would prove him correct.*
2. *Zacchaeus (Luke 19:1-10), the "wee little man" of Jericho*
3. *Felix (Acts 24:24-26)*

4. Joseph *(Genesis 41:25, 34)*

5. King Menahem *(2 Kings 15:19-20)*

6. Peter *(Matthew 17:24-27)*

7. Samuel's *(1 Samuel 8:1-3)*

8. A Pharisee *(Luke 18:9-14)*

9. His birthright *(Genesis 25:29-34)*

10. Thirty pieces of silver *(Matthew 26:14-16)*

11. Levi *(Luke 5:27-32)*

12. To collect no more than was legal *(Luke 3:12-13)*

13. The lords of the Philistines *(Judges 16:4-5)*

14. The chief priests *(Matthew 28:11-15)*

15. A half shekel each *(Exodus 30:12-16)*

16. Caesar *(Matthew 22:17-22)*

17. Jehoiakim *(2 Kings 23:33-35)*

18. Solomon *(1 Kings 12:1-14)*

19. Hoshea *(2 Kings 17:3)*

20. King Ahasuerus *(Esther 10:1)*

21. Jehoshaphat *(2 Chronicles 17:11)*

22. Artaxerxes *(Ezra 7:21-24)*

23. Caesar Augustus *(Luke 2:1-7)*

24. Samson's *(Judges 14:15)*

25. Levi (or Matthew) *(Luke 5:29-32)*

 ## IT'S A STEAL!

Since the very beginning, humans have been "light-fingered," forgetting there is a line between "mine" and "yours." In fact, one of Jesus' own disciples was dipping his hands into the group treasury. The Bible is full of stories of thieving types, some of them filching things from their own families. By the way, "legal theft" by the government—taxation, that is—is such a big topic that it has a set of questions all to itself.

1. In the Bible's first recorded theft, who stole idols from her father?
2. Which robber was released from prison on the day of Jesus' crucifixion?

3. According to Malachi, what were the people of Judah stealing from God?
4. Who was stoned for stealing booty during the battle for Ai?
5. Which Epistles say that the Day of the Lord will come like a thief?
6. Which disciple of Jesus stole from the treasury?
7. In the time of the judges, what man stole 1,100 pieces of silver from his own mother?
8. What did Joseph accuse his brothers of stealing?
9. Which prophet condemns people who pile up stolen goods?
10. Numerically, which of the Ten Commandments forbids stealing?
11. What wayward son of King David "stole the hearts of the men of Israel"?
12. According to Proverbs, what kind of thief is not despised?
13. Who claimed that Jesus' disciples had stolen his body from the tomb?
14. Which prophet lamented that the "princes are rebels, the companions of thieves"?
15. What book of the Bible states that if a thief is killed during a burglary, the defender is not guilty of bloodshed?
16. What was Jesus doing when he lamented that his Father's house had been made into a "den of thieves"?
17. According to the Old Testament, what was the penalty for one who stole a sheep and sold it?
18. What book of the Bible states that "stolen waters are sweet"?
19. Who urged people to store up "treasures in heaven . . . where thieves do not break in and steal"?
20. Who stated that thieves and swindlers would not inherit the Kingdom of God?
21. In which of Jesus' parables is a man robbed, beaten, and left half-dead by the roadside?
22. When Jesus referred to the thief who "comes only to steal and destroy," to whom was he referring?
23. Which prophet quotes God as saying, "I hate robbery and iniquity"?
24. Where was Jesus when he was placed between two robbers?

IT'S A STEAL! (ANSWERS)

1. Rachel (Genesis 31:19), wife of Jacob, who stole the household idols from her father, Laban

2. Barabbas (John 18:40). Bible scholars think that Barabbas was probably an anti-Roman political agitator, and many of these were notorious for robbing (and killing) Roman officials. So Barabbas was more than just a petty thief.

3. The tithes they owed (Malachi 3:8)

4. Achan (Joshua 7:10-26)

5. 1 Thessalonians (5:2) and 2 Peter (3:10)

6. Judas Iscariot (John 12:4-6)

7. Micah (Judges 17:1-4). He was not the same as the prophet Micah.

8. His silver cup (Genesis 44:1-17)

9. Habakkuk (Habakkuk 2:6)

10. Number eight (Exodus 20:15)

11. Absalom (2 Samuel 15:2-6). More important, he was trying to steal the throne from his dad.

12. One who steals because of hunger (Proverbs 6:30)

13. The chief priests of the Jews (Matthew 28:11-13)

14. Isaiah (Isaiah 1:23)

15. Exodus (22:2)

16. Driving the money changers out of the Temple (Mark 11:15-17)

17. He had to pay the owner back with four sheep (Exodus 22:1).

18. Proverbs (9:17)

19. Jesus (Matthew 6:19-20)

20. Paul (1 Corinthians 6:10)

21. The Good Samaritan (Luke 10:30)

22. Satan (John 10:10)

23. Isaiah (Isaiah 61:8)

24. On the cross, of course, with the two thieves crucified on either side of him (Matthew 27:38)

"I WANT YOURS!"

Here's a bit of trivia for you: Nine of the Ten Commandments have to do with actions, but one has to do with intentions. We're talking about "Thou shalt not covet." This is the last commandment, but a very important one because lots of folks who would never consider murder or stealing have no qualms about coveting. After all, who knows what we're thinking? (Answer: God does.)

1. In the commandment not to covet, what is listed first among things your neighbor has that you must not covet?
2. In Genesis, what is the first thing man coveted?
3. Which apostle boasted, "I have not coveted anyone's silver or gold or clothing"?
4. Complete this saying of Jesus: "What is a man profited, if he gain the whole world and lose his own _____?"
5. Which Old Testament book says that "the eye is not satisfied with seeing, nor the ear filled with hearing"?
6. Jesus told people to lay up for themselves treasures in _____.
7. Who told people to set affection on things above, not on things on the earth?
8. Which prophet recorded God's lament that "everyone from the least to the greatest is given to covetousness"?
9. Complete this verse from Proverbs: "He that is greedy of gain troubles his own _____."
10. Which magician coveted the apostles' power of bestowing the Holy Spirit?
11. In which Epistle does Paul say that a bishop must "not be given to filthy lucre"?
12. What Old Testament book asks the question, "Wilt thou set thine eyes upon that which is not"?
13. Which prophet lamented that people "covet fields, and take them by violence"?
14. What wicked king of Israel coveted the vineyard of Naboth so much that he had him executed in order to get it?
15. Which companion of Paul forsook him "for love of this world"?

"I WANT YOURS!" (ANSWERS)

1. *His house (Exodus 20:17)*

2. *The forbidden fruit in Eden, of course (Genesis 3:4-6). More accurately, it was the godlike power that the serpent promised Adam and Eve if they ate the fruit.*

3. *Paul (Acts 20:16-33)*

4. *Soul (Matthew 16:26)*

5. *Ecclesiastes (1:8)*

6. *Heaven (Matthew 6:20)*

7. *Paul (Colossians 3:2)*

8. *Jeremiah (Jeremiah 6:13)*

9. *House (Proverbs 15:27)*

10. *Simon (Acts 8:9-23), who then tried to buy the power from them*

11. *Titus (1:7)*

12. *Proverbs (23:5)*

13. *Micah (Micah 2:2)*

14. *Ahab (1 Kings 21)*

15. *Demas (2 Timothy 4:10)*

 THE ROOT OF ALL EVIL? (PART 2)

More questions about money and its usually negative effects on human beings . . .

1. According to Jesus, what is easier than a rich man entering the Kingdom of Heaven?
2. Who was given money to say that Jesus' disciples had stolen his body from the tomb?
3. What church was becoming smug and lazy because of its wealth?
4. Who were the first wealthy men to set eyes on Jesus?
5. Which king of Israel became legendary for both his wealth and his wisdom (and a lot of wives, to boot)?
6. What man did Jesus tell to sell all his possessions and give the proceeds to the poor?
7. Omri, king of Israel, paid 6,000 pieces of silver to buy the land to build what famous city?

8. What pagan military officer was willing to pay 30,000 pieces of silver and 6,000 pieces of gold to be cured of leprosy?

9. When Joseph sent his 11 brothers back to Canaan, which brother did he supply with 300 pieces of silver and five changes of clothes?

10. During the Syrians' siege of Samaria, what peculiar food was selling for the outrageous price of 80 pieces of silver?

11. Which book of the Bible contains the lament of a wealthy man who was not satisfied with his money?

12. What good king of Judah was stupid enough to display his treasures to the ambassadors from Babylon?

13. Who uttered the famous words "Woe to you who are rich"?

14. Which Old Testament book offers this wise advice: "He that loveth silver shall not be satisfied with silver; nor he that loveth abundance with increase"?

15. Does the Bible approve of a graduated tax system?

16. According to Psalms, what type of moneylender would be considered pure enough to enter the Lord's Temple?

17. Which prophet condemned the rich of Israel for selling out the poor for money?

18. In which book of prophecy would you find these words: "The silver is mine, and the gold is mine, saith the Lord of hosts"?

19. What neighbor nation of Israel is most often condemned for being such wheeler-dealers in money?

20. According to 1 Timothy, what type of man should not be a lover of money?

21. Which of Jesus' disciples had charge of the group's money?

22. According to Proverbs, what type of money dwindles away?

23. What soothsaying slave girl made a great deal of money for her owners?

24. Which New Testament Epistle advises, "Keep your lives free from the love of money, and be satisfied with what you have"?

25. What type of people were the Jews allowed to lend money to with interest?

26. Which king held a grand feast to show off his vast wealth?

27. What 80-year-old rich man lamented that he could no longer taste food nor hear the voices of singers?

28. Who was the shortest wealthy man in the Bible?

29. In Jesus' parable of the sower and the seed, what symbolizes the people whose love of money keeps them from becoming believers?

30. Which prophet lamented that the people of Israel had made their wealth by cheating their customers?

31. What was one of the unfortunate results of good King Jehoshaphat of Judah becoming wealthy?
32. What nasty Persian official boasted to his friends about how wealthy he was?
33. What young king pleased the Lord by praying for wisdom instead of for wealth?
34. The book of Proverbs states, "Give me neither poverty nor riches." What, instead, is requested?
35. In Jesus' parable, what happened to the rich man who had to build bigger storehouses in which to keep all his wealth?
36. Whom did Paul praise for being as generous as rich people, even though they were poor?
37. Which of the psalms contains the "can't take it with you" philosophy?
38. Which New Testament epistle of Paul's instructs the rich to be "rich in good works"?
39. What great city, famous for its wealth (and vice), is destroyed in the book of Revelation?
40. Who confronted King David with an incriminating parable about a rich man who takes away a poor man's prized possession?
41. What foreign visitor was deeply impressed with King Solomon's wealth?
42. Which New Testament book says that a rich man's wealth will vanish like a wildflower withering?
43. What name do the Gospels use for the worship of money?
44. The original Greek text of the New Testament mentions a coin called an *assarion*. How does the English Bible translate this?
45. When Paul wrote "The love of money is the root of all evil," the Greek word translated "money" actually refers to a metal. Which one?
46. In only one place in the Bible is a coin's appearance referred to. Whose face was on the coin?
47. According to Jeremiah, a rich man should not boast of his riches, but boast of what?
48. Which group of Jews, reputed to be very religious, are referred to in Luke's Gospel as "money-lovers"?

THE ROOT OF ALL EVIL? (PART 2) (ANSWERS)

1. A camel going through the eye of a needle (Matthew 19:24)

2. The Roman soldiers (Matthew 28:1-15)

3. The church at Laodicea (Revelation 3:14-18)

4. Probably the wise men, or magi. Because they brought expensive gifts (gold, frankincense, myrrh) and had traveled a long way, they were undoubtedly well-heeled.

5. Solomon

6. The rich young nobleman, who is not mentioned by name (Matthew 19:16-22). The young man did not take Jesus up on his offer.

7. Samaria, which he made the capital of his kingdom (1 Kings 16:24)

8. Naaman, the Syrian who was eventually cured by the prophet Elisha (2 Kings 5:5)

9. Benjamin, who was his only full brother of the large brood (Joseph and Benjamin being the two sons of Jacob and Rachel) (Genesis 45:22)

10. A donkey's head (2 Kings 6:25). We have to assume that the Samaritans were on the verge of starvation.

11. Ecclesiastes (2:1-11), which supposedly was written by rich King Solomon

12. Hezekiah (Isaiah 39:2). Later on, the Babylonians attacked Jerusalem and carried off all the treasures.

13. Jesus (Luke 6:9-24)

14. Ecclesiastes (5:10)

15. Apparently not, because Exodus 30:11-16 describes a tax in which the rich and the poor pay the same amount.

16. One who had not charged interest (Psalm 15:5). Consider that when you look at the interest rate on your credit card statement.

17. Amos (Amos 8:6)

18. Haggai (2:8)

19. The people of the seacoast city of Tyre, which was renowned in ancient times for being a city of merchants. It is mentioned dozens of times in the Old Testament.

20. A church's bishop (or "overseer" or "leader," depending on the translation you have) (1 Timothy 3:3). For that matter, no Christian is supposed to be a lover of money.

21. Judas (John 13:29)

22. Money obtained dishonestly (Proverbs 13:11)

23. The fortune-teller of Philippi. She lost her ability when Paul exorcised the demon that gave her this ability (Acts 16:16-18).

24. Hebrews (13:5)

25. Foreigners—that is, non-Jews (Deuteronomy 23:20). Jews could not charge interest to a fellow Jew.

26. Ahasuerus, the Persian king who later married the Jewish girl Esther (Esther 1:2-4)

27. Barzillai, a good friend of King David (2 Samuel 19:32-35)

28. Probably Zacchaeus, the wealthy tax collector of Jericho, who was so short he had to climb a tree to see Jesus passing through (Luke 19:1-10)

29. The seeds that fall among the thorns, the thorns symbolizing wealth (Matthew 13:18-23)

30. Hosea, who mentions using "false scales" to falsify business transactions (Hosea 12:7)

31. He married off one of his children to the family of wicked King Ahab of Israel (2 Chronicles 18:1).

32. Haman, the official who plotted to have all the Jews exterminated (Esther 5:11)

33. Solomon, who ended up being both rich and wise (1 Kings 3:5-15)

34. Food (Proverbs 30:8)

35. He died (Luke 12:16-21).

36. The Christians in Macedonia (2 Corinthians 8:1-4)

37. Psalm 49. All 20 verses are directed against the foolishness of trusting in riches. Most of the psalm dwells on the idea that even the rich man must die, leaving his wealth to someone else.

38. 1 Timothy (6:17-19)

39. Babylon (which may be a sort of code name for the city of Rome) (Revelation 18:21)

40. The prophet Nathan. He was chastising David for his adultery with Bathsheba, whose husband had been killed at David's command (2 Samuel 12:1-25).

41. The queen of Sheba, who was herself rather well-heeled (1 Kings 10:4-7)

42. James (1:10-11)

43. Mammon, who is not a god, though Jesus uses the words "You cannot serve both God and mammon" (Matthew 6:24)

44. "Penny" in most modern versions (Matthew 10:29; Luke 12:6). The King James Version (reflecting its British origin) has "farthing." An assarion, a penny, and a farthing are all very small coins.

45. Silver. The Greek word is philarguria, literally the "love of silver."

46. Caesar's, meaning that it was a Roman coin (Matthew 22:18-21)

47. That he knows the Lord (Jeremiah 9:23)

48. The Pharisees (Luke 16:14)

PART 4

BAD COMPANY

HANGIN' WITH THE WRONG CROWD

What comes easier to human beings—following the small group that behaves itself or following the crowd that seriously misbehaves? A no-brainer, isn't it? You might say that caving in to peer pressure is a kind of moral laziness, taking the easy path in life. It's usually just a small group—the Bible uses the word *remnant*—that manages to resist the temptations of bad companions.

1. What book of the Bible opens with the words, "Blessed is the man that walks not in the counsel of the ungodly"?
2. Complete this verse from Exodus: "You shall not follow a crowd to do _____."
3. What Christian writer quoted the old proverb "Bad companions corrupt good morals"?
4. According to Proverbs, a companion of _____ shames his father.
5. Who split the kingdom of Israel in two by following the advice of his arrogant young friends?
6. From what corrupt city was Lot and his family delivered by God's angels?
7. Complete this famous verse from Romans: "Be not conformed to this world, but be _____ by the renewing of your mind."
8. What book of the Bible is the source of this verse: "I had rather be a doorkeeper in the house of my God than to dwell in the tents of wickedness"?
9. Which apostle noted that the pagans thought it strange that Christians no longer followed them in immorality?
10. Who noted that "wide is the gate, and broad is the way, that leads to destruction and many there are which go in there"?
11. Complete this verse from Proverbs: "He that walks with wise men shall be wise, but a companion of fools shall be _____."
12. Which prophet observed that his nation's princes were "companions of thieves"?
13. Who referred to sin as a little leaven that leavens the whole lump?
14. In what book of the Bible does God say, "Come out of her, my people, and be not partakers of her sins"?
15. According to Paul, Christians should not be "unequally _____ together with unbelievers."
16. Complete this verse from Proverbs: "The righteous is more excellent than his neighbor, but the way of the wicked _____ them."

17. Which prophet lamented that he dwelled "in the midst of a people of unclean lips"?
18. In the Old Testament, wicked people are often referred to as "sons of _____."
19. Which prophet said of his nation, "They are all adulterers, an assembly of treacherous men"?
20. According to Paul, Christians should "have no fellowship with the unfruitful works of _____."
21. What book of the Bible says, "Depart from me, all you workers of iniquity"?
22. In Jeremiah, God tells people to "flee out of the midst of" what wicked city?
23. Complete this saying of Paul: "Come out from among them, and be _____."
24. According to the book of Numbers, evil neighbors will prove to be "_____ in your sides."
25. Which king let his hundreds of wives and concubines lead him into worshipping false gods?
26. What book of the Bible tells people to "make no friendship with an angry man, and with a furious man thou shalt not go"?
27. Which group of Christians did Paul accuse of being "bewitched" by false teachers?

HANGIN' WITH THE WRONG CROWD (ANSWERS)

1. Psalms
2. Evil (Exodus 23:2)
3. Paul (1 Corinthians 15:33)
4. Riotous men (Proverbs 28:7)
5. Rehoboam, Solomon's son (1 Kings 12)
6. Sodom, of course (Genesis 19:1-29)
7. Transformed (Romans 12:2)
8. Psalms (Psalm 84:10)
9. Peter (1 Peter 4:3-4)
10. Jesus (Matthew 7:13)
11. Destroyed (Proverbs 13:20)
12. Isaiah (Isaiah 1:23)

13. *Paul (1 Corinthians 5:6). Leaven is yeast, of course. Sin is like yeast working through a lump of bread dough.*

14. *Revelation (18:4)*

15. *Yoked (2 Corinthians 6:14)*

16. *Seduces (Proverbs 12:26)*

17. *Isaiah (Isaiah 6:5)*

18. *Belial. Roughly, this means "sons of worthlessness."*

19. *Jeremiah (Jeremiah 9:2)*

20. *Darkness (Ephesians 5:11)*

21. *Psalms (Psalm 6:8)*

22. *Babylon (Jeremiah 51:6)*

23. *Separate (2 Corinthians 6:17)*

24. *Thorns (Numbers 33:55). Obviously, the Bible is the source of "thorn in one's side."*

25. *Solomon (1 Kings 11:3-4)*

26. *Proverbs (22:24)*

27. *The Galatians (3:1)—"O foolish Galatians!"*

 ## ENEMIES LISTS

Here's something that ought to be obvious: In a sinful world, good people make enemies, sometimes very powerful ones. Could you name a certain person if you saw a list of that person's enemies and opponents? Give it a try. In the left column below are various groupings of enemies. In the right column are the "good guys" (not necessarily perfect, but good) whom the enemies opposed. Match each group of enemies on the left to the correct person on the right. And note that the various enemies in each group weren't necessarily working together or at the same time.

1. Judas, Caiaphas, Herod
2. Absalom, Goliath, Ziba
3. Pharaoh, Dathan, Korah
4. Judah, Reuben, Simeon
5. Ahab, Jezebel
6. Sennacherib, Rabshakeh, Rabsaris
7. Demetrius, Alexander, Ananias

a. Paul
b. Nehemiah
c. Hezekiah
d. John the Baptist
e. Jeremiah
f. Elijah
g. Jesus

8. Sanballat, Tobiah, Geshem
9. Herod, Herodias
10. Pashur, Hananiah, Jehoiakim

h. Moses
i. Joseph
j. David

ENEMIES LISTS (ANSWERS)

1. *g., Jesus*

2. *j., David*

3. *h., Moses*

4. *i., Joseph*

5. *f., Elijah*

6. *c., Hezekiah*

7. *a., Paul*

8. *b., Nehemiah*

9. *d., John the Baptist*

10. *e., Jeremiah*

 BAD SEED: KIDS GONE WILD

Can good people raise rotten kids? Definitely. (So can bad people, but that's pretty obvious.) In a few cases, rotten parents produce good kids. The sad truth is, we have no way of knowing how our kids will turn out. The Bible simply commands parents to do the best they can, which includes being strict, not indulgent. The questions below deal not only with bad kids, but also with parents whose lousy parenting skills are also condemned in the Bible.

1. Which king with many wives and many children almost lost his throne to his rebellious son Absalom?
2. What wicked king of Israel had 70 sons?
3. What good man made sacrifices in case any of his children had sinned?
4. Which Epistle advises, "Children, obey your parents in the Lord"?
5. According to Malachi, which prophet will come back to earth to turn the hearts of the children to their fathers?
6. To whom did Paul advise that a bishop must be able to control his own children?

7. In which Gospel did Jesus say that children rebelling against their parents would be a sign of the end times?

8. Which of the Ten Commandments states that children will be punished for their parents' sins?

9. Who advised young Christians to stop thinking like children?

10. What book of the Bible says that a child raised up in the right way will not depart from it?

11. Which priest was too indulgent toward his spoiled sons?

12. Which prophet had dishonest sons who took bribes?

13. Which king grieved and wailed over his wayward son?

14. According to the Law, what was the penalty for anyone who attacked his mother or father?

15. Which prophet talked about children dishonoring their parents, so that a man's enemies are in his own household?

16. According to Deuteronomy, what should be done to a rebellious son who would not submit to discipline?

17. Which of Gideon's (Jerubbaal) 70 sons (the youngest) was the only one to escape the plot of his scheming brother, Abimelech?

18. What book of the Bible says that children will not be put to death for their parents' sins?

19. Which Epistle advises fathers not to exasperate their children?

20. Which prophet said that a son would not share the guilt of the father?

21. Manasseh, one of the rottenest kings of Judah, was the son of what virtuous father?

22. Complete this famous verse from Ezekiel: "The fathers have eaten sour _____, and the children's teeth are set on edge."

23. Josiah, one of the finest kings of the entire Bible, was the son and grandson of what two wicked kings?

24. Athaliah, the murderous queen of Judah, had what wicked king and queen as parents?

25. Which son of the godly king Jehoshaphat had all his brothers killed by the sword when he came to the throne?

BAD SEED: KIDS GONE WILD (ANSWERS)

1. *David (2 Samuel 15–18)*

2. *Ahab (2 Kings 10:1)*

3. *Job (Job 1:5)*

4. Ephesians (6:1)

5. Elijah (Malachi 4:5-6)

6. Timothy (1 Timothy 1:2; 3:2-4)

7. Mark (13:4, 12)

8. The second (against graven images) (Exodus 20:4-5)

9. Paul (1 Corinthians 1:1; 14:20)

10. Proverbs (22:6)

11. Eli (1 Samuel 3:12-13)

12. Samuel (1 Samuel 8:1-3)

13. David (2 Samuel 18:24, 33), who lamented loud and long over the death of the rebellious Absalom

14. Death (Exodus 21:15)

15. Micah (Micah 1:1; 7:6)

16. He should be stoned (Deuteronomy 21:18-21).

17. Jotham (Judges 9:1-5)

18. Deuteronomy (24:16)

19. Ephesians (6:4)

20. Ezekiel (Ezekiel 18:20)

21. Hezekiah (2 Kings 20:21–21:18)

22. Grapes (Ezekiel 18:2)

23. Son of Amon, grandson of Manasseh (2 Kings 21:18, 25-26)

24. Ahab and Jezebel (2 Kings 11)

25. Jehoram (2 Chronicles 21:4), who also married the wicked Athaliah, daughter of Ahab and Jezebel

 ## BROTHERLY LOVE (HA!)

According to Proverbs, there is a type of friend who "sticks closer than a brother." Well, considering how brothers often treat each other, we can only say, "We hope so!" For all our talk about "brotherly love," real brothers seem more inclined to quarrel and hate than to love. (Proverbs is more realistic about brother relations when it states that "an offended brother is more unyielding than a fortified city.") And, of course, the original brother-against-brother story goes all the way back to the very first brothers on the planet.

1. Whose sulking older brother refused to attend the joyous welcome-home party?
2. Which son of Gideon (Jerubbaal) killed 70 of his brothers at once?
3. Which judge, an illegitimate son, was thrown out of the house by his brothers?
4. Who hated his brother for taking away his birthright?
5. What did Moses rebuke his brother, Aaron, for?
6. Who was the first man to murder his brother?
7. Who hated his brother Amnon for what he had done to Tamar?
8. What dreamy boy was hated for being his father's favorite?
9. What older brother of David chewed him out for coming to watch the Israelites fighting the Philistines?
10. What nasty king of Judah had his brothers killed with the sword after he came to the throne?

BROTHERLY LOVE (HA!) (ANSWERS)

1. The Prodigal Son's (Luke 15:20-28)

2. Abimelech (Judges 8:35; 9:1-5)

3. Jephthah (Judges 11:1-2)

4. Esau (Genesis 27:41)

5. Making the gold calf (Exodus 32:19-22)

6. Cain (Genesis 4:8), who also happened to be the first man to have a brother

7. Absalom (2 Samuel 13:22)

8. Joseph (Genesis 37:1-4)

9. Eliab (1 Samuel 17:28-29)

10. Jehoram (2 Chronicles 21:4)

 ## SOME SO-CALLED FRIENDS

The Bible presents us with some truly great friendships—David and Jonathan, Ruth and Naomi, Paul and Barnabas, Jeremiah and Baruch, and many others. It also has a lot to say (especially in Proverbs) about the value of loyal friends. Alas, there is the flip side of all this: so-called friends who give bad advice, turn traitorous, and otherwise behave abominably.

1. Before Jesus' arrest, to what treacherous man did he say, "Friend, wherefore art thou come"?
2. Which king of Israel was accused of loving his enemies and hating his friends?
3. What suffering man received no comfort from his three talkative (and critical) friends?
4. What two unscrupulous rulers became friends after they met Jesus?
5. Who gave his Philistine wife to his best man?
6. What pitiful man lamented, "My friends scorn me: but mine eye poureth out tears unto God"?
7. Which New Testament Epistle warns that friendship with the world is enmity with God?
8. What lecherous son of David had a calculating friend who devised a scheme in which the prince would rape his half sister?
9. Who warned his followers that they would be betrayed by their friends and relatives?
10. Who warned the Israelites against letting friends seduce them into worshipping false gods?
11. Who scolded Job's three friends for not speaking the whole truth about God?
12. According to Proverbs, what type of person causes best friends to go their separate ways?
13. Which prophet predicted that friends would eat one another's flesh during a siege of Jerusalem?
14. Which prophet warned against trusting a friend?
15. Who was accused of being "a friend of tax collectors and sinners"?

SOME SO-CALLED FRIENDS (ANSWERS)

1. Judas Iscariot (Matthew 26:50), who betrayed him with a kiss. "Friend," indeed!

2. David, who was so accused because of the grief he showed over his rebellious son Absalom (2 Samuel 18:24; 19:4-7).

3. Job, whose friends were Zophar, Eliphaz, and Bildad (Job 2:11)

4. Herod and Pilate (Luke 23:6-12)

5. Samson (Judges 14:20). Some translations simply refer to this person as "friend," though in this context it more specifically means "friend and best man."

6. Job (Job 16:20)

7. James (4:4)

8. Amnon, whose friend Jonadab concocted the scheme for Amnon to seduce Tamar (2 Samuel 13)

9. Jesus (Luke 21:16)

10. Moses (Deuteronomy 5:1; 13:6-8)

11. God (Job 42:7)

12. A whisperer (Proverbs 16:28)

13. Jeremiah (Jeremiah 19:9)

14. Micah (Micah 7:5)

15. Jesus (Luke 7:34). It was true, of course, but the accusation shows that Jesus' enemies had no concept of God's love and compassion.

 # NEXT OF KIN

Would you recognize famous Bible characters by hearing their relatives named? For example: Wife was Eve, sons were Cain and Abel. Answer: Adam (of course). Keep in mind that the people below weren't "all bad all the time." Some were real villains, others were good folks who wandered from the right path.

1. Father was Kish, son was Jonathan
2. Wife was Jezebel, father was Omri, son was Ahaziah
3. Brother was Jacob, mother was Rebecca, father was Isaac
4. Brothers were Abel and Seth
5. Wife was Herodias, father was Herod the king
6. Father was Solomon, grandfather was David, son was Abijam
7. Father was Noah, brothers were Shem and Japheth
8. Father was Judah, wife was Tamar, brother was Onan
9. Father was Ethbaal, husband was Ahab, daughter was Athaliah
10. Father was David, brother was Absalom, sister was Tamar
11. Father was Gideon (Jerubbaal), brother was Jotham
12. Brother was Abiram, father was Eliab
13. Father was Josiah, mother was Hamutal, brother was Eliakim
14. Brothers were Moses and Aaron

15. Father was Ahab, mother was Jezebel, sister was Athaliah
16. Father was Hezekiah, son was Amon

NEXT OF KIN (ANSWERS)

1. *King Saul*

2. *Ahab, wicked king of Israel*

3. *Esau*

4. *Cain*

5. *Herod Antipas (not the Herod at the time of Jesus' birth, but the second Herod, who executed John the Baptist and met with the arrested Jesus)*

6. *Rehoboam, whose arrogance split Israel into two kingdoms (1 Kings 12)*

7. *Ham (Genesis 9:18)*

8. *Er (Genesis 38:6-7), killed by God for his wickedness*

9. *Jezebel*

10. *Amnon (2 Samuel 13)*

11. *Abimelech, who murdered all his 70 brothers, except Jotham (Judges 9:1-6)*

12. *Dathan, one of the lead rebels against Moses (Numbers 16)*

13. *Jehoahaz, king of Judah (2 Kings 23:31-34)*

14. *Miriam, who (along with Aaron) briefly rebelled against Moses (Numbers 12)*

15. *Ahaziah, king of Israel (2 Kings 1)*

16. *Manasseh, king of Judah (2 Kings 21)*

MARRIAGES MADE IN HEAVEN . . . OR ELSEWHERE

"Love and marriage go together. . . ." Well, that's what the song tells us, anyway. The reality is sometimes different, and the Bible is definitely grounded in reality. Human beings aren't perfect, and neither are most marriages. In fact, you might say that things have been going wrong with marriage ever since Adam and Eve.

1. What wealthy king was led into idol worship by his many foreign wives?
2. Who made a wedding feast before giving the wrong bride to Jacob?

3. What gruesome objects did Saul require from David as dowry for his daughter?
4. Who prompted the Jews after the Babylonian exile to divorce their foreign wives?
5. Who made a seven-day marriage feast but never married the woman?
6. When Shechem the Hivite asked to marry Dinah, what did her brothers ask as a dowry?
7. What evil king of Israel was under the thumb of his equally evil, foreign-born wife?
8. What unscrupulous king divorced his first wife to marry his brother's wife?
9. Who was the first polygamist?
10. Who said that Moses allowed divorce because of people's hardness of heart?
11. Where does the Bible prohibit polygamy?
12. Which prophet spoke about Jews who divorced their wives to marry pagan women?
13. Who was thrown into prison for criticizing the marriage of a king?
14. Who married a prostitute named Gomer?
15. What wicked Persian official had a wife named Zeresh?
16. What husband and wife lied to the apostles about their finances?
17. Whose disobedient wife turned into a pillar of salt?
18. What unnamed wife urged her husband to curse God?
19. What wicked priest had a wife who would become a harlot?
20. What marital sin did Paul condemn in 1 Corinthians 5?
21. Who made it very clear that married people are no longer married to each other in the afterlife?
22. Which Old Testament book contains detailed regulations about incest?
23. What book of the Bible states that it is "better to dwell in a corner of the housetop than with a brawling woman in a wide house"?
24. Who said that any man who divorces his wife and marries another commits adultery?
25. Who told Christians that it was permissible for a believer to let go of an unbelieving spouse?
26. Which Epistle says that "whoremongers and adulterers God will judge"?
27. Which daughter of a king married one man, was taken from him, married another, then returned to the first husband?

28. Who received a threatening dream from God because he had taken Abraham's wife Sarah into his harem?
29. Which king was told by a prophet that the child born of his adulterous affair with another man's wife would die?
30. What book of the Bible notes that "the eye of the adulterer waits for the twilight"?
31. Which Old Testament book is filled with warnings against the adulterous woman?
32. Which prophet lamented that "the land is full of adulterers"?
33. What brief New Testament book warns against "going after strange flesh"?
34. Who sent the servant woman Hagar away at his wife's urging?

MARRIAGES MADE IN HEAVEN . . . OR ELSEWHERE (ANSWERS)

1. Solomon (1 Kings 11:3-8)

2. Laban, Jacob's crafty uncle (Genesis 29:22-26)

3. A hundred Philistine foreskins (1 Samuel 18:25-27)

4. Ezra (Ezra 10)

5. Samson (Judges 14:10-20)

6. That all of Shechem's men be circumcised (Genesis 34). While they were recovering from the ordeal, they were murdered by Dinah's brothers.

7. Ahab, who, with his wife Jezebel, might well qualify as the wickedest married couple in the Bible (1 Kings 18–22).

8. Herod (Matthew 14:3-4)

9. Lamech (Genesis 4:19)

10. Jesus (Matthew 19:8)

11. It doesn't.

12. Malachi (Malachi 2:10-16)

13. John the Baptist (Matthew 14:3-4)

14. Hosea (Hosea 1:1-3)

15. Haman (Esther 5:12-14; 6:13)

16. Ananias and Sapphira (Acts 5:1-11)

17. Lot's wife (Genesis 19:26), who disobeyed the Lord's command not to look back at the burning city of Sodom

18. Job's wife (Job 2:3-10)

19. Amaziah (Amos 7:10-17)

20. *A man was sleeping with his father's wife. Presumably this was not his own mother, but his father's second wife.*

21. *Jesus (Matthew 22:39-30). This is certainly a piece of good news for people unhappily married.*

22. *Leviticus, (18:1-18)*

23. *Proverbs (21:9)*

24. *Jesus (Luke 16:1, 18)*

25. *Paul (1 Corinthians 7:13-17)*

26. *Hebrews (13:4)*

27. *Michal, daughter of Saul. She married David, then Phaltiel, but David insisted on having her back, much to the distress of Phaltiel (1 Samuel 24:44; 2 Samuel 3:13-16).*

28. *Abimelech, who, to his credit, was not aware that the two were married (Genesis 20:3)*

29. *David, who had committed adultery with Bathsheba (2 Samuel 12:1-14)*

30. *Job (24:15)*

31. *Proverbs (especially chapter 7)*

32. *Jeremiah (Jeremiah 23:10)*

33. *Jude, (1:7)*

34. *Abraham (Genesis 21:9-14), whose wife, Sarah, regretted suggesting that Abraham father a child by Hagar*

 ## PARTNERS IN CRIME: SINNING IN PAIRS

Most of us don't need anyone to egg us on to do bad things. We do just fine sinning solo! But it's always easier to fall into sin if you have someone else giving you a nudge—while you nudge in return. Some of the pairs/couples/duos below are well-known, others less so. All were "sin partners."

1. What married couple died after lying to the apostles about the value of the possessions they had sold?
2. What two women brought about the execution of John the Baptist?
3. What two brothers killed Hamor and Shechem for seducing their sister Dinah?

4. Which priests—two of Aaron's sons—were killed because they offered "strange fire" to the Lord?
5. What two gluttonous priests were notorious for keeping the sacrificial meat for themselves?
6. Who requested special places for themselves in Jesus' Kingdom?
7. What two sinful cities were destroyed by fire and brimstone from heaven?
8. What were the names of two of the magicians in Pharaoh's court at the time of Moses?
9. What married couple were the Bible's original villains?
10. In Revelation, who is the evil companion of the Beast?
11. Absalom—the handsome, rebellious son of King David—was egged on to his treachery by what evil counselor?
12. What great leader of Israel had to face a near-rebellion by his own brother and sister?
13. What two sisters got their father drunk and slept with him?
14. What two brothers helped lead a rebellion against Moses in the wilderness?
15. Which king and which prophet of Moab tried but failed to put a lasting curse on the Israelites?
16. What two political enemies got chummy following the trial of Jesus?
17. Which Jew revealed the murder plot of two of the Persian king's eunuchs against their king?
18. What brutal punishment was inflicted on Zimri while he lay with his Midianite mistress?
19. What army leader conspired with Ish-bosheth, Saul's son, to make Ish-bosheth king instead of David?
20. What two kings of Midian were defeated in battle by the judge Gideon?
21. Which son of David had a scheming friend named Jonadab who plotted the seduction of David's daughter Tamar?
22. What wicked queen was killed when two of her eunuchs pushed her out a window?
23. What two priests led the Jewish opposition to Jesus?
24. The soldier Joab and the priest Abiathar joined in an attempt to make which son of David king?
25. What two evil kings, united in a military alliance, were assassinated by the future king Jehu?
26. Which rebuilder of Jerusalem was opposed in his work by Sanballat and Tobiah?

27. What saintly leader of Israel had two corrupt sons who scandalized the Israelites?
28. At Jesus' trial before the council, what did the two false witnesses accuse him of?
29. What two Christian women of Philippi were asked by Paul to stop their quarreling?
30. Which king of Judah was assassinated through the plotting of Zabad and Jehozabad?

PARTNERS IN CRIME: SINNING IN PAIRS (ANSWERS)

1. Ananias and Sapphira (Acts 5:1-11)

2. Herodias and her daughter (Mark 6:22-29)

3. Levi and Simeon (Genesis 34:1-26). Depending on how you look at it, the two were either defending the family honor or behaving like violent creeps.

4. Nadab and Abihu (Numbers 3:4). We aren't quite sure what "strange fire" was, but we know it did not please God.

5. Hophni and Phinehas (1 Samuel 2:16-17, 34)

6. James and John (Mark 10:35-41). On this occasion their pride and ego got the better of them.

7. Sodom and Gomorrah (Genesis 19:24)

8. Jannes and Jambres (2 Timothy 3:8). These are not, by the way, named in the book of Exodus. The names in 2 Timothy are from Jewish folklore.

9. Adam and Eve, both of them disobeying God and being expelled from Eden

10. The false prophet, who performs miracles on behalf of the Beast (Revelation 16:13-14; 19:19-20)

11. Ahitophel, who had once been a trusted counselor of David. When Absalom's revolt failed, Ahitophel hung himself (2 Samuel 17:1-23).

12. Moses, who faced down the opposition of Miriam and Aaron (Numbers 12)

13. The daughters of Lot, who became the ancestors of the Moabites and the Ammonites (Genesis 19:30-38)

14. Dathan and Abiram, who, along with the other rebels, were destroyed when the earth opened up to swallow them (Numbers 16)

15. Balak (the king) and Balaam (the prophet). After a fateful encounter with an angel, Balaam ended up blessing Israel (Numbers 23–24).

16. Pilate and Herod (Luke 23:12)

17. *Mordecai, who passed the information on to his cousin Esther, the king's wife (Esther 2:21-23)*

18. *Phinehas, Aaron's grandson, drove a spear through both of them (Numbers 25:1-8).*

19. *Abner (2 Samuel 2:8-9)*

20. *Zebah and Zalmunna (Judges 8:4-13)*

21. *Amnon, whose rape of his half sister is one of the more sordid stories in the Bible (2 Samuel 13)*

22. *Jezebel (2 Kings 9:30-33)*

23. *Annas and Caiaphas (John 18:12-24)*

24. *Adonijah (1 Kings 1:5-53). The coup failed, and Solomon became king.*

25. *Jehoram of Israel and Ahaziah of Judah (2 Kings 9:24-27)*

26. *Nehemiah (Nehemiah 4; 6)*

27. *Samuel, whose sons were Joel and Abiah (1 Samuel 8:1-3)*

28. *Saying he would destroy the Temple and rebuild it in three days (Matthew 26:60-61)*

29. *Euodias and Syntyche (Philippians 4:2)*

30. *Joash (2 Chronicles 24:25-26). If you knew this answer you are very, very well read in the Bible.*

 ## THREE'S MISERY: THE POLYGAMY PROBLEM

It's pretty clear in Genesis that God's original intention for marriage was one man for one woman. It wasn't long, however, before things changed, with men taking multiple wives and having children by them, creating blended families that didn't always blend, creating jealous wives, and generally proving that the original one-man-for-one-woman plan was best. Even though some of the great men of the Bible were polygamists—David and Solomon, to name the most prominent—those great men's lives were dreadfully complicated by having more than one wife. No wonder that, by the time of Jesus, polygamy had almost died out in Israel.

1. What man in Genesis 4 was the first to have more than one wife?
2. What wise and wealthy king of Israel had hundreds of foreign wives who led him into idol worship?
3. What book of the Bible warns against what happened in question 2?

4. What crafty character in Genesis created an unhappy home by marrying two sisters?
5. What book of the Bible specifically forbids marrying two sisters?
6. What book of the Bible says that when a man marries a second wife, he must not deprive the first one of food, clothing, or sex?
7. What name was given to servant women who had sexual relations with their masters and often had children by them?
8. Which servant did Abraham father a child by, creating strife in his home?
9. Who was Jacob's favorite wife?
10. Who grieved his parents by marrying two Hittite women named Judith and Bashemath?
11. What book of the Bible tells husbands they must not show preferential treatment to the sons of the wife they happen to love most?
12. What great leader was the son of a long-childless woman who had been taunted by a rival wife?
13. What great king had Michal as the first of his many wives?
14. Which prophet predicted a horrible future time when seven women would gladly make themselves the wife of one man?
15. Which kingdom-splitting king had 18 wives and 60 concubines?
16. What man with many wives had an adulterous fling with the wife of one of his captains?
17. What Persian king got a warning from God while dining with his wives, concubines, and nobles?
18. Which son of David fell in love with, then raped, his half sister?
19. What became of that son of David?
20. According to Paul's letter to Timothy, what church officials must have only one wife?
21. Which son of the judge Gideon murdered his 70 brothers?
22. Which judge of Israel was denied his inheritance by his many brothers?
23. Which patriarch in Genesis took Keturah as his third wife?
24. What evil king, much influenced by his dominating foreign wife, also had other wives?
25. What foreign king dumped his disobedient wife and married a Jewish girl?
26. What woman, given as wife to Phaltiel by her father, was later reclaimed by David?

THREE'S MISERY: THE POLYGAMY PROBLEM (ANSWERS)

1. Lamech, who had two wives (Genesis 4:19-24)

2. Solomon, described as having 700 wives "of royal birth" (1 Kings 11), but being foreign-born they led him away from fully serving the true God

3. Deuteronomy (17:17): "Neither shall he [the king] multiply wives to himself, that his heart turn not away."

4. Jacob, whose family affairs fill up Genesis 29 through 37

5. Leviticus (18:18), which, alas, was written after the time of Jacob and his wives

6. Exodus (21:10). Apparently this law was designed to make polygamy at least a little compassionate.

7. Concubines. The line between "wife" and "concubine" was pretty thin. Generally the children of a concubine could expect to inherit less than a wife's children.

8. Hagar, mother of Ishmael (Genesis 16). This led to conflict with Abraham's childless wife, Sarah, even though the Hagar-Abraham connection was Sarah's idea!

9. The lovely Rachel. However, Jacob was tricked by her father into marrying her less attractive sister, Leah. Jacob married both, but at least we can say he was an unwilling polygamist.

10. Esau, Jacob's brother (Genesis 26:34). It was assumed (usually correctly) that foreign wives would lead a man into idolatry.

11. Deuteronomy (21:15-17), which is pretty blunt about admitting that men can father children by women they don't love

12. Samuel, son of Hannah and Elkanah. Poor Hannah had long suffered the teasing of Elkanah's other wife, Peninnah, who had borne many children (1 Samuel 1).

13. David (1 Samuel 18:27). It was to prove a mostly unhappy marriage, as you can see in 2 Samuel 6:20-23.

14. Isaiah (Isaiah 4:1)

15. Rehoboam, Solomon's son (2 Chronicles 11:21; 12), whose arrogance split Israel into two kingdoms

16. David, who had an affair with Bathsheba, wife of Uriah the Hittite (2 Samuel 11–12)

17. Belshazzar (Daniel 5). We can assume that the ruler of the vast Persian Empire had a very large harem.

18. Amnon, who raped, then threw aside Tamar (2 Samuel 13)

19. He was murdered by his half brother (and Tamar's full brother) Absalom (2 Samuel 13:22-39). This story of David's "blended" family is the classic illustration of the evil effects of polygamy.

20. Bishops (or "overseers" in some translations) and deacons (1 Timothy 3:2, 12)

21. *Abimelech (Judges 9). Note that Gideon (Jerubbaal) had many wives, and that Abimelech was the son of a concubine. His jealousy of his brothers got out of hand, to say the least.*

22. *Jephthath, who was the son of Gilead and a prostitute. His half brothers, sons of Gilead and his wife, drove him away (Judges 11:1-3).*

23. *Abraham (Genesis 16:3; 23:19; 25:1)*

24. *Ahab (1 Kings 16:29-31; 20:2-3), whose best-known wife was the evil Jezebel*

25. *Ahasuerus, who married Esther (Esther 1:10-12; 2:1-17)*

26. *Michal, daughter of Saul (1 Samuel 25:44; 2 Samuel 3:13-16)*

THE ARCHTRAITOR AND SOME OTHER TREACHEROUS FOLK

Call someone a Judas, and people know just what you mean: a traitor, a turncoat. Judas Iscariot, the disciple who sold out his master, Jesus, is probably the greatest traitor of history. But the Bible has several more treacherous types, many of whom paid the price for their treason and trickery. Not all the traitors were bad boys—in fact, quite a few were plotters against wicked oppressors.

1. What infamous Philistine woman tricked Samson into revealing the secret of his strength?
2. Which son of David led a major revolt against his father?
3. When Pekah the usurper reigned in Israel, who murdered him and took over the throne?
4. What fiery chariot driver slew the kings of Israel and Judah and later had Queen Jezebel murdered, after which he reigned as king in Israel?
5. Hazael of Syria usurped the throne after he murdered the king, Ben-hadad. What unusual method did he use for the murder?
6. Which traitor murdered Elah, king of Israel, and then later, after a seven-day reign, committed suicide?
7. Who murdered Shallum and took his place on the throne of Israel?
8. When Judas appeared in Gethsemane to betray Jesus, he was accompanied by a crowd. What were the people of the crowd carrying?
9. Which prophet asked God, "Why do you tolerate the treacherous"?

10. What wicked queen screamed out, "Treason! Treason!" when she realized there was a plot against her?
11. Which prophet said, "With treachery the treacherous betray"?
12. In Judges, what wicked ruler was the victim of treachery by the people of Shechem?
13. In what book of the Bible does an oppressed man call upon God to "show no mercy to wicked traitors"?
14. Who predicted that people of faith would be betrayed even by their own family members?

THE ARCHTRAITOR AND SOME OTHER TREACHEROUS FOLK (ANSWERS)

1. Delilah (Judges 16:1-20)

2. Absalom (2 Samuel 15–18)

3. Hoshea (2 Kings 15:30)

4. Jehu (2 Kings 9). Here was a case where Jehu, though technically a traitor against his king and others, was a finer character than those he plotted against.

5. He took a thick cloth, dipped it in water, and smothered the king (2 Kings 8:9-15).

6. Zimri (1 Kings 16:8-18)

7. Menahem (2 Kings 15:14)

8. Swords and clubs (Mark 14:43)

9. Habakkuk (Habakkuk 1:13)

10. Athaliah (2 Kings 11:13-14)

11. Isaiah (Isaiah 24:16)

12. Abimelech (Judges 9:23)

13. Psalms (59:5)

14. Jesus (Luke 21:16)

PART 5

THE FLESH IS WEAK (VERY!)

NOT G-RATED: SEXUAL SINS IN THE BIBLE

If you filmed the entire Bible, the film would definitely not be G-rated, for there is an abundance of illicit sex in the Bible. How could it be otherwise since the Bible depicts the human race "warts and all," and forbidden sexual activity is definitely part of mankind's depravity? Adultery, promiscuity, prostitution, incest, homosexuality—it's all here. (Prostitution is mentioned so often in the Bible that there is a separate set of questions devoted to it.) But unlike contemporary books and videos, the Bible does not use this kind of sexual material to entertain the reader but to warn him: This behavior isn't pleasing to God, and it will get you in serious trouble. In pleasing the body, you can kill your soul.

1. Who had two daughters who got him drunk and committed incest?
2. What church in Greece had a member who was cohabiting with his stepmother?
3. How many times had the immoral Samaritan woman, who was living with her present lover, been married?
4. Which son of David forced his half sister to have sexual relations with him?
5. What book of the Old Testament mentions a gang rape of a concubine belonging to a Levite?
6. Which daughter-in-law of Judah enticed him to have relations with her?
7. Which Israelite sinned in the wilderness by taking a Midianite woman as his harlot companion?
8. Which daughter of Jacob was raped by Shechem?
9. Who was killed by God because he spilled his seed on the ground rather than father a child by his brother's wife?
10. What sin were the men of Gibeah hoping to commit when they stormed the house of a man who had taken in a traveler?
11. Which priest had two sons who slept with the women who worked at the entrance of the Tabernacle?
12. What beautiful woman (married to someone else) committed adultery with David?
13. Which son of Jacob had sexual relations with one of his father's concubines?

14. Who had sex with his father's concubines on the palace roof in full view of anyone?
15. Which prophet's wife was a harlot before marriage and an adulteress afterward?
16. What New Testament church was home to a sexually immoral woman named Jezebel?
17. Which king did John the Baptist call an adulterer?
18. What sexual sin did Paul say was a result of not worshipping the true God?
19. According to the Law, what was the punishment for committing adultery?

NOT G-RATED: SEXUAL SINS IN THE BIBLE (ANSWERS)

1. Lot (Genesis 19:30-38)

2. The church in Corinth (1 Corinthians 5:1)

3. Five (John 4:4-30)

4. Amnon (2 Samuel 13:1-14)

5. Judges (19:22-28)

6. Tamar (Genesis 38:12-18)

7. Zimri (Numbers 25:6-15)

8. Dinah (Genesis 34:1-2)

9. Onan (Genesis 38:8-9)

10. Homosexual rape (Judges 19:22)

11. Eli (1 Samuel 2:22)

12. Bathsheba (2 Samuel 11:2-4)

13. Reuben (Genesis 35:22)

14. Absalom (2 Samuel 16:22)

15. Gomer, wife of Hosea (Hosea 1–2)

16. Thyatira (Revelation 2:18-20)

17. Herod (Mark 6:17-18)

18. Homosexuality (Romans 1:21-27)

19. Death (Leviticus 20:10)

IT'S TEMPTING . . .

The great tempter in the Bible is the original bad guy, Satan. There are also plenty of human tempters, people who enjoy leading the innocent astray—or trapping them in a difficult situation. But in the grand scheme of things, tempters show just what people are made of, whether they have the inner strength that is needed in an immoral world. Although the tempters are usually bad guys, temptation also is a way of showing that sometimes the "good" people aren't as good as they thought.

1. Who tempted Abraham by asking him to sacrifice his son Isaac?
2. Who tempted Jesus with the question, "Is it lawful for a man to put away his wife"?
3. How many days was Jesus tempted by Satan? (Hint: The temptation took much longer than the Gospels seem to indicate.)
4. Who advised husbands and wives not to go overboard on sexual abstinence, because it might lead to temptation?
5. According to James, what does the man who endures temptation receive?
6. "Lead us not into temptation" is from what famous Bible passage?
7. Who tempted Jesus by asking him to show a sign from heaven?
8. To whom did Jesus say, "Thou shalt not tempt the Lord thy God"?
9. According to the Epistle of James, we are not tempted by God but by what?
10. Which New Testament letter mentions that Jesus was like all human beings in that he was subject to temptation?
11. Which letter claims that God will always make a way to escape temptation?
12. What couple died after they tempted the Spirit of the Lord?

IT'S TEMPTING . . . (ANSWERS)

1. *God did (Genesis 22:1-2). Apparently the word* tempt *here means "test," as it often does in the Bible. Abraham passed the test admirably.*
2. *The Pharisees (Mark 10:2)*
3. *Forty (Mark 1:13; Luke 4:1-13)*
4. *Paul (1 Corinthians 7:5)*
5. *The crown of life (James 1:12)*

6. *The Lord's Prayer (Matthew 6:13)*

7. *The Pharisees and the Sadducees (Matthew 16:1)*

8. *Satan (Luke 4:6, 12)*

9. *Our own lusts (James 1:13-14). No mention of Satan!*

10. *Hebrews (2:9, 18)*

11. *1 Corinthians (10:13)*

12. *Ananias and Sapphira, who had lied to the apostles (Acts 5)*

 ## LET'S GET PHYSICAL: THE ANATOMY LESSON

Here is a big grab bag of questions about (you guessed it) the human body. Some of the questions deal with the numerous sins that all parts of the body can commit. Others deal with various sins and crimes committed against the body. Get the idea? Have fun, and don't strain your brain—which, by the way, is an organ that is not mentioned in the Bible, because the ancients believed that thoughts originated in the heart, not the mind.

1. What happened to the children who made fun of Elisha's bald head?
2. Which Epistle says that blessing and cursing should not come out of the same mouth?
3. Which son of Saul was murdered by two servants who stabbed him in the belly and carried his severed head to David?
4. Which king executed John the Baptist after his stepdaughter asked for John's head on a platter?
5. Who cut off the ear of Malchus, the high priest's servant?
6. What rebel against David was beheaded, with his head thrown over the city wall?
7. Which king received 70 human heads in baskets?
8. According to Jesus, what bodily organ should you pluck out if it causes you to sin?
9. What evil queen "painted her face" before meeting with the rebellious King Jehu?
10. What blind father recognized Jacob's voice but was deceived by his glove-covered hands?
11. Which Old Testament book says that anyone who scorns his parents will have his eyes pecked out by ravens?

12. What gruesome object did the Philistines fasten in the temple of Dagon?
13. Which wife of King David gave him a tongue-lashing for dancing in the streets?
14. According to the Law, if a man was attacked by another man, what part of the assailant's body was the woman forbidden to touch?
15. Whose teeth were set on edge when the fathers ate sour grapes?
16. In what place will sinners "gnash their teeth"?
17. Which king had a "jealous eye"?
18. Which prophet mentions a lustful woman infatuated with men's privates?
19. What sort of lips does the Lord detest?
20. Which prophet lamented that he was a man of "unclean lips"?
21. How did God deal with this prophet's unclean lips?
22. According to Jesus, what should we do when someone strikes us on the right cheek?
23. Who were promised that their "eyes would be opened" if they would disobey God?
24. What book of the Old Testament contains the "eye for an eye" rule?
25. According to Jesus, what people loaded heavy burdens onto men's shoulders, but would not help carry them?
26. Which Christian's preaching caused the Jews to gnash their teeth in rage?
27. For what crime could a man have his shoe taken off and his face spit in?
28. What part of the body are we supposed to cut off if it causes us to sin?

LET'S GET PHYSICAL: THE ANATOMY LESSON (ANSWERS)

1. They were torn apart by two bears (2 Kings 2:23-24).

2. James (3:10)

3. Ish-bosheth, slain by Rechab and Baanah (2 Samuel 4:5-8)

4. Herod (Mark 6:14-28). He was so entranced by the girl's dance that he offered to give her anything she asked for.

5. Peter (John 18:10), who was zealous to keep Jesus from being arrested. Jesus then healed the man's ear.

6. Sheba (2 Samuel 20:21-22)

7. *Jehu (2 Kings 10:1-7). They were the heads of evil King Ahab's family members, a dynasty that Jehu effectively eliminated.*

8. *Your eye (Mark 9:47)*

9. *Jezebel, widow of evil King Ahab (2 Kings 9:30)*

10. *Isaac, who was deceived by his wily son Jacob (Genesis 27:22). The gloves were intended to make Isaac believe that he was touching the hands of Jacob's hairy-bodied brother, Esau.*

11. *Proverbs (30:17)*

12. *The head of Israel's King Saul, whom they had defeated in battle (1 Chronicles 10:10)*

13. *Michal (2 Samuel 6). David replied that he was dancing spontaneously and joyously because the Ark of the Covenant had been returned to the Israelites.*

14. *His genitals. Her punishment for doing so was to have her hand cut off (Deuteronomy 25:11-12).*

15. *The children's (Ezekiel 18:2). The meaning is that the punishment for sin is passed on to the next generation. Ezekiel makes this statement as if it were a common proverb among the people—then goes on to say that it is no longer true.*

16. *Hell (Matthew 8:12; 13:42; 24:51). "Gnashing of teeth" is an indication of anguish and rage.*

17. *Saul, who kept his "jealous eye" on his rival, David (1 Samuel 18:9)*

18. *Ezekiel, who is speaking figuratively. The "woman" is actually Jerusalem, which spiritually speaking has left her true husband (God) and has become promiscuous (worshipping false gods) (Ezekiel 23:20).*

19. *Lying lips (Proverbs 12:22)*

20. *Isaiah (Isaiah 6:5), who also stated that his whole nation had unclean lips*

21. *An angel touched Isaiah's lips with a coal from the Temple's altar (Isaiah 6:6-7). This is a vision, not an actual burning of flesh.*

22. *Turn the left cheek toward the person (Matthew 5:39). The idea is that we don't repay evil with evil.*

23. *Adam and Eve, who believed the serpent's lie (Genesis 3:5-7)*

24. *Exodus (21:24)*

25. *The Pharisees. He was speaking figuratively—not actual physical burdens, but rules and regulations that were too difficult to live by (Matthew 23:4).*

26. *Stephen's (Acts 7:54)*

27. *Refusing to marry the widow of his deceased brother (Deuteronomy 25:9)*

28. *The hand, according to Jesus (Matthew 5:30)*

INNOCENT (NOT!) AMUSEMENTS

Refer to someone as "religious," and people often think of some sour-faced killjoy, someone who would take all the fun out of life. Well, there may be such people (probably not many), but Christianity is not really antipleasure, nor is the Bible. Some pleasures are quite innocent, but let's face it, many of the things that are considered "fun" in our culture aren't innocent at all, and the same was true in Bible times.

1. Which of Jesus' parables refers to the "cares and riches and pleasures of this life" that hinder spiritual growth?
2. Where was Moses when the Israelites indulged in wild religious revelry?
3. Which Epistle speaks of suffering along with the people of God rather than enjoying "the pleasures of sin for a season"?
4. Complete this verse from Ecclesiastes: "The heart of the wise is in the house of mourning; but the heart of fools is in the house of _____."
5. Which Epistle warned Christians that their pagan neighbors would mock them for not indulging in the sinful pleasures they had enjoyed in the past?
6. What great man was referred to as a "glutton and a winebibber"?
7. Which prophet condemned selfish pleasure-seekers who say to themselves, "I am, and none else beside me"?
8. What Hebrew hero was mocked while the Philistines held a wild party in honor of their god Dagon?
9. In what book of the Bible would you find this verse: "He that loveth pleasure shall be a poor man: he that loveth wine and oil shall not be rich"?
10. At whose fateful birthday party did a young woman ask for (and get) the head of John the Baptist on a platter?
11. Who urged Christians not to behave as the unbelievers did, "in the vanity of their mind"?
12. Which Epistle condemned those who "have lived in pleasure on the earth, and been wanton"?
13. Which of Paul's letters contains a list of wicked behaviors that can keep a person from entering the Kingdom of God?
14. Which prophet spoke out against those who enjoyed feasting to music, "but they regard not the work of the Lord"?

15. Which Epistle laments people who are such pleasure-lovers that they "riot in the daytime"?
16. Complete this verse from 1 Timothy: "She that liveth in pleasure is _____ while she liveth."
17. In 2 Timothy, Paul lamented that in the end times, people would be lovers of pleasure rather than lovers of _____.

INNOCENT (NOT!) AMUSEMENTS (ANSWERS)

1. The parable of the sower (Luke 8:14)

2. On Mount Sinai, receiving the Ten Commandments. The Israelites were having their wild party around the golden calf Aaron had made (Exodus 32).

3. Hebrews (11:25)

4. Mirth (Ecclesiastes 7:4)

5. 1 Peter (4:4)

6. Jesus (Matthew 11:19). He wasn't, but we can assume he was no killjoy either.

7. Isaiah (Isaiah 47:8)

8. Samson, who literally brought the house down on them (Judges 16)

9. Proverbs (21:17)

10. Herod's (Matthew 14:1-12)

11. Paul (Ephesians 4:17)

12. James (5:5)

13. Galatians (5:19-21)

14. Isaiah (Isaiah 5:12)

15. 2 Peter (2:13)

16. Dead (1 Timothy 5:6)

17. God (2 Timothy 3:4)

 ## PUI (PEOPLE UNDER THE INFLUENCE)

If you're looking for a Bible verse that tells people to abstain from alcohol, sorry, there isn't one. Jews and Christians took wine for granted as a normal part of life, and John's Gospel records that Jesus' first miracle was turning water into wine. (We can safely assume that he intended people to drink it.) Still, the Bible does have some harsh words to say about drunkenness—as well as some pretty sordid stories about how certain people behaved while under the influence.

1. What righteous man was, rather surprisingly, the Bible's first drunk?
2. What man was seduced by his two daughters while he was drunk?
3. Who dropped dead as a stone on hearing bad news the morning after being drunk?
4. Absalom wanted to avenge the rape of his sister, Tamar, so he waited until the rapist was very drunk. Who was this man, later slain by Absalom's men?
5. This king of Israel, who ruled barely two years, was assassinated while drunk. Who was he?
6. What Syrian king was getting drunk at a time when he was supposed to be waging war on the Samaritans?
7. Nehemiah waited until this Persian king was softened up with wine before he asked the king to let the Jews return to their homeland. Who was the king?
8. What Persian queen refused to obey her drunken husband's order that she appear before his besotted guests?
9. Job's sons and daughters were so busy eating and drinking that they failed to notice that disaster was about to strike. What killed them?
10. The arrogant Babylonian king Belshazzar, drunk at his feast, committed an outrage when he asked for new drinking vessels to be brought in. What were these vessels that led to so much trouble for the king?
11. Which husband, the victim of David's adulterous scheming, was made drunk by the king?
12. What book of the Bible describes a woman who is "drunk with the blood of the saints"?
13. According to Proverbs, what people, along with drunkards, become poor?
14. What pagan city, according to Jeremiah, "made the whole earth drunk"?
15. What righteous man was accused of being a "glutton and a wine-guzzler"?
16. Which prophet lamented over people who got their neighbors drunk in order to gaze upon their nakedness?

17. What group of people, filled with the Spirit, were accused of being drunk early in the day?
18. Which prophet described the earth as "reeling like a drunkard"?
19. According to Ephesians, Christians should be filled with _____ instead of wine?
20. In Deuteronomy, what penalty is prescribed for a rebellious, drunken son?
21. In what book of the Bible does a persecuted man lament that he has become the "song of the drunkards"?
22. According to 1 Timothy, what sort of person should definitely not be a heavy drinker?
23. In Revelation, what wicked city had made the whole world drunk with "the maddening wine of her adulteries"?
24. Who advised Christians to behave decently, "not in orgies and drunkenness"?

PUI (PEOPLE UNDER THE INFLUENCE) (ANSWERS)

1. Noah, who "planted a vineyard" in his post-Flood days, made some wine, and let it go to his head (Genesis 9:21)
2. Lot (Genesis 19:30-36)
3. Nabal, Abigail's husband (1 Samuel 25:36-37)
4. Amnon, Absalom's half brother (2 Samuel 13:28)
5. Elah (1 Kings 16:8-10)
6. Ben-hadad (1 Kings 20:12-20)
7. Artaxerxes (Nehemiah 2:1)
8. Vashti (Esther 1:3-12)
9. A great windstorm (Job 1:13-19)
10. Vessels from the Temple in Jerusalem (Daniel 5:1-5)
11. Uriah, the husband of Bathsheba (2 Samuel 11:13)
12. Revelation (17:6), describing the "great harlot" who symbolizes the evil forces that persecute the saints
13. Gluttons (Proverbs 23:21)
14. Babylon (Jeremiah 51:7)
15. Jesus, believe it or not (Matthew 11:19)
16. Habakkuk (Habakkuk 2:15)
17. Jesus' apostles, on the Day of Pentecost (Acts 2:13-15)

18. *Isaiah (Isaiah 24:20)*

19. *The Spirit (Ephesians 5:18)*

20. *Death by stoning (Deuteronomy 21:20-21)*

21. *Psalms (Psalm 69:12). The idea is that the man has become a laughingstock.*

22. *A Christian bishop (or "overseer" in many translations) (1 Timothy 3:2-3)*

23. *Babylon, which is a symbol of human wickedness (Revelation 18:2-3)*

24. *Paul (Romans 13:13). Because he was writing to the Christians in Rome, we can assume they were all-too-familiar with orgies and drunkenness.*

 ## FAT OF THE LAND

In the diet-conscious, weight-conscious 21st century, fat is considered a bad thing, especially on the human body. Sometimes a fat person is looked upon as more loathsome than a sexually immoral person. The Bible isn't very concerned about human appearance, because the inner person is more important than the outer. In the Bible, the sin is not the bulging waistline, but the habit of living for the belly, as if the spirit didn't matter.

1. The book of Proverbs tells you to "put a _____ to your throat if you are given to gluttony."
2. What pagan king, assassinated by one of Israel's judges, is the first fat man mentioned in the Bible?
3. Which prophet predicted a time when the fat of Israel would waste away?
4. According to the book of Job, what sort of man has a fat neck and a bulging waistline?
5. In Ezekiel's parable of God judging between the fat sheep and the lean sheep, who were the fat sheep?
6. Which prophet condemned the rich of Israel for lying on ivory beds and dining on fattened calves?
7. Which priest of Israel was chastised for allowing his greedy sons to grow fat on the people's sacrificial animals?
8. According to Ezekiel, what guests would be invited to dine on the blood and fat of aristocrats?
9. What great man was accused of being "a glutton and a drunkard"?
10. According to Proverbs, what is the fate of drunkards and gluttons?

11. Which prophet spoke out against people who "have grown fat and sleek . . . their evil deeds have no limit"?
12. Which apostle lamented that some people were so materialistic that "their god is their belly"?
13. Which parable of Jesus concerned a well-fed man who said to himself, "Eat, drink, and be merry"?
14. The famous phrase "Let us eat and drink, for tomorrow we shall die" is taken from what book of the Bible?

FAT OF THE LAND (ANSWERS)

1. *Knife (Proverbs 23:2). We can assume this wasn't meant to be taken literally.*

2. *Eglon, the king of Moab who was stabbed to death by the Israelite judge Ehud (Judges 3:12-26)*

3. *Isaiah (Isaiah 17:4)*

4. *The wicked man (Job 15:20-27)*

5. *The leaders of Israel—specifically, the priests and prophets who had not cared for the people (Ezekiel 34)*

6. *Amos (Amos 6:4)*

7. *Samuel's mentor, Eli, whose greedy sons were Hophni and Phinehas (1 Samuel 2:29)*

8. *The birds and wild animals (Ezekiel 39:17-18). Ezekiel was prophesying judgment on the godless rulers of mankind.*

9. *Jesus, believe it or not (Matthew 11:19)*

10. *They become poor (Proverbs 23:21).*

11. *Jeremiah (Jeremiah 5:28)*

12. *Paul (Philippians 3:19)*

13. *The parable of the rich fool, who accumulated so many material things, then died and went to hell (Luke 12:19-20)*

14. *Isaiah (22:13)*

 ## HA-HA AND CHA-CHA: LAUGHING AND DANCING

Laughing and dancing aren't bad things . . . are they? Considering what passes for "comedy" today in TV and movies and the type of dancing seen in pop-music videos, you might wonder. Well, the Bible doesn't condemn laughing or dancing. In fact, the Bible is very much "pro-joy." Some verses in the Bible provide the assurance that victims of oppressors will someday weep instead of laugh. On the other hand, much of the laughter spoken of in the Bible isn't the ha-ha laughter of relief or merriment, but the cruel laughter of mockery. And though dancing is usually associated with innocent merrymaking, in a few memorable instances, dancing was connected to some really horrible events.

1. Who was snickered at for claiming that a dead girl was only asleep?
2. What woman's entrancing dance proved fatal for John the Baptist?
3. Who danced with all his might when the Ark of the Covenant was brought to Jerusalem, then was cut down to size by his catty wife?
4. Who laughed when she heard she would bear a son in her old age?
5. Whose ill-fated daughter came out dancing after his victory over the Ammonites?
6. Who had his decree for a Passover celebration laughed at by the men of Israel?
7. What is the only book in the Bible to mention God laughing?
8. Which Epistle tells Christians to turn their laughter to mourning?
9. According to Psalm 126, what caused laughter among the Jews?
10. What old man laughed at God's promise that he would father a child in his old age?
11. What group of enemies were busy dancing and partying when David caught up with them?
12. What famous idol did the Israelites dance in front of while Moses was away?
13. What book of the Bible says there is a time to weep and a time to laugh?
14. To whom in the Beatitudes does Jesus promise laughter?
15. What book of the Bible says that even in laughter the heart can be sorrowful?
16. In a famous event in Elijah's life, who danced wildly around the altar of their false god?
17. What book of the Bible says, "Our dance is turned into mourning"?
18. According to Job, whose children dance about and make music?
19. What Old Testament character's name means "laughter"?
20. Complete this verse from Psalms: "Thou hast turned my _____ into dancing."
21. What book of the Bible says that laughter is foolishness?

22. Which prophet told King Hezekiah that Jerusalem would laugh at the mighty conqueror Sennacherib?
23. What book of the Bible says that "the just upright man is laughed to scorn"?
24. Complete this verse from Ecclesiastes: "As the crackling of thorns under a pot, so is the laughter of the _____."
25. Who laughed at Nehemiah's plans to rebuild Jerusalem?

HA-HA AND CHA-CHA: LAUGHING AND DANCING (ANSWERS)

1. *Jesus (Matthew 9:23-25). When Jesus raised the girl to life, those who had snickered were put to shame.*

2. *The daughter of Herodias (Matthew 14:6-8). When her stepfather offered her anything she wanted as a reward for her dance, she asked for John's head on a platter.*

3. *David (2 Samuel 6:14, 20)*

4. *Sarah (Genesis 18:10-12). As it turned out, she did indeed bear a child.*

5. *Jephthah's (Judges 11:34). Alas, he had promised to sacrifice the first thing he saw after his victory, and it turned out to be the daughter.*

6. *Hezekiah (2 Chronicles 30:5, 10)*

7. *Psalms (2:4; 37:13; 59:8). God laughs at the wicked.*

8. *James (4:8-9)*

9. *Bringing the captives back to Jerusalem (Psalm 126:1-2)*

10. *Abraham (Genesis 17:17)*

11. *The Amalekites (1 Samuel 30:16-18)*

12. *The gold calf made by Aaron (Exodus 32:19)*

13. *Ecclesiastes (3:4)*

14. *Those who weep (Luke 6:21)*

15. *Proverbs (14:13)*

16. *The priests of Baal (1 Kings 18:26)*

17. *Lamentations (5:15), which is a dirge over the capture of Jerusalem by the Babylonians*

18. *The children of the wicked (Job 21:7-12)*

19. *Isaac (Genesis 21:3-6)*

20. *Mourning (Psalm 30:11)*

21. *Ecclesiastes (2:2)*

22. *Isaiah (2 Kings 19:21)*

23. *Job (12:4)*

24. *Fool (Ecclesiastes 7:6)*

25. *Sanballat, Tobiah, and Geshem (Nehemiah 2:19)*

HARLOTS, OR WHATEVER YOU WISH TO CALL THEM . . .

Depending on your translation, your Bible may refer to "harlots" or "prostitutes" or "whores" or even "loose women." In fact, such women are referred to quite often in the Bible, maybe because prostitution seems to be a fixture of human history. (No wonder it has been referred to as "the world's oldest profession.") Though a few of the harlots of the Bible seem to have the proverbial "heart of gold," the Bible definitely does not glamorize prostitution the way our contemporary culture does, nor does it have a high opinion of the men who keep the prostitutes in business.

1. In Judges, what mighty warrior of Israel was a prostitute's son?
2. What two New Testament Epistles speak of the righteousness of the prostitute Rahab?
3. Which king served as judge when two prostitutes fought over a child?
4. Who had a vision of a prostitute with a city's name engraved on her head?
5. What character in a parable wasted his money on prostitutes?
6. According to Jesus, which prophet had prostitutes and tax collectors as followers?
7. Which prophet did the Lord tell about two prostitutes named Aholah and Aholibah?
8. Where did the prostitute Rahab live?
9. Who ordered his daughter-in-law Tamar burned because she had acted like a prostitute?
10. Who married a faithless woman named Gomer?
11. Who went on a killing spree when their sister Dinah was treated like a prostitute?
12. Who tricked the people of Gaza by leaving a prostitute's house earlier than they expected?
13. Which Epistle warns Christians against patronizing prostitutes?

14. Which prophet warned the priest Amaziah that his wife would become a prostitute?
15. According to tradition, what follower of Jesus had been a prostitute, though the Bible does not refer to her as one?
16. Which prophet lamented that his people had "traded boys for prostitutes"?
17. Which prophet stated that the earnings of a prostitute had been used to purchase idols?

HARLOTS, OR WHATEVER YOU WISH TO CALL THEM . . . (ANSWERS)

1. Jephthah (Judges 11:1)
2. James (2:25) and Hebrews (11:31)
3. Solomon (1 Kings 3:16)
4. John (Revelation 17:5)
5. The Prodigal Son (Luke 15:30)
6. John the Baptist (Matthew 21:32)
7. Ezekiel (Ezekiel 23:1-21)
8. Jericho (Joshua 2:1-6)
9. Judah (Genesis 38:24)
10. Hosea (Hosea 1–3)
11. Levi and Simeon (Genesis 34:25-31)
12. Samson (Judges 16:1-3)
13. 1 Corinthians (6:15-18)
14. Amos (Amos 7:17)
15. Mary Magdalene
16. Joel (Joel 3:3)
17. Micah (Micah 1:7)

 ## DOWN BY THE LAZY RIVER

Ask employers if it's hard to find good help these days, and they'll shout out, "Yes!" The old work ethic—"Keep your nose to the grindstone"—has been replaced by the new play ethic—"Why work if you don't have to?" There were lazy folks in Bible times, often referred to by the old word *sluggards,* and the Bible condemns them heartily. The next time you start complaining about poor service and poor quality, consider that sluggards are largely responsible.

1. What busy creature does the book of Proverbs tell the sluggard to stop and consider?
2. What New Testament author told Christians, "If any would not work, neither should he eat"?
3. According to Ecclesiastes, "By much slothfulness the _____ decays, and through idleness of hands the _____ falls through."
4. Proverbs tells us that the "soul of the sluggard desires, and has _____."
5. Which New Testament Epistle tells Christians to "be not slothful"?
6. Which of Jesus' parables is concerned with several diligent servants and one very lazy servant?
7. According to Proverbs, "Whoever is slack in his work is a brother to him who _____."
8. In what Greek city did Paul find that people had nothing better to do than gossip and exchange news?
9. What famous wicked city did Ezekiel say had "abundance of idleness" as one of its chief sins?
10. Which prophet accused Israel's leaders of being lazy dogs, "dreaming, lying down, loving to slumber"?
11. Proverbs says that "in all labor there is profit, but mere talk leads to _____."
12. Which of Paul's epistles says that "he who sows sparingly shall also reap sparingly"?
13. According to Ecclesiastes, "The sleep of a laboring man is _____."
14. What Christian boasted that he had supported himself by the work of his own hands?

DOWN BY THE LAZY RIVER (ANSWERS)

1. *The ant, of course (Proverbs 6:6)*

2. *Paul (2 Thessalonians 3:10)*

3. *Building, house (Ecclesiastes 10:18)*

4. *Nothing (Proverbs 13:4)*

5. *Hebrews (6:12)*

6. *The parable of the talents (Matthew 25:14-30)*

7. *Destroys (Proverbs 18:9)*

8. *Athens (Acts 17:21)*

9. *Sodom (Ezekiel 16:49)*

10. *Isaiah (Isaiah 56:10)*

11. *Poverty (Proverbs 14:23)*

12. *2 Corinthians (9:6)*

13. *Sweet (Ecclesiastes 5:12)*

14. *Paul (Acts 20:34)*

PART 6

HELLO, CRUEL WORLD

MURDER, THEY DID

Here's a tidbit to tuck away in your memory bank: In the Ten Commandments, "Thou shalt not kill" is not the correct translation. The Hebrew word actually means "murder," not "kill." In fact, if you browse the Old Testament, you'll see that some forms of killing—notably capital punishment—were legal and even approved by God. But murder was, and is, always wrong. Not only were some of the Bible's utterly despicable characters guilty of murder, but so—on occasion—were some of its better ones.

1. Who was the world's first murderer?
2. What great leader of Israel killed an Egyptian for abusing a Hebrew slave?
3. Which of his military men did David have murdered by sending him into the thick of battle?
4. In Genesis, which character boasted that he had killed a young man who had injured him?
5. Which two sons of Jacob slaughtered Shechem and his kin while they were recovering from circumcision?
6. What book of the Bible records the sordid story of a poor woman who was literally raped to death by a group of men?
7. What man in the life of Jesus was in prison for being both a revolutionary and a murderer?
8. What obese king of Moab was murdered in a sneaky way by the Israelite judge Ehud?
9. Which captain of King Saul murdered Asahel by ramming a spear through his belly?
10. Which half brother (who wanted to seize the throne) did Solomon have murdered?
11. Who killed off the dynasty of King Baasha of Israel, then committed suicide after seven days?
12. What means did the woman Jael use to murder the Canaanite captain Sisera who rested in her tent?
13. Which son of David avenged his sister's rape by murdering his drunk half brother Amnon?
14. Which son of the judge Gideon murdered 70 of his own half brothers?
15. Which captain of David's avenged his brother's murder by stabbing Abner in the belly?

16. Who did Jesus say was a "murderer from the beginning"?
17. The Jewish Sanhedrin stoned what saintly man for blasphemy?
18. What cruel king of Judah had all his brothers killed by the sword?
19. Which king of Israel's dynasty was entirely wiped out by Baasha?
20. What was Joab doing to Amasa when he suddenly stabbed Amasa in the belly?
21. Which king of Sennacherib was murdered by two of his own sons while worshipping in the temple of his god?
22. Which of the apostles was beheaded by wicked Herod?
23. Which son of King Saul was stabbed in the belly then beheaded by Reca and Baanah?
24. What evil royal couple had Naboth executed because he refused to sell them his family's vineyard?
25. What good king of Judah was murdered on the road by two of his own officials?
26. What wicked king's assassins were all killed by the people of Judah?
27. Which king of Aram was murdered by being smothered with a wet cloth over his face?
28. Which king's seven sons and grandsons were murdered and exposed on a hillside by the Gibeonites?
29. What evil king of Judah "shed so much innocent blood that he filled Jerusalem from end to end"?
30. What wicked queen, the daughter of Ahab and Jezebel, almost exterminated her husband's entire family after he died?
31. What evil son of the judge Gideon (Jerubbaal) was mortally wounded when a woman dropped a millstone on his head?
32. What wounded king tried to get his armor bearer to kill him so he wouldn't die at the hands of the Philistines?
33. Which son of David was speared three times while he dangled in midair, his head caught in a tree?
34. Which king of Judah had the prophet Zechariah stoned to death because he predicted disaster for him?
35. What persecutor of Christians was "breathing out murderous threats against the Lord's disciples"?
36. What Babylonian ruler killed the king of Judah's sons right before the king's eyes, then had him blinded?
37. Which apostle wrote that "anyone who hates his brother is a murderer"?
38. Who lamented that God's prophets and wise men were always persecuted and murdered?

39. Which apostle was assumed to be an escaped murderer when a venomous snake bit him on the hand?
40. What evil king of Israel killed everyone in the city of Tiphsah, even ripping open its pregnant women?

MURDER, THEY DID (ANSWERS)

1. Cain, who killed his brother, Abel (Genesis 4)

2. Moses (Exodus 2:12)

3. Uriah the Hittite, husband of Bathsheba, with whom David fathered a child (2 Samuel 11:15-17)

4. Lamech (Genesis 4:23)

5. Simeon and Levi (Genesis 34:25-31)

6. Judges (19:25-28)

7. Barabbas (Luke 23:18-19)

8. Eglon (Judges 3:12-30)

9. Abner (2 Samuel 2:22-23)

10. Adonijah (1 Kings 2:23-25)

11. Zimri (1 Kings 16:11-19)

12. Drove a tent peg through his head (Judges 4:21)

13. Absalom (2 Samuel 13:23-29)

14. Abimelech (Judges 9:5)

15. Joab (2 Samuel 3:27)

16. The devil (John 8:44)

17. Stephen (Acts 6:11-15)

18. Jehoram (2 Chronicles 21:4)

19. Jeroboam's (1 Kings 15:27-29)

20. Kissing him (as a greeting, that is) (2 Samuel 20:9-10)

21. Sennacherib (2 Kings 19:36-37)

22. James (Acts 12:2)

23. Ish-bosheth (2 Samuel 4:5-8)

24. Ahab and Jezebel (1 Kings 21:10-24)

25. Joash (2 Kings 12:20)

26. Amon (2 Kings 21:23-24)

27. *Ben-hadad (2 Kings 8:7-15)*

28. *Saul's (2 Samuel 21:1-9)*

29. *Manasseh (2 Kings 21:16)*

30. *Athaliah (2 Kings 11:1)*

31. *Abimelech (Judges 9:52-53)*

32. *Saul (1 Samuel 31:4-6)*

33. *Absalom (2 Samuel 18:9-15)*

34. *Joash (2 Chronicles 24:20-22)*

35. *Saul (Acts 9:1), who later became the great apostle Paul*

36. *Nebuchadnezzar (Jeremiah 39:5-7)*

37. *John (1 John 3:15).*

38. *Jesus (Matthew 23:37)*

39. *Paul (Acts 28:4)*

40. *Menahem (2 Kings 15:16)*

 ## AH, SWEET REVENGE!

When Jesus told people to "turn the other cheek" when someone struck them, he was turning the world's standards upside down. Whether he meant his words literally or not, he was telling people that their "natural" response to injury is all wrong. Instead of getting mad—and worse, getting even—the Bible holds up a higher standard. Of course, no one said this was easy, and the Bible itself has ample examples of vengeful people.

1. How did Samson get vengeance on the Philistines for binding and blinding him?
2. What handsome young son of David brutally avenged the rape of his sister Tamar?
3. Which prophet did Queen Jezebel promise to kill as revenge for his slaying of her Baal prophets?
4. For what slight did the Persian official Haman plot the extermination of all the Jews living in Persia?
5. What book of the Bible says, "He who digs a pit shall fall into it, and he who rolls a stone, it will roll back on him?"

6. How did King Ahab get even with the prophet Micaiah for prophesying his defeat in battle?

7. Which nation did the prophet Ezekiel condemn because it had acted vengefully toward the Jews?

8. What act led Simeon and Levi to slaughter the men of Shechem while the men were recovering from circumcision?

9. Which apostle wrote, "Recompense no man evil for evil"?

10. Which two disciples of Jesus wanted to call down fire from heaven to destroy a Samaritan village?

11. Which prophet lost his head because he had spoken out against Herodias marrying her husband's brother?

12. In which book of the Bible do the souls of martyred saints call out, "How long, O Lord, before you avenge our blood"?

13. In which book of the Bible does God say the famous words, "Vengeance is mine; I will repay"?

14. What book of the Bible says that when you give food to a hungry enemy, you are "heaping burning coals on his head"?

15. Who prophesied that Jesus would return to earth "in flaming fire taking vengeance on those who know not God"?

16. Which parable did Jesus tell to show that God will in due time avenge the suffering of his people?

17. In which little-read Old Testament book would you find these words: "Do not seek revenge or bear a grudge against one of your people, but love your neighbor as yourself."

18. What man would David not harm, even though he hoped that the Lord would avenge him for the wrongs that man had done?

19. What man was ordered to destroy the dynasty of Ahab in revenge for Ahab's killing of the Lord's prophets?

20. Which apostle did a group of Jews plot to ambush, swearing not to eat or drink until he was dead?

21. Which son of the judge Gideon was killed in revenge for the slaughter of his 70 brothers?

22. Which captain of David killed Abner in revenge for the killing of his brother Asahel?

AH, SWEET REVENGE! (ANSWERS)

1. *Killed thousands of them by tearing down their temple (Judges 16:28-31)*

2. *Absalom, who murdered his half brother Amnon for his dirty deed (2 Samuel 13:23-33)*

3. Elijah (1 Kings 19:1-2)

4. The Jew Mordecai had failed to bow down to him (Esther 3).

5. Proverbs (26:27)

6. Ahab put him in prison, with bread and water rations (1 Kings 22:26-28).

7. Edom (Ezekiel 25:12)

8. The rape of their sister Dinah (Genesis 34:25-27)

9. Paul (Romans 12:17)

10. James and John, who were angry that the town had rejected Jesus (Luke 9:52-55). Needless to say, Jesus did not destroy the town.

11. John the Baptist (Mark 6:19-24)

12. Revelation (6:9-11)

13. Deuteronomy (32:35)

14. Proverbs (25:21-22), a verse also quoted in Romans 12:20

15. Paul (2 Thessalonians 1:6-8)

16. The parable of the persistent widow and the unjust judge (Luke 18:1-8)

17. Leviticus (19:18)

18. Saul (1 Samuel 24:9-12)

19. Jehu (2 Kings 9:5-7)

20. Paul (Acts 23:12-16)

21. Abimelech (Judges 9:24)

22. Joab (2 Samuel 3:27)

 BLOODY MESS

The Bible isn't squeamish about the subject of blood. This shouldn't be surprising, because the people in Bible times were familiar with the slaughtering of animals for food and ritual as well as the frequent violence that led to the shedding of human blood. Interestingly, the loss of blood, an idea that most people find unpleasant, was transformed by Jesus' death into a symbol of love and forgiveness.

1. What woman was "drunk with the blood of the saints"?
2. What Roman official killed some Galileans and mixed their blood with their sacrifices?

3. What wicked king shed so much blood that he "filled Jerusalem from one end to another"?
4. What murdered man's blood "cried out from the earth"?
5. What evil queen's blood spattered on King Jehu's horses?
6. What guilty man said, "I have sinned in that I have betrayed innocent blood"?
7. Which prophet said, "Woe to him that buildeth a town with blood"?
8. Which king was Shimei cursing when he said, "Thou bloody man"?
9. Whose wife referred to him as a "bloody husband"?
10. What was the name of the field purchased by Judas' 30 pieces of silver?
11. To whom did God give the edict "Whoso sheddeth man's blood, by man shall his blood be shed"?
12. Which of Joseph's 11 brothers advised the others not to shed his blood?
13. According to the law of Moses, who was supposed to avenge a murder?
14. What did Israel suffer because of Saul's shedding the blood of the Gibeonites?
15. What wicked king died, with his blood running out of the chariot he was riding in?
16. What wicked queen fell to her death, with her blood spattering on the walls?
17. When Jesus mentioned the shedding of righteous blood, what man from the book of Genesis did he hold up as an example of righteousness?
18. Whose blood, according to Jesus, had been shed by wicked men since the foundation of the world?
19. Which rebel against King David was killed and "wallowed in blood in the midst of the highway"?
20. David told his son Solomon to execute what person because he had shed blood in peacetime as well as in wartime?
21. The book of Nahum is directed against a certain "bloody city." What great pagan city is it?
22. What was the name of the places where people who had unintentionally shed blood could flee?
23. What beloved king was not allowed to build the Lord's Temple because he was a "man of blood"?

BLOODY MESS (ANSWERS)

1. The great harlot (Revelation 17:4-6), who probably represents Rome.

2. Pilate (Luke 13:1)

3. Manasseh (2 Kings 21:16)

4. Abel's, after being killed by his brother, Cain (Genesis 4:10)

5. Jezebel (2 Kings 9:33)

6. Judas Iscariot (Matthew 27:4)

7. Habakkuk (Habakkuk 2:12)

8. David (2 Samuel 16:6-7)

9. Moses' wife Zipporah, who said, "A bloody husband thou art " (Exodus 4:25). This was connected to the incident of circumcising their son.

10. The Field of Blood (Matthew 27:8)

11. Noah (Genesis 9:6)

12. Reuben, who advised throwing him into a pit in the wilderness instead (Genesis 37:22)

13. The "revenger of blood" (Numbers 35), a person (presumably a close relative) who was responsible for killing the murderer

14. A three-year famine (2 Samuel 21:1)

15. Ahab (1 Kings 22:35, 40)

16. Jezebel, Ahab's wife (2 Kings 9:33)

17. Abel, who was killed by his brother, Cain (Matthew 23:35)

18. The prophets' (Luke 11:50)

19. Amasa, captain of the rebel forces under David's son Absalom (2 Samuel 20:12)

20. Joab, the commander-in-chief (1 Kings 2:5-7)

21. Nineveh, the capital of Assyria. The Assyrians were regarded by the Hebrews (and everyone else) as extremely cruel.

22. Cities of refuge (Numbers 35:11; Deuteronomy 19), six of them in all. These were provided to protect a person until his case could be properly tried. They were not designed to protect willful murderers.

23. David (1 Chronicles 22:7-8)

HAULING A LOAD OF HATE AROUND

Regarding holding grudges, comic Buddy Hackett said, "While you're holding a grudge, they're out dancing." By hating, you probably do more harm to yourself than those you hate. Besides, according to the Bible, hate is just *wrong*. We can hate sin but not sinners.

1. Who warned his followers that "you shall be hated by all men for my name's sake"?
2. According to Proverbs, "Hatred stirs up quarrels, but _____ covers all sins."
3. Who despised her husband after she saw him dancing joyfully in the streets of Jerusalem?
4. Who hated his crafty brother for receiving their father's blessing?
5. Which daughter of David was hated and abandoned by the half brother who raped her?
6. What wicked king of Israel hated Micaiah, the one prophet in his court who spoke the truth?
7. What spoiled son was hated so much by his older brothers that they sold him as a slave?
8. Which Old Testament book commands, "You shall not hate your neighbor in your heart"?
9. What servant woman conceived a child by her master and afterward despised his childless wife?
10. Which son of David hated his brother so much that he murdered him?
11. Who commanded people to love their enemies instead of hating them?
12. Which New Testament Epistle says that rich Christians should not despise the poor?
13. What early king of Israel was despised by men who doubted whether he could lead the nation?
14. What book of the Bible commands people to give aid to a fallen animal that belongs to someone who hates them?
15. Which Epistle says that anyone who hates his brother is a murderer?
16. According to Proverbs, "The bloodthirsty hate the _____."
17. Who stated that if we do not forgive people their offenses, God will not forgive us?

18. In which book of the Bible does a man lament, "They that hate me without cause are more than the hairs of my head"?
19. According to the Epistle of James, "He that has shown no mercy shall have _____ without mercy."
20. Who classified hatred as among the "works of the flesh"?

HAULING A LOAD OF HATE AROUND (ANSWERS)

1. Jesus (Matthew 10:22)

2. Love (Proverbs 10:12)

3. Michal, wife of King David (2 Samuel 6:16)

4. Esau, brother of Jacob (Genesis 27:41)

5. Tamar, raped by Amnon (2 Samuel 13:10-15)

6. Ahab (1 Kings 22:8)

7. Joseph (Genesis 37)

8. Leviticus (19:17)

9. Hagar, servant of Abraham and Sarah (Genesis 16:4)

10. Absalom, who murdered Amnon for raping Tamar (2 Samuel 13)

11. Jesus (Matthew 5:44)

12. James (2:6)

13. Saul (1 Samuel 10:26-27)

14. Exodus (23:5)

15. 1 John (3:15)

16. Upright (Proverbs 29:10)

17. Jesus (Matthew 6:15)

18. Psalms (Psalm 69:4)

19. Judgment (James 2:13)

20. Paul (Galatians 5:19-20)

 ## ANGER DANGER

The two words don't rhyme, but they are closely related, because angry people are a danger to themselves and others. The violence we see in the world tells us that a lot of people are angry and not dealing with it constructively. While anger isn't always bad (some saintly people, including Jesus himself, got angry on occasion), it usually is, because it's usually rooted in ego—something like "How dare they do that to ME!" Some people seem to be constantly angry, on the verge of exploding, and the Bible has some harsh words for such people and their behavior.

1. What very bad boy is the Bible's first recorded angry man?
2. What wise Old Testament book says that "wrath kills the foolish man, and envy slays the simpleminded one"?
3. Complete this verse from the Epistle of James: "Be swift to hear, slow to speak, slow to wrath, for the wrath of man works not the _____ of God."
4. Who warned that being angry with someone without cause puts a person in danger of judgment?
5. According to Ecclesiastes, anger rests in the _____ of fools.
6. Who advised Christians to "not let the sun go down upon your wrath"?
7. What two sons of Jacob were hot with anger when their sister Dinah was raped by Shechem?
8. What pagan prophet got very angry with his stubborn donkey who kept veering off the path?
9. Where was Jesus when he got "whipping mad" at some people?
10. What wicked king grew angry and pouted because he could not buy the plot of land he wanted?
11. What Christian made the Jews so angry that they "gnashed their teeth" and then stoned him?
12. What group of travelers angered wicked King Herod by deceiving him?
13. What saintly king of Judah on one occasion became angry with a prophet who reproved him?
14. What disobedient wife made her royal husband angry by not appearing before his party guests?
15. What world conqueror grew angry at three young Jewish men who would not bow down to his idol?
16. What Christian leader reminded his readers of the Old Testament verse, "'Vengeance is mine, I will repay,' says the Lord"?
17. According to Proverbs, what kind of answer turns away wrath?
18. Where was Jesus when he read from the Scriptures and the people "were filled with wrath"?

19. Which prophet was angry because the gourd vine that sheltered him from the sun withered away?
20. Complete this verse from Proverbs: "He that is slow to anger is better than the _____."
21. Which prophet predicted that "their princes shall fall by the sword for the rage of their tongue"?
22. Who listed anger among the "works of the flesh" that can keep a person from entering heaven?
23. What leper from a foreign land was angry because the prophet Elisha told him to go wash in the waters of the Jordan River?
24. What book of the Bible states that "a stone is heavy, and the sand weighty, but a fool's wrath is heavier than them both"?
25. What book of the Bible tells people to "cease from anger and forsake wrath"?
26. What man was Jonathan angry with for persecuting his bosom friend, David?
27. What wicked Persian official was angry because the Jew Mordecai would not salute him?
28. What young man was angry with the three friends who condemned Job, believing he had sinned?
29. What angry king felt leprosy break out on his face while he was in a rage?
30. When Moses came down from Mount Sinai with the Ten Commandments, what angered him so much that he broke the stone tablets with the commandments?

ANGER DANGER (ANSWERS)

1. *Cain, who was angry that his sacrifice was not accepted by God (Genesis 4:6). His brother Abel soon learned just how angry Cain was.*

2. *Job (5:2)*

3. *Righteousness (James 1:19-20)*

4. *Jesus (Matthew 5:22)*

5. *Bosom (Ecclesiastes 7:9)*

6. *Paul (Ephesians 4:26)*

7. *Simeon and Levi, who took revenge on the whole family of the rapist (Genesis 34:1-25)*

8. *Balaam, who could not see the angel that the donkey saw (Numbers 22:27-29)*

9. The Temple courts, where he used a whip to drive out the money changers (John 2:14-16)

10. Ahab (1 Kings 21:4)

11. Stephen, the first Christian martyr (Acts 7:54-58)

12. The wise men, who were wise enough not to report where they had found the baby Jesus (Matthew 2:16)

13. Asa (2 Chronicles 16:10)

14. Vashti, the wife of Ahasuerus, ruler of Persia (Esther 1:12)

15. Nebuchadnezzar (Daniel 3:13-19)

16. Paul (Romans 12:19)

17. A soft one (Proverbs 15:1)

18. Nazareth, his hometown (Luke 4:28)

19. Jonah (Jonah 4:1-11)

20. Mighty (Proverbs 16:32)

21. Hosea (Hosea 7:16)

22. Paul (Galatians 5:19-20)

23. Naaman, the Syrian who was (as Elisha said) cured by the waters (2 Kings 5:9-12)

24. Proverbs (27:3)

25. Psalms (Psalm 37:8)

26. Saul, Jonathan's father (1 Samuel 20:34)

27. Haman (Esther 3:5)

28. Elihu (Job 32:2-3)

29. Uzziah (2 Chronicles 26:19)

30. The Israelites were engaging in an idolatrous party at the foot of the mountain (Exodus 32:19).

 ## BURNING DESIRE

Or, more accurately, the desire to burn. Arson is nothing new in human history, nor is the use of fire in warfare. In fact, fire is one of humanity's oldest weapons. Like anything else, fire can do very good things for human beings (warm them, cook their food), but it can also do great harm as well.

1. Who burned the Philistines' crops by tying torches to the tails of foxes and turning them loose in the fields?
2. What Babylonian official burned Jerusalem?
3. What Canaanite city was burned down by the men of Dan?
4. Which Israelite had his goods burned after he had been stoned to death?
5. Which group of people burned David's city of Ziklag?
6. Which king committed suicide by burning down his palace with himself inside?
7. Which judge killed about 1,000 people when he burned down the tower of Shechem?
8. Which tribe of Israel sacked Jerusalem and burned it?
9. In the days of the judges, which tribe had its cities burned by the other tribes?
10. What Israelite city was burned by Pharaoh?
11. Who burned Joab's barley field just to get his attention?
12. What group of Christian converts burned their books of magic?

BURNING DESIRE (ANSWERS)

1. Samson (Judges 15:4-5)

2. Nebuzaradan (2 Kings 25:9)

3. Laish (Judges 18:26-27)

4. Achan (Joshua 7:24-25)

5. The Amalekites (1 Samuel 30:1)

6. Zimri (1 Kings 16:18)

7. Abimelech (Judges 9:49)

8. Judah (Judges 1:8)

9. Benjamin (Judges 20:48)

10. Gezer (1 Kings 9:16)

11. Absalom (2 Samuel 14:28-33)

12. The Ephesians (Acts 19:17-19). Obviously this was a case of fire being put to good use, not bad.

HEADS ARE GONNA ROLL

Beheading seems like a horrible means of execution, but it's a lot more humane (meaning faster) than crucifixion, stoning, and other methods. In the Bible, it was sometimes used on people who deserved it, but it was often used by evil people to get rid of their enemies. The questions below deal with bad guys who were sometimes the punished, sometimes the punisher.

1. Which of Jesus' apostles was the first to be martyred when Herod had him beheaded with a sword?
2. What saintly relative of Jesus was beheaded, with his head brought in to his executioner on a platter?
3. Which judge of Israel was sent the heads of the Midianite leaders Oreb and Zeeb?
4. What book of the Bible mentions those who were beheaded "because of their testimony for Jesus"?
5. Which son of Saul was stabbed in the belly and then beheaded before his head was brought to David?
6. What rebel against King David was beheaded, with his head thrown over the city wall?
7. Which prophet did the king of Israel swear to behead?
8. What evil king's 70 sons were beheaded, with their heads put in baskets and piled up at the city gates?
9. What braggart Philistine warrior had his head cut off with his own sword?
10. What fallen king had his head cut off by the Philistines?
11. What cursing man did David's soldier Abishai threaten to go and behead?
12. Which New Testament Epistle pays tribute to the martyrs who were stoned, sawn in two, or beheaded?
13. According to tradition, what Bible author was beheaded during the reign of the Christian-persecuting emperor Nero?

HEADS ARE GONNA ROLL (ANSWERS)

1. *James (Acts 12:1-2)*
2. *John the Baptist (Matthew 14:10-11)*
3. *Gideon (Jerubbaal) (Judges 7:25)*

4. *Revelation (20:4)*
5. *Ish-bosheth (2 Samuel 4:5-8)*
6. *Sheba (2 Samuel 20:21-22)*
7. *Elisha (2 Kings 6:30-31)*
8. *Ahab's (2 Kings 10:1-8)*
9. *Goliath (1 Samuel 17:8, 46-51)*
10. *Saul (1 Samuel 31:8-9)*
11. *Shimei (2 Samuel 16:5-9)*
12. *Hebrews (11:37)*
13. *Paul*

 ## GRISLY EXECUTIONS

According to Genesis, it wasn't God's original intention for man to die. Death was Adam's punishment for disobedience. So in a way, all human death is "unnatural," not something God built into the original order of the world. Even so, the human race grew accustomed to the hard truth that we must die, most from old age or disease. But the questions below deal with some very unusual deaths in the Bible, all of them involving punishment for evil.

1. What two cities were rained on by fire and brimstone?
2. What devoured Aaron's sons, Nadab and Abihu, when they offered "strange fire" to the Lord?
3. What Canaanite captain was killed when Jael, a Hebrew woman, drove a tent peg through his skull?
4. Who was killed for touching the Ark of the Covenant?
5. The Lord sent a pestilence on Israel that killed 70,000 people. What act of King David brought this on?
6. God sent fire from heaven to kill the soldiers who came to capture which prophet?
7. What husband and wife dropped dead after it was revealed they had lied about the price of the possessions they had sold?
8. Who was hanged on the very gallows he had prepared for Mordecai?
9. What people were killed by great hailstones from heaven?

10. Who, along with his household, was swallowed up by the earth for rebelling against Moses?
11. What man, reluctant to produce children with his widowed sister-in-law, was slain by God?
12. Who was the first individual who was killed by God for being wicked?
13. What did God do when the Israelites began to complain about the death of Korah and his followers?
14. In the Exodus story, what was the last plague sent upon the Egyptians?

GRISLY EXECUTIONS (ANSWERS)

1. Sodom and Gomorrah (Genesis 19:24)

2. Fire from God (Leviticus 10:1-2). Translators still puzzle over what exactly is meant by "strange fire," though clearly God considered it wicked, whatever it was.

3. Sisera (Judges 4:18-21)

4. Uzzah (2 Samuel 6:6-7)

5. He numbered the people of Israel (2 Samuel 24:1-5).

6. Elijah (2 Kings 1:9-12)

7. Ananias and Sapphira (Acts 5:1-10)

8. Haman (Esther 7:10)

9. Amorites (Joshua 10:8-14)

10. Korah (Numbers 16)

11. Onan (Genesis 38:8-10)

12. Er (Genesis 38:7)

13. He sent a plague that killed 14,700 Israelites (Numbers 16:41-50).

14. The deaths of the firstborn (Exodus 12:29)

 ## DYING IN DROVES

"Weapons of mass destruction" has become a catchphrase in our modern world. Technology has advanced, and we possess the means to harm a lot of people in a small amount of time. Though there were no nuclear or chemical warheads in ancient times, there were still many instances of people dying by the thousands—sometimes through a lot of human effort, sometimes by the power of God. In most cases (but not all), the victims were getting what they deserved.

1. What book of the Bible records the killing of 75,000 Persians by the Jews?
2. Which judge and his men killed 120,000 Midianites?
3. When the Israelites lost 30,000 soldiers during the time of Samuel, who were they fighting?
4. Which king headed up the slaying of 47,000 Syrians?
5. What nation saw 185,000 of its soldiers slaughtered by an angel of the Lord?
6. Which king of Israel killed 20,000 men of Judah in one day because they had forsaken the Lord?
7. For what offense did the Lord kill 50,070 men of Beth Shemesh?
8. For what sin of David did the Lord kill 70,000 Israelites with a plague?
9. Which king of Judah led an army that killed 500,000 soldiers of Israel?
10. What Syrian king fled when 100,000 of his soldiers were killed by the people of Israel?

DYING IN DROVES (ANSWERS)

1. Esther (9:15-16)
2. Gideon (Judges 8:7-10)
3. The Philistines (1 Samuel 4:10)
4. David (1 Chronicles 19:18)
5. Assyria (2 Kings 19:35)
6. Pekah (2 Chronicles 28:6)
7. For looking into the Ark of the Covenant (1 Samuel 6:19)
8. For taking a census (2 Samuel 24:10, 15)
9. Abijah (2 Chronicles 13:17)
10. Ben-hadad (1 Kings 20:29-30)

DEPARTMENT OF DEFENSE (AND SOMETIMES OFFENSE)

Bible times were violent, and lots of men went to war. In the good guys column were those who fought Israel's enemies and stood up for what was right. In the bad guys column were some cruel types who loved violence for its own sake and abused their authority.

1. Who was spit on, beaten, and mocked by Roman soldiers?
2. Which apostle was sleeping between two soldiers when he was miraculously delivered?
3. What loyal Hittite soldier was put on the front lines of battle so David could take his wife?
4. Who was commander of the rebel army when Absalom rebelled against David?
5. What Philistine soldier was slain by a boy carrying a bag of stones?
6. What Gittite soldier supported David during the rebellion of Absalom?
7. Which soldier led a revolt against King Elah, made himself king, and then committed suicide after a seven-day reign?
8. What foreign king had Nebuzaradan as commander of his troops?
9. Which Gospel mentions the Roman soldiers gambling to see who got the robe of Jesus?
10. Which prisoner had a nephew that informed the Roman soldiers of a plot to kill him?
11. What Canaanite commander was murdered by a woman named Jael?
12. Where was Paul when a Roman soldier stopped him from being murdered by an angry mob?
13. Which judge from Gilead was called to be a commander against the Ammonites?
14. What irate soldier falsely accused Jeremiah of deserting to the Babylonians and had him arrested?
15. Which commander (and later king) led a successful revolt against the ill-fated King Zimri?
16. What army commander was anointed by a prophet and told to stamp out Ahab's evil dynasty?
17. What Assyrian field commander tried to intimidate King Hezekiah by speaking propaganda to the people of Jerusalem?
18. What Babylonian soldier was ordered to execute Daniel and his friends?

19. Which soldier (David's oldest brother) picked on David for coming to the battle lines?
20. Which brother of Joab was famous for having killed 300 enemy soldiers in battle?
21. Which prophet told Roman soldiers to be content with their pay and to avoid taking money by force?

DEPARTMENT OF DEFENSE (AND SOMETIMES OFFENSE) (ANSWERS)

1. Jesus (Matthew 27:28-31)

2. Peter (Acts 12:6-11)

3. Uriah (2 Samuel 11:3, 15), husband of Bathsheba. Here was a case of good soldier, bad commander in chief.

4. Amasa (2 Samuel 17:25)

5. Goliath (1 Samuel 17:23, 48-54)

6. Ittai (2 Samuel 15:19)

7. Zimri (1 Kings 16:9-18)

8. Nebuchadnezzar (2 Kings 25:8)

9. John (19:23-24)

10. Paul (Acts 23:16-22)

11. Sisera (Judges 4:2, 21), killed when Jael drove a tent peg through his skull

12. Outside the Temple (Acts 21:30-32)

13. Jephthah (Judges 11:5-6)

14. Irijah (Jeremiah 37:13-15)

15. Omri (1 Kings 16:16)

16. Jehu (2 Kings 9:1-7)

17. Rabshakeh (2 Kings 18:17-37)

18. Arioch (Daniel 2:13-14)

19. Eliab (1 Samuel 17:28)

20. Abishai (1 Chronicles 11:20)

21. John the Baptist (Luke 3:14)

STONE COLD KILLERS

Stoning strikes us as a kind of primitive way to execute someone, but people in ancient Israel probably didn't see it that way. They lived in a stony place filled with plenty of supplies for execution. (Plus they didn't have the technology for electric chairs or gas chambers.) Many of the people in the questions below were bad folks who got what they deserved, whereas some others were quite innocent, meaning that it was the bad boys who were doing the stoning.

1. Which deacon became the first Christian martyr when the Jews stoned him?
2. What owner of a vineyard was stoned after being falsely accused before the people?
3. Which son of a priest was stoned to death by order of King Joash?
4. Who was stoned by an irate mob while trying to carry out the orders of King Rehoboam?
5. Which of Jesus' parables talks about the stoning of a landowner's servant?
6. Who was in danger of being stoned after the Amalekites dragged off the wives and children of Ziklag?
7. What shepherd boy felled a giant with a single stone?
8. Who stoned the Amorites while Joshua led an attack on them?
9. Who was stoned for holding back some of the loot from Jericho?
10. For what seemingly minor offense did the Israelites stone a man while in the wilderness?
11. In which city did some Jews persuade the people to stone Paul?
12. Who fled from Iconium when they heard of a plot to stone them?
13. Who pelted David and his men with stones while he accused David of being a violent man?
14. Which Gospel mentions Jesus miraculously passing through a crowd that intended to stone him?
15. Who intended to stone the woman caught in adultery?
16. In what humiliating way was Abimelech murdered?
17. What shepherd boy went into battle with a bag of stones?
18. In Leviticus, what was the crime of the man who was stoned by the Israelites?

STONE COLD KILLERS (ANSWERS)

1. *Stephen (Acts 7:59)*

2. *Naboth (1 Kings 21:13). He had refused to sell his family vineyard to the king, so Ahab resorted to dirty dealing to get it.*

3. *Zechariah (2 Chronicles 24:20-22)*

4. *Adoram (1 Kings 12:18)*

5. *The parable of the tenants (Matthew 21:35)*

6. *David (1 Samuel 30:6)*

7. *David (1 Samuel 17:48-50)*

8. *The Lord (Joshua 10:11)*

9. *Achan and his family (Joshua 7:24-25)*

10. *Gathering sticks on the Sabbath (Numbers 15:32-36)*

11. *Lystra (Acts 14:8-19)*

12. *Paul and Barnabas (Acts 14:5-6)*

13. *Shimei (2 Samuel 16:5-6)*

14. *John (8:59; 10:31, 39)*

15. *The scribes and the Pharisees (John 8:3-11)*

16. *A woman dropped a millstone on his head (Judges 9:53-54).*

17. *David (1 Samuel 17:49). Because one of them killed the giant Goliath, we can safely say that David knew his weapons well.*

18. *Blasphemy (Leviticus 24:23)*

V IS FOR *VIOLENCE*

The ancient world (like our modern world) was an extremely violent place, and what the ancients lacked in technology, they made up for in grit. Reflecting the human condition, the Bible is full of stories of violent people. Admittedly, some of these are heroes sent by God to deliver his people from violent oppressors. The Bible has words of praise for valiant warriors like Joshua, Gideon (Jerubbaal), Samson, and David. But on the whole the Bible is antiviolence—maybe because, on the whole, violent people are bad folks, delighting not in helping others but in being mean because they enjoy it. It's no surprise that in the Bible (as in real life), violent people often came to a violent end.

1. What oversized warrior had brass armor weighing over 125 pounds (5,000 shekels)?
2. What Roman official in Jerusalem bowed to the wishes of an uncontrollable mob?
3. In which city in Greece did a group of Jews whip up a company of thugs to cause an anti-Paul riot?
4. Who carried only five smooth stones as his weapons?
5. What did the judge Ehud use to kill fat King Eglon of Moab?
6. Who killed 600 Philistines with an ox goad?
7. What did Jael use to murder Sisera?
8. Which rebel was killed by three darts shot into his heart by Joab?
9. Which prophet was commanded to make a model of Jerusalem and set battering rams against it?
10. Who threw a javelin at David?
11. In which city was Jesus almost killed by an angry mob?
12. Which city had a riot on behalf of the goddess Artemis?
13. Which king fortified Jerusalem with catapults for throwing stones?
14. Which apostle was almost done in by 40 men waiting to ambush him at Jerusalem?
15. Who drew the army of Ai out of the city while another group ambushed the city and destroyed it?
16. What paranoid king ordered the execution of the infants in Bethlehem?
17. Who killed Abner?
18. What evil king of Judah was killed by his servants?
19. What Christian witness was killed by the people of Pergamos?
20. Who killed Ben-hadad with a wet cloth?
21. What two women brought about the execution of John the Baptist?
22. Which king of Israel had the whole dynasty of Ahab murdered?
23. What former member of the Egyptian court killed an Egyptian official?
24. Whom did Rechab and Baanah murder to try to get in good with David?
25. Which king of Assyria was murdered at worship by his two sons?
26. What good king of Judah was murdered by his court officials?
27. What saintly deacon was murdered by the Jewish elders for his testimony?

28. Who had one of his army men killed in order to cover up an adulterous affair?
29. Who killed Hamor and Shechem for raping their sister Dinah?
30. What Old Testament figure boasted to his two wives that he had killed a young man?
31. Which son of Abraham was supposed to have been against everyone, and everyone against him?
32. Who caused a riot when people thought he had taken a Gentile into the Temple?
33. Which tribe was ambushed at Gibeah by the other tribes of Israel?
34. In the time of the judges, what did a Levite do when his concubine had been savagely abused by the men of Gibeah?
35. Who killed Amasa after holding his beard and kissing him?
36. What rebel killed Gedaliah, the governor of Judah, after Judah fell to the Babylonians?
37. Where did Cain kill Abel?
38. Which king was critically wounded by Philistine arrows?
39. Who slew 1,000 men with the jawbone of a donkey?
40. Who carried a staff that was as big as a weaver's beam?
41. Who pelted King David with stones while telling him what a violent king he was?
42. What book of the Bible states that "the robbery of the wicked shall destroy them"?

V IS FOR VIOLENCE (ANSWERS)

1. Goliath (1 Samuel 17:4-6)

2. Pilate (Matthew 27:23-24)

3. Thessalonica (Acts 17:1-5)

4. David (1 Samuel 17:39-40)

5. A two-edged dagger (Judges 3:16-21)

6. Shamgar (Judges 3:31)

7. A tent peg through his temples (Judges 4:17-21)

8. Absalom (2 Samuel 18:14)

9. Ezekiel (Ezekiel 4:1-2)

10. Saul (1 Samuel 18:10-11)

11. Nazareth (Luke 4:24-29)

12. *Ephesus (Acts 19:28-29)*

13. *Uzziah (2 Chronicles 26:14-15)*

14. *Paul (Acts 23:21-23)*

15. *Joshua (Joshua 8:12-22)*

16. *Herod (Matthew 2:16)*

17. *Joab (2 Samuel 3:27)*

18. *Amon (2 Kings 21:23)*

19. *Antipas (Revelation 2:12-13)*

20. *Hazael (2 Kings 8:7, 15)*

21. *Herodias and her daughter (Mark 6:21-28)*

22. *Jehu (2 Kings 9)*

23. *Moses (Exodus 2:12)*

24. *Ish-bosheth (2 Samuel 4:6-8)*

25. *Sennacherib (2 Kings 19:36-37)*

26. *Joash (2 Kings 12:20-21)*

27. *Stephen (Acts 7:58-59)*

28. *David (2 Samuel 12:9)*

29. *Levi and Simeon (Genesis 34:26)*

30. *Lamech (Genesis 4:23)*

31. *Ishmael (Genesis 16:12)*

32. *Paul (Acts 21:30-35)*

33. *Benjamin (Judges 20:29-33)*

34. *He cut her into 12 pieces and sent a piece to each tribe of Israel (Judges 20:6).*

35. *Joab (2 Samuel 20:9-10). This is not Abraham's son.*

36. *Ishmael (2 Kings 25:25)*

37. *Out in the fields (Genesis 4:8)*

38. *Saul (1 Samuel 31:3)*

39. *Samson (Judges 15:15)*

40. *Goliath (1 Samuel 17:7)*

41. *Shimei (2 Samuel 16:5-8)*

42. *Proverbs (21:7)*

JEEPERS, WEEPERS!

Bad folks may or may not weep, but they do cause *others* to weep. You might call this the victims of bad boys chapter, and it's a fairly long one, considering that the Bible's bad folks sure caused a lot of tears to be shed.

1. Who wept over the death of his rebellious son, Absalom?
2. Whose second husband, Phaltiel, wept as he watched her return to her first husband, David?
3. Who wept because her husband's other wife taunted her for being childless?
4. Who said, "Depart from me, all ye workers of iniquity; for the Lord hath heard the voice of my weeping"?
5. In what foreign land did Jewish exiles weep "when they remembered Zion"?
6. What book of the Bible states that there is "a time to weep, and a time to laugh; a time to mourn, and a time to dance"?
7. According to Psalms, "They that sow in tears shall reap in _____."
8. What book of the Bible prophesies a time when "God shall wipe away all tears from [his people's] eyes"?
9. What victim of his brother's sneakiness cried as he begged Isaac for his rightful blessing?
10. Which Old Testament book laments that the oppressed weep but have no comforter?
11. Complete this verse from Psalms: "I am weary with my groaning . . . I water my _____ with my tears."
12. What sensitive prophet said, "Oh, that my head were waters, and mine eyes a fountain of tears"?
13. Jacob wept with love and joy over what beautiful woman?
14. Who cried in Egypt when his brothers did not recognize him?
15. Which judge's wife wept in front of him?
16. What three men wept when they saw Job's misery?
17. Which prophet mentions women weeping for the god Tammuz?
18. Which New Testament Epistle mentions the priest Melchizedec weeping?
19. Whom did Jesus tell not to weep for him?
20. Which king's decree for extermination caused the Jews to weep?
21. Who said, "Mine eye poureth out tears to God"?
22. Which king of Israel wept in front of the prophet Elisha?

23. What two male friends wept together?
24. When Saul was king, what caused the people of Gibeah to wail in despair?
25. Which prophet cried when he realized what Hazael of Syria would do to the people of Israel?
26. Which king of Judah cried because of his terrible illness?
27. Who wept with relief when he realized that not all his sons had been killed?
28. The elders of which church wept over Paul?
29. Where was Paul when his friends wept at hearing the prophecy that Paul would be handed over to the Gentiles?
30. Who wept bitterly after denying Jesus?
31. What baby was crying when he was discovered by a princess?
32. Who wept at her husband's feet and tried to dissuade him from listening to the advice of his assistant?
33. Who was reading the words of the law when the people began to weep?
34. To whom did Jesus say, "Weep not"?
35. What friend did Jesus mourn for?
36. Which king received approval from God after weeping and tearing his clothes in repentance?
37. Who wept and said to Jesus, "I believe; help thou my unbelief"?
38. Who wept upon seeing what the Amalekites had done to the people of Ziklag?
39. Who discovered the widows of Joppa weeping over the dead Tabitha?
40. Where was Jesus when the sinful woman washed his feet with her tears?
41. Who wept at thinking her son would die of thirst in the desert?
42. What Old Testament woman is pictured as "weeping for her children and refusing to be comforted"?
43. At whose death did Abraham weep?
44. Who wept at seeing the new Temple that was built after the exiles' return from Babylon?
45. What caused Nehemiah to weep?
46. Who wept because he realized David did have a chance to kill him but chose not to?
47. Who wept when he thought Joseph was dead?

JEEPERS, WEEPERS! (ANSWERS)

1. *David (2 Samuel 18:33)*
2. *Michal's (2 Samuel 3:14-16)*
3. *Hannah (1 Samuel 1:6-7)*
4. *David, believed to be the author of Psalm 6*
5. *Babylon (Psalm 137:1)*
6. *Ecclesiastes (3:4)*
7. *Joy (Psalm 126:5)*
8. *Revelation (7:17; 21:4)*
9. *Esau (Genesis 27:38)*
10. *Ecclesiastes (4:1)*
11. *Couch (Psalm 6:6)*
12. *Jeremiah (Jeremiah 9:1)*
13. *Rachel (Genesis 29:11)*
14. *Joseph (Genesis 42:8, 24)*
15. *Samson's (Judges 14:16)*
16. *Eliphaz, Bildad, and Zophar (Job 2:11-12)*
17. *Ezekiel (Ezekiel 8:14)*
18. *Hebrews (5:6-7)*
19. *The daughters of Jerusalem (Luke 23:28)*
20. *Ahasuerus's (Esther 4:3)*
21. *Job (Job 16:20)*
22. *Joash (2 Kings 13:14)*
23. *David and Jonathan (1 Samuel 20:40-41)*
24. *The threat of attack by the Ammonites (1 Samuel 11:1-4)*
25. *Elisha (2 Kings 8:11-12)*
26. *Hezekiah (2 Kings 20:1-3)*
27. *David (2 Samuel 13:35-36)*
28. *The church at Ephesus (Acts 20:17, 37)*
29. *Caesarea (Acts 21:1-14)*
30. *Peter (Matthew 26:75)*
31. *Moses (Exodus 2:6-10)*
32. *Esther (Esther 8:3)*

33. *Ezra (Nehemiah 8:9)*

34. *The widow from Nain (Luke 7:11-13)*

35. *Lazarus (John 11:34-37)*

36. *Josiah (2 Chronicles 34:1, 27)*

37. *The father of the boy with an evil spirit (Mark 9:21-24)*

38. *David (1 Samuel 30:1-4)*

39. *Peter (Acts 9:39-40)*

40. *The home of Simon the Pharisee (Luke 7:36-40)*

41. *Hagar, mother of Ishmael (Genesis 21:9-16)*

42. *Rahel (Jeremiah 31:15)*

43. *Sarah's (Genesis 23:2)*

44. *Old men who remembered the glory of Solomon's Temple (Ezra 3:12)*

45. *He heard the walls of Jerusalem were still in ruins (Nehemiah 1:4).*

46. *Saul (1 Samuel 24:11-16)*

47. *Jacob (Genesis 37:33-35)*

 ## UNBLESSED ARE THE STRIFEMAKERS

"Blessed are the peacemakers" is one of the most famous sayings of the Bible. The opposite idea is also shown—many times in many ways—in the Bible: Shame on those who stir up strife. Sad, isn't it, in a world with so much strife and conflict, that there really are people who delight in creating more quarrels?

1. According to Proverbs, "Only by _____ comes contention."
2. Who lamented that some Christians "are still carnal, for there is among you envying and strife and division"?
3. What caused a quarrel among Jesus' disciples?
4. What rebellious son of David almost split the kingdom in two by his conspiracy?
5. Proverbs says that "hatred stirs up quarrels, but _____ covers all sins."
6. Who had to send his many brothers on a journey with the reminder not to quarrel along the way?
7. Who claimed that he came not to send peace on the earth but a sword of division?

8. What caused an ugly quarrel between David and his wife Michal?
9. Who urged Christians to settle their differences among themselves, not in the law courts?
10. Which relative did Abraham almost quarrel with over the matter of grazing rights?
11. Who had to face down some quarrelsome Israelites who demanded water?
12. Which king had to decide a famous case of two women arguing over a child?
13. What suffering man desired to argue his case directly with the Almighty?
14. What Old Testament site got its name because it was a place where the Israelites had quarreled with Moses and the Lord?
15. Who commanded Christians to "do everything without complaining or arguing"?
16. In Acts, a group of Jews known as the Freed Slaves argued with what saintly man?
17. What Syrian soldier did the king of Israel believe was trying to pick a quarrel with him?
18. According to Paul, what church leader should be gentle, not quarrelsome?
19. In Acts, what vain and wicked king had a long quarrel with the people of Tyre and Sidon?
20. Complete this verse from Proverbs: "A perverse man sows strife, and a _____ separates chief friends."
21. Which New Testament Epistle says, "You desire to have, and cannot obtain, so you fight and war"?
22. Who told believers to "tell it to the church" when they had a dispute with a fellow believer?
23. Complete this saying of Paul's: "If it be possible, live _____ with all men."
24. Which prophet looked forward to a future time when "nation will not take up war against nation"?
25. Complete this saying from Proverbs: "A _____ answer turns away wrath, but grievous words stir up anger."
26. What two officials had been quarreling but became friends after both of them encountered the accused Jesus?

UNBLESSED ARE THE STRIFEMAKERS (ANSWERS)

1. Pride (Proverbs 13:10)

2. Paul (1 Corinthians 3:3)

3. Which of them would be the greatest (Luke 22:24)

4. Absalom (2 Samuel 15–18)

5. Love (Proverbs 10:12)

6. Joseph (Genesis 45:24)

7. Jesus (Matthew 10:34-36). He was referring to the way that the gospel would divide families.

8. She mocked him for dancing in the streets when the Ark was brought to Jerusalem (2 Samuel 6:16-23).

9. Paul (1 Corinthians 6:1-3)

10. His nephew, Lot (Genesis 13:8)

11. Moses (Exodus 17:2)

12. Solomon (1 Kings 3:16-28)

13. Job (Job 13:3)

14. Meribah, which is Hebrew for "quarreling" (Numbers 20:3-13)

15. Paul (Philippians 2:14)

16. Stephen (Acts 6:9)

17. Naaman (2 Kings 5:6-7), who in fact only wanted his leprosy cured

18. A bishop (or "overseer" in some versions) (1 Timothy 3:2-3)

19. Herod Agrippa (Acts 12:20)

20. Whisperer (Proverbs 16:28)

21. James (4:2)

22. Jesus (Matthew 18:17)

23. Peaceably (Romans 12:18)

24. Micah (Micah 4:3)

25. Soft (Proverbs 15:1)

26. Herod and Pilate (Luke 23:11-12)

SELF-MURDERING

Is suicide a sin? Historically, Christians have believed that it is. In the past, some churches would not allow a person who had committed suicide to be buried in their cemeteries. Christian theologians taught that every human life was God's, and only God could take it away. But the Bible makes no specific judgment on suicide. It is worth noting, however, that most of the seven suicides in the Bible weren't particularly admirable characters.

1. Which king of Israel killed himself by falling on his own sword?
2. According to Matthew's account, Judas committed suicide by hanging himself. How, according to Acts, did Judas die?
3. Which king of Israel, who reigned only seven days, killed himself by burning down the palace with himself inside?
4. Which judge of Israel had his armor bearer kill him so he would avoid the disgrace of being killed by a woman?
5. Which strongman killed himself along with a houseful of Philistines?
6. Which friend of Absalom was so disgraced when Absalom did not follow his advice that he hanged himself?
7. Who refused to obey the king's request to kill him, then followed the king in committing suicide?

SELF-MURDERING (ANSWERS)

1. Saul (1 Samuel 31:4)
2. He fell headlong in a field and burst open (Acts 1:18).
3. Zimri (1 Kings 16:18)
4. Abimelech, who had a millstone dropped on his head by a woman of Thebez (Judges 9:53-54)
5. Samson (Judges 16:29-30)
6. Ahithophel (2 Samuel 17:23)
7. Saul's armor bearer (1 Samuel 31:5)

PARDON ME: FORGIVENESS AND UNFORGIVENESS

"To err is human, to forgive divine"—so said the poet Alexander Pope, though many people think those words come from the Bible. Pope's words do nicely sum up the Bible's teaching about forgiveness. People are expected to forgive, just as God does. Why not, since our own sins and failings ought to make us willing to overlook the sins of others? Unfortunately, in the Bible (as in our own lives) there are many examples of *not* forgiving.

1. What wild young man confessed his riotous living to his forgiving father? (Hint: It's a parable.)
2. According to Jesus, how many times are we supposed to forgive someone?
3. What is the one sin that cannot be forgiven?
4. Who asked the prophet Elisha's forgiveness for worshipping in the temple of the god Rimmon?
5. Who was the first man recorded as forgiving those who had wronged him?
6. To whom did Jesus say, "Your sins are forgiven"?
7. Who was Jesus' immediate predecessor in preaching the forgiveness of sins?
8. In which Gospel does Jesus say from the cross, "Father, forgive them, for they know not what they do"?
9. According to the Epistle to the Hebrews, what is required if sins are to be forgiven?
10. According to Deuteronomy, what sin cannot be forgiven?
11. Who begged David's forgiveness for her husband's boorish behavior?
12. What abused prophet prayed that God would not forgive his enemies' many plots against him?
13. What happens to people who will not forgive their enemies?
14. According to Jesus, what was poured out for the forgiveness of men's sins?
15. According to Mark's Gospel, what activity should we cease from until we have forgiven our brothers?
16. What woman loved much because she had been forgiven much?

PARDON ME: FORGIVENESS AND UNFORGIVENESS (ANSWERS)

1. *The Prodigal Son (Luke 15:11-32)*

2. *Seventy times seven (Matthew 18:21-22). Peter had assumed (wrongly) that seven times was adequate.*

3. *Blasphemy against the Holy Spirit (Matthew 12:31)*

4. *Naaman, the Syrian soldier whom Elisha healed of leprosy (2 Kings 5:17-18)*

5. *Joseph, who had been so badly treated by his brothers (Genesis 50:17)*

6. *The paralytic man whom he healed (Matthew 9:2)*

7. *His kinsman, John the Baptist (Mark 1:4)*

8. *Luke (23:34)*

9. *The shedding of blood (Hebrews 9:22)*

10. *Leading others into idolatry (Deuteronomy 29:16-20)*

11. *Abigail, the wife of surly Nabal. After Nabal died, Abigail became one of David's many wives (1 Samuel 25:23-28).*

12. *Jeremiah (Jeremiah 18:23)*

13. *They will not be forgiven by God (Matthew 6:15).*

14. *His blood (Matthew 26:28)*

15. *Praying (Mark 11:25)*

16. *The immoral woman who anointed Jesus' feet with precious ointment (Luke 7:36-47)*

PART 7

JUST DESSERTS

"H-E-DOUBLE-TOOTHPICKS"

Hell isn't a popular idea these days. Many people wonder how a loving, compassionate God could allow people to suffer eternally. The Bible looks at hell from a different angle: The mystery is that God would choose to save anyone at all, given the rotten way human beings treat one another. Though the idea of hell is unfashionable right now, there's no doubt that the first Christians had very solid beliefs in both eternal bliss (heaven) and eternal agony (hell).

1. Who said that the way that leads to destruction is "broad"?
2. Which Old Testament prophet proclaimed that God takes no pleasure in the death of the wicked but desires that all people would turn from their evil ways?
3. According to Jesus, who would gather up all the wicked and toss them into a furnace of fire?
4. What sin, which can never be forgiven, leads to eternal damnation?
5. What does a person in hell do with his teeth?
6. If your hand causes you to sin, what should you do with it?
7. In a famous parable, which patriarch of Israel had a conversation with a rich man in hell?
8. Which Gospel says that some men are condemned because they loved darkness rather than light?
9. Which apostle stated that God cast sinning angels into hell?
10. What book of the Bible speaks of eternal torment in a "lake of fire"?
11. What is the "brimstone" that is part of hell?
12. What people did Jesus refer to as a "generation of vipers" that was in serious danger of hell?
13. Which Old Testament book expresses a definite belief in hell and heaven?
14. Which Epistle cites the fiery destruction of Sodom and Gomorrah as examples of sin being destroyed by fire?
15. Which Old Testament book ends with a passage describing a fire that will never be quenched?
16. According to Jesus, what becomes of trees that do not bear good fruit?
17. Who warned that Jesus is coming to "burn up the chaff with unquenchable fire"?

18. In which Gospel does Jesus say that "whoever rejects the Son will not see life"?

19. Who was Jesus speaking about when he said, "Fear him who is able to destroy both soul and body in hell"?

20. What, according to Jesus, is easier than a rich man entering the Kingdom of God?

21. Who stated that the "wages of sin is death"?

22. According to James, what bodily organ is "set on fire by hell"?

23. According to Jude, what sort of people will end up in "blackest darkness" forever?

24. What book of the Bible speaks of the "great winepress of God's wrath"?

25. What is the "second death" spoken of in Revelation?

26. What is *annihilationism*?

"H-E-DOUBLE-TOOTHPICKS" (ANSWERS)

1. *Jesus (Matthew 7:13)*

2. *Ezekiel (Ezekiel 33:11)*

3. *The angels (Matthew 13:41-43)*

4. *Blaspheming against the Holy Spirit (Mark 3:29). This is a mystery in itself, because Christians have never been quite sure just what blaspheming against the Spirit involves.*

5. *Gnashes, or grinds them, an image used several times by Jesus in the Gospels. The idea is that a person in agony and regret would grind his teeth.*

6. *Cut it off. It's better to be maimed than to go to hell, according to Mark 9:43. The Bible isn't literally suggesting cutting one's hand off, but it's making the point that whatever causes us to sin is a serious problem.*

7. *Abraham, who was in heaven with the poor beggar Lazarus (Luke 16:19-26)*

8. *John (3:18-19)*

9. *Peter (2 Peter 2:4)*

10. *Revelation (20:10)*

11. *Probably burning sulfur, mentioned in Revelation 21:8. "Fire and brimstone" are what destroyed the sinful cities of Sodom and Gomorrah (Genesis 19:24).*

12. *The Pharisees and teachers of the law (Matthew 23:2, 33)*

13. *Daniel, which predicts a time when some will be raised for everlasting life, others for everlasting contempt (12:2)*

14. *Jude (1:7)*

15. *Isaiah (66:24)*

16. *They are cut down and thrown into the fire (Matthew 7:19). The trees are human beings, of course.*

17. *John the Baptist (Luke 3:15-17)*

18. *John (3:36)*

19. *God (Matthew 10:28). Some people think it refers to Satan, but it is pretty clear in the context that this isn't so.*

20. *A camel passing through the eye of the needle (Mark 10:25)*

21. *Paul (Romans 6:23)*

22. *The tongue, which can do all kinds of evil things (James 3:6)*

23. *False teachers (Jude 1:8-13)*

24. *Revelation (14:19). That passage is, by the way, the source of the phrase "grapes of wrath" in the "Battle Hymn of the Republic."*

25. *The eternal lake of fire (Revelation 2:11; 20:6; 21:8). The "first death" is to the normal physical death of a person.*

26. *The belief that the wicked are simply snuffed out, not punished eternally. It is difficult to square annihilationism with the Bible's rather blunt words about eternal punishment.*

 ## MAKING GOD REALLY MAD

You probably haven't heard many "wrath of God" sermons lately. We modern folks like to concentrate on God's love, not his anger. The fact is, the God of the Bible is loving and forgiving and merciful . . . but also angry at evil. The reason the Bible mentions God's wrath so often is that humans need reminding that their sins are serious. One of the great mysteries of the Bible is not that God is often angry, but that he isn't *more* angry at humanity.

1. Who warned his followers to avoid the "outer darkness," where there would be "weeping and gnashing of teeth"?
2. Why was the Lord angry with King Solomon?
3. In what book of the Bible does God warn that "your wives shall be widows, and your children fatherless"?
4. In what book do people drink "the wine of the wrath of God"?
5. Complete Psalm 103:8: "The Lord is merciful and gracious, _____ to anger."

6. Whom did God ask, "How long will this people provoke me"?
7. What object had Uzzah touched that made the Lord very angry with him?
8. In the Old Testament, the Lord was often angry because the Israelites are a _____-necked people.
9. According to 2 Kings, what one tribe of Israel remained after the Lord vented his anger on the nation?
10. According to Psalm 110, what people will God strike down on the day of his wrath?
11. In Jeremiah, the people are told to put on what type of cloth to turn away the Lord's anger?
12. What entire book of the Bible is a lament about the Lord's anger being poured out on Jerusalem?
13. Which Epistle says that the wrath of God is revealed against all man's ungodliness?
14. In which book of the Bible do people beg to be delivered from the wrath of the Lamb?
15. In which book of the Bible does God say, "Take this wine cup of fury at my hand"?
16. Who warned a "brood of vipers" against God's wrath to come?
17. Which apostle told people not to be vengeful, but to "leave room for God's wrath"?
18. According to John's Gospel whoever rejects the _____ will face the wrath of God.

MAKING GOD REALLY MAD (ANSWERS)

1. Jesus (Matthew 22:13), who also had a lot to say about God's love

2. Solomon had let his pagan wives lead him away from the Lord (1 Kings 11:9).

3. Exodus (22:24)

4. Revelation (14:10)

5. Slow

6. Moses (Numbers 14:11). The Israelites were notorious ingrates.

7. The Ark of the Covenant (2 Samuel 6:6-7)

8. Stiff. To be "stiff-necked" means to be proud, not willing to bow down to God.

9. Judah, the one tribe not conquered by the Assyrians (2 Kings 17:18). Later, however, Judah was faithless enough that God allowed it to be conquered by the Babylonians.

10. Kings (Psalm 110:5)

11. *Sackcloth, coarse cloth like burlap and a symbol of sorrow and repentance (Jeremiah 4:8). The meaning is that the repentance, not the cloth itself, will change the Lord's mind.*

12. *Lamentations*

13. *Romans (1:18)*

14. *Revelation (6:16-17). The Lamb is Christ, pouring out his anger on the wicked.*

15. *Jeremiah (25:15)*

16. *John the Baptist (Matthew 3:7). The "vipers" are the Pharisees and Sadducees.*

17. *Paul (Romans 12:19)*

18. *Son, that is, Christ (John 3:36)*

 ## GOD BATTLING THE BAD

In the Bible, Israel was a tiny nation surrounded by greedy, oppressive, war-loving empires. It seemed almost inevitable that in any military encounter, Israel had to be the loser. But history has plenty of examples of small forces defeating larger ones, and so does the Bible. Tiny David whipped the hulking Goliath, and the small army of Israel whipped the big battalions of the mighty empires—particularly when the Lord was on Israel's side.

1. Which nation's army was defeated when an angel of the Lord struck down 185,000 soldiers?
2. What nation's army was destroyed in the Red Sea?
3. What nation was Israel fighting when Moses' arms, held aloft, caused Israel to win?
4. What weather phenomenon did the Lord use to defeat the Amorites when Joshua and his men were fighting them?
5. Which prophet's word caused the Aramean soldiers to be struck blind?
6. When Samuel was offering a sacrifice, what did the Lord do to rattle the Philistines?
7. What occurred when Jonathan and his armor bearer attacked the Philistines?
8. What made the Syrians flee, thinking the Israelites had joined forces with Egyptians and Hittites?

9. Whom were the Judeans fighting when God helped them slaughter 500,000 soldiers?
10. Which king led the people in singing and praising God, leading God to destroy the men of Ammon, Moab, and Mount Seir?

GOD BATTLING THE BAD (ANSWERS)

1. *Assyria's (2 Kings 19:35)*
2. *Egypt's (Exodus 14:13-31)*
3. *Amalek (Exodus 17:11)*
4. *Large hailstones (Joshua 10:6-13)*
5. *Elisha's (2 Kings 6:18-23)*
6. *Thundered from heaven (1 Samuel 7:10)*
7. *An earthquake (1 Samuel 14:11-15)*
8. *The Lord made a sound like a thundering army (2 Kings 7:6-7).*
9. *Israel (2 Chronicles 13:15-16)*
10. *Jehoshaphat (2 Chronicles 20:21-22)*

L-DAY: THE "DAY OF THE LORD"

Both the Old and New Testaments refer to a "Day of the Lord." At times it seems to refer to any moment when God suddenly appears to punish sin and wickedness. But there are also passages that seem to refer to one final dramatic moment at the end of time, the day of final judgment on all humanity—good news for the saints, bad news for the bad folks.

1. The apostle Paul predicted that the Day of the Lord would arrive like a "_____ in the night."
2. Which prophet proclaimed that the Day of the Lord would come "like destruction from the Almighty"?
3. Which prophet predicted that silver and gold would be no help at all on the day of the Lord's wrath?
4. Which apostle foretold that on the Day of the Lord the heavens would disappear with a roar?

5. According to Malachi, which prophet would return to earth as a forewarning of the Day of the Lord?
6. Who had to remind Christians that the Day of the Lord had not yet arrived?
7. According to Zephaniah, what would consume the whole earth on the Day of the Lord?
8. In Peter's famous Pentecost sermon, what did he say would happen to the sun on the Day of the Lord?
9. What book of the Bible laments that "in the day of the Lord's anger none escaped or remained"?
10. Who prophesied that the Day of the Lord would be "a day of clouds, a time of doom for the nations"?
11. According to Joel, the Day of the Lord would arrive in what valley?
12. Which prophet warned, "Woe to you who long for the day of the Lord!"?
13. Who asked the question, "The day of the Lord is great . . . Who can endure it"?
14. According to Zephaniah, what might provide a shelter on the Day of the Lord?
15. Who prophesied that the Day of the Lord would be a time when all nations would be paid back for all they had done?
16. Who foretold the looting of Jerusalem on the Day of the Lord?
17. According to Isaiah, who would be destroyed on the Day of the Lord?
18. Who prophesied that on the Day of the Lord, God would be like "a refiner's fire"?

L-DAY: THE "DAY OF THE LORD" (ANSWERS)

1. Thief (1 Thessalonians 5:2)
2. Isaiah (Isaiah 13:6) and Joel (Joel 1:15) use almost precisely the same words.
3. Ezekiel (Ezekiel 7:19)
4. Peter (2 Peter 3:10)
5. Elijah (Malachi 4:5)
6. Paul (2 Thessalonians 2:2)
7. Fire (Zephaniah 1:18)
8. It would be darkened (Acts 2:20).
9. Lamentations, appropriately enough (2:22)

10. *Ezekiel (Ezekiel 30:3)*

11. *The valley of decision (Joel 3:14)*

12. *Amos (Amos 5:18)*

13. *Joel (Joel 2:11)*

14. *Humility and righteousness (Zephaniah 2:3)*

15. *Obadiah (1:15)*

16. *Zechariah (Zechariah 14:1-2)*

17. *Sinners (Isaiah 13:9), a theme echoed throughout the Bible*

18. *Malachi (Malachi 3:2). If these words sound familiar, it might be because they are included in George Frideric Handel's Messiah.*

 ## CALLED ON GOD'S CARPET

God the Almighty is accommodating enough to human weakness (and boldness and foolhardiness) to allow us to question him. On other occasions, however, the Almighty himself is the questioner—which, if you think about it, seems appropriate, since the Creator has every right to call his creatures on the carpet, especially when they are behaving badly. See if you can guess who God is questioning in these quotes.

1. "How long will this people provoke me?" (Hint: a leader)
2. "Have I any pleasure at all that the wicked should die?" (Hint: a prophet)
3. "Doest thou well to be angry?" (Hint: a reluctant prophet)
4. "Who told thee that thou wast naked?"
5. "Why is thy countenance fallen? If thou doest well, shalt thou not be accepted?" (Hint: a farmer)
6. "How long wilt thou mourn for Saul, seeing I have rejected him from reigning over Israel?" (Hint: a judge and prophet)
7. "Shall seven years of famine come unto thee in thy land? Or wilt thou flee three months before thine enemies?" (Hint: a king)
8. "Should I not spare Nineveh, that great city?" (Hint: a prophet)
9. "Hast thou an arm like God? Or canst thou thunder with a voice like him?" (Hint: a righteous man)
10. "Why is this people of Jerusalem slidden back by a perpetual backsliding?" (Hint: a prophet)
11. "Hast thou killed, and also taken possession?" (Hint: a king)

CALLED ON GOD'S CARPET (ANSWERS)

1. *Moses (Numbers 14:11). The people referred to are the rebellious, griping Israelites, of course.*

2. *Ezekiel (Ezekiel 18:23)*

3. *Jonah (Jonah 4:9)*

4. *Adam (Genesis 3:11)*

5. *Cain (Genesis 4:6-7)*

6. *Samuel (1 Samuel 16:1)*

7. *David (2 Samuel 24:11-14)*

8. *Jonah (Jonah 4:11)*

9. *Job (Job 40:9)*

10. *Jeremiah (Jeremiah 8:4-5)*

11. *King Ahab (1 Kings 21:19)*

 ## EYES YOU CAN'T ESCAPE

Have you ever looked at the back of a U.S. one-dollar bill? On its left side is a pyramid with an eye at the top. That old symbol is, of course, intended to represent the eye of God, watching over all the doings of humanity. Although God does not possess physical eyes, the Bible makes it clear that he is aware of everything that happens, so the eyes of the Lord are mentioned numerous times. Bad folks can't hide from the eyes of the Almighty.

1. According to Judges, the Israelites did evil in the eyes of the Lord by serving what false gods?
2. According to Samuel, what request of Israel was evil in the eyes of the Lord?
3. What famous rich and wise man did evil in the eyes of the Lord by catering to his wives' religions?
4. What wicked king was told by Elijah that he had done evil in the eyes of the Lord?
5. What form of sacrifice was condemned as evil in the eyes of the Lord in 2 Kings 17?

6. What kind of man is a disgrace in the eyes of God, according to Psalm 52?
7. According to Proverbs 15, where are the eyes of God?
8. Which prophet lamented that the people believed that those who did evil were good in the eyes of the Lord?
9. What famous (and arrogant) building project did God "come down" from heaven to look at?
10. In which book of the Bible does God say, "I will hide my eyes from you"?
11. Which prophet said that God's eyes were too pure to look upon wickedness?
12. What does God look upon to remind himself never to flood the earth again on account of human evil?
13. What foreign army did God "look down upon" before throwing its men into confusion?
14. Who was the first person who made a sacrifice that the Lord looked upon with favor?
15. What leader was told by God that "man looks at the outward appearance, but the Lord looks at the heart"?
16. What book of the Bible states that the Lord looked on the Israelites and was concerned?
17. According to Psalm 14, what does the Lord hope to see when he looks down from heaven?
18. When the world was almost completely corrupt, what good man "found favor in the eyes of the Lord"?

EYES YOU CAN'T ESCAPE (ANSWERS)

1. Baal and Asherah, the false gods of Canaan (Judges 2:11; 3:7)
2. Their request for a king to rule over them (1 Samuel 12:17)
3. Solomon (1 Kings 11:5-16)
4. Ahab (1 Kings 21:20)
5. Sacrifice of children (17:17), commonly practiced by the pagan nations but forbidden in Israel
6. A mighty man (52:1), that is, one who uses his power to oppress others
7. Everywhere (15:3)
8. Malachi (Malachi 2:17)
9. The tower of Babel (Genesis 11:5)
10. Isaiah (Isaiah 1:15), referring to God ignoring the prayers of the wicked

11. *Habakkuk (Habakkuk 1:13)*

12. *The rainbow (Genesis 9:15-16)*

13. *The Egyptian troops that pursued the Israelites (Exodus 14:24)*

14. *Abel (Genesis 4:4)*

15. *Samuel (1 Samuel 16:7)*

16. *Exodus (2:25)*

17. *People who seek him (14:2)*

18. *Noah (Genesis 6:8)*

 ## PRESCRIBING THE PENALTY

We modern folks read the laws of the Old Testament and think, *Wow, things were pretty strict in those days!* Indeed they were. Ancient people believed strongly in what we now call the "deterrent effect" of the law. If you saw someone being stoned to death for blasphemy or adultery, it would definitely have an effect on you. The good news about legal punishments in the Bible is the bad boys were often punished. The bad news is, the innocent were sometimes destroyed by the not-so-innocent.

1. What was the first punishment imposed in the Bible?
2. What was the first punishment imposed on a *human* in the Bible?
3. What was the penalty for doing work on the Sabbath?
4. The basic principle of "eye for eye, tooth for tooth" is found in which Old Testament books?
5. To what man did God deliver the edict "Whoever sheds the blood of man, by man shall his blood be shed"?
6. For stealing a sheep or an ox, what was the thief required to pay back to the owner?
7. The guilt offering for a person who sinned unintentionally was what sacrifice?
8. If a bull gored a person to death, what was done to the bull?
9. Stoning was the penalty prescribed for anyone who sacrificed his child to what foreign god?
10. What form of capital punishment was mandated for a man who married both a woman and her mother?
11. What was the penalty for a man who slept with a virgin engaged to another man?

12. What punishment—imposed by God, not by man—was imposed on a man who married his brother's wife?
13. When a flogging was imposed, what was the maximum number of lashes that could be given?
14. What form of capital punishment was the penalty for being a medium or spiritist?
15. A thief who could not pay restitution for his theft suffered what punishment?
16. What book of the Bible records the stoning of a man who violated the Sabbath by gathering wood on that day?
17. Because priests and their families were expected to be holy, what was done to a priest's daughter who became a prostitute?
18. What name was given to the towns where a person who killed someone accidentally could flee for sanctuary?
19. How many witnesses were required for the death penalty to be imposed?
20. When a person was stoned to death, who had to cast the first stones?
21. If a master blinded a servant or knocked out his or her tooth, what was the penalty?
22. If a man seduced a virgin, what did he have to do besides marry her?
23. Which Gospel tells the story of an adulterous woman who would have been stoned to death if not for Jesus?
24. What punishment was imposed on a woman who grabbed the privates of a man her husband was fighting with?
25. What type of offender could not be ransomed, but was required to be executed?
26. What book of the Bible states that contempt of court was punishable by death?
27. In Genesis, what form of execution was imposed on the pharaoh's baker?
28. What wicked king had Naboth stoned to death after accusing him (falsely) of cursing God and the king?
29. Which apostle was flogged five times?
30. On what occasion did the Levites go through the Israelite camp, killing 3,000 of the people?
31. What punishment was imposed on Jesus prior to his crucifixion?

32. When criminals were crucified, what was often done to hasten their deaths?
33. In the laws of Moses, what was the penalty for attacking one's father or mother?
34. What was the time limit on exposing the body of an executed criminal?
35. What city did Jesus say was notorious for its stoning of God's prophets?
36. Which New Testament Epistle says that some people had been executed by being sawed in two?
37. Which king punished the Ammonites he conquered by sentencing them to hard labor?
38. After King Amaziah defeated the Edomites in battle, how did his army execute 10,000 of them?
39. Which leader of Israel hung the king of Ai after burning the city down?
40. In which book of the Bible would you find these words: "It is not good to punish the just man, or to flog officials for their integrity"?
41. Which apostle once escaped a flogging by reminding the flogger that he was a Roman citizen?
42. Who warned his followers that they would be "flogged in the synagogues"?
43. What tactless young king told the people of Israel, "My father scourged you with whips, but I will scourge you with scorpions"?
44. After the apostles were flogged by the Jewish authorities, what were they ordered not to do?
45. What punishment, mentioned several times in the laws of Moses, is interpreted to mean excommunication or banishment?

PRESCRIBING THE PENALTY (ANSWERS)

1. The serpent that tempted Adam and Eve was made to crawl on its belly and "eat dust" (Genesis 3:14).
2. Eve was sentenced to suffer pains in childbirth and to be dominated by her husband (Genesis 3:16).
3. Death (Exodus 35:2)
4. Exodus (21:23), Leviticus (24:20), and Deuteronomy (19:21)
5. Noah (Genesis 9:1-6)
6. Five oxen for one ox, four sheep for one sheep (Exodus 22:1)

7. *A ram (Leviticus 5:14-19)*

8. *It was stoned to death, and its meat could not be eaten (Exodus 21:28).*

9. *Molech (Leviticus 20:2)*

10. *Burning (Leviticus 20:14)*

11. *Both man and girl would be stoned—unless the girl had screamed for help, in which case only the man was stoned (Deuteronomy 22:23-27).*

12. *The two would be childless (Leviticus 20:21).*

13. *Forty (Deuteronomy 25:3)*

14. *Stoning (Leviticus 20:27)*

15. *He would be sold as a slave (Exodus 22:2).*

16. *Numbers (15:32-36)*

17. *She was burned to death (Leviticus 21:9).*

18. *Cities of refuge (Numbers 35:6)*

19. *At least two (Deuteronomy 17:6)*

20. *The witnesses (Deuteronomy 17:5-7)*

21. *He had to free the servant (Exodus 21:26-27).*

22. *Pay her father 50 shekels of silver (Deuteronomy 22:28-29)*

23. *John (8:7-11)*

24. *Her hand was cut off (Deuteronomy 25:11-12).*

25. *A murderer (Numbers 35:31)*

26. *Deuteronomy (19:15-21)*

27. *Hanging (Genesis 40:22)*

28. *Ahab (1 Kings 21:13)*

29. *Paul (2 Corinthians 11:24)*

30. *After the orgy around the gold calf idol (Exodus 32:25-28)*

31. *Flogging, also called scourging (Mark 15:15)*

32. *Their legs were broken (John 19:32).*

33. *Death (Exodus 21:15)*

34. *It had to be taken down at sunset (Deuteronomy 21:23).*

35. *Jerusalem (Luke 13:34)*

36. *Hebrews (11:37)*

37. *David (2 Samuel 12:29-31)*

38. *Threw them off a cliff (2 Chronicles 25:12)*

39. *Joshua (Joshua 8:29)*

40. *Proverbs (17:26)*

41. *Paul (Acts 22:25)*

42. *Jesus (Matthew 10:17)*

43. *Rehoboam (1 Kings 12:6-11), whose foolish words caused the kingdom to be split in two.*

44. *Not to preach the message of Jesus anymore (Acts 5:40). But read Acts 5:42 to see if they obeyed that order.*

45. *Being "cut off" from Israel, mentioned in Exodus 12:15; 30:33; Leviticus 20:2-3; and elsewhere*

 ## PUNISHED IN MOST PECULIAR WAYS

Yes, Bible times were violent, and a lot of people in the Bible died suddenly and dramatically. Jesus Christ was the classic case of an innocent man whose execution was totally undeserved, but in a number of cases, the people who were punished got what they deserved, often in dramatic—and sometimes odd—ways.

1. What Canaanite captain was killed when Jael, a Hebrew woman, drove a tent peg through his skull?
2. Which son of Saul was murdered by two servants who stabbed him in the belly and carried his severed head to David?
3. What devoured Aaron's sons, Nadab and Abihu, when they offered "strange fire" to the Lord?
4. Who was killed for touching the Ark of the Covenant?
5. The Lord sent a pestilence on Israel that killed 70,000 people. What act of King David brought this on?
6. God sent fire from heaven to kill the soldiers who came to capture which prophet?
7. Which husband and wife dropped dead after it was revealed they had lied about the price of the possessions they had sold?
8. Who was hanged on the very gallows he had prepared for Mordecai?
9. What people were killed by great hailstones from heaven?
10. Who, along with his household, was swallowed up by the earth for rebelling against Moses?

11. What man, reluctant to produce children with his widowed sister-in-law, was slain by God?
12. What two cities were rained on by fire and brimstone?
13. What did God do when the Israelites began to complain about the death of Korah and his followers?
14. What was the last plague sent upon the Egyptians?
15. Who was the first individual killed by God for being wicked?

PUNISHED IN MOST PECULIAR WAYS (ANSWERS)

1. Sisera (Judges 4:18-21). Jael really had him pegged (sorry!).
2. Ish-bosheth, slain by Recab and Baanah (2 Samuel 4:5-8)
3. Fire from God (Leviticus 10:1-2)
4. Uzzah (2 Samuel 6:6-7)
5. He numbered the people of Israel (2 Samuel 24:1-15).
6. Elijah (2 Kings 1:10, 12)
7. Ananias and Sapphira (Acts 5:1-10)
8. Haman (Esther 7:10)
9. Amorites (Joshua 10:11-12)
10. Korah (Numbers 16:1-33)
11. Onan (Genesis 38:9-10)
12. Sodom and Gomorrah (Genesis 19:24-25)
13. He sent a plague that killed 14,700 Israelites (Numbers 16:41-50).
14. The death of the firstborn in each family (Exodus 12:29)
15. Er (Genesis 38:7)

THE BACK OF GOD'S HAND

No, God doesn't literally have hands, but the Bible often speaks of his hands doing amazing things, including punishing the wicked ones. In some way God's holiness has to administer a "spanking" (or something much worse) to people who behave badly.

1. Whom did Moses warn that the hand of the Lord would send a plague on livestock?

2. In the lifetime of the prophet Samuel, the Lord's hand was against what foreign nation?
3. What poor man lamented that he had been struck by the hand of God?
4. What book of the Bible speaks of the Lord's hand holding a full cup of foaming wine?
5. Which prophet stated that Jerusalem had drunk "a cup of wrath" from the hand of the Lord?
6. What shyster was struck blind by the hand of God?
7. Who told Pharaoh that the plagues on Egypt were done by "the finger of God"?
8. Who claimed that he drove out demons "by the finger of God"?
9. Complete this verse from Hebrews: "It is a _____ thing to fall into the hands of the living God."
10. What book of the Bible says that because of the Israelites' faithlessness, "the hand of the Lord was against them to defeat them"?

THE BACK OF GOD'S HAND (ANSWERS)

1. *The Egyptian pharaoh (Exodus 9:1-3)*

2. *The Philistines (1 Samuel 7:13)*

3. *Job (Job 19:21)*

4. *Psalms (Psalm 75:8)*

5. *Isaiah (Isaiah 51:17)*

6. *Elymas, the fake sorcerer (Acts 13:6-12)*

7. *His court magicians (Exodus 8:19)*

8. *Jesus (Luke 11:20)*

9. *Fearful (or, in some translations, "dreadful") (Hebrews 10:31)*

10. *Judges (2:15)*

PART 8

SINS OF THE SPIRIT

THE PREENING OF THE PROUD

Flying the pennants of one's accomplishments did not go over well with the writers of the Bible; pride was considered a serious sin. In fact, the original sin of humanity was pride, when Adam and Eve succumbed to the temptation to "be like gods." Self-worship and narcissism were condemned constantly by the prophets and men of wisdom, but just as now, people refused to listen.

1. Complete this familiar verse from Proverbs: "Pride goeth before destruction and a _____ spirit before a fall."
2. In the Old Testament, the proud are often referred to as being _____-necked.
3. Which prophet condemned people for being proud of their jewels?
4. According to James, what type of Christian should rejoice in his high position?
5. What did Jesus say would happen to proud people?
6. Which organ of the body is pride associated with?
7. According to Proverbs, what does pride breed?
8. In the book of Revelation, who uttered proud words and blasphemies?
9. According to Jeremiah, what is the one thing a person should boast about?
10. Which king of Judah met his downfall after he became proud?
11. According to Moses, what great event would be forgotten because the Hebrews had become proud?
12. The Christians of Corinth were proud of what sinful deed?
13. What (formerly) proud king of Babylon praised God for being humbled?
14. What book of the Bible repeatedly uses the phrase "all is vanity"?
15. According to 1 Corinthians 13, what wonderful thing is not proud?
16. Complete this verse from Psalms: "Though the Lord be high, he has respect unto the _____, but the proud he knoweth afar off."
17. According to Ecclesiastes, what is better than pride?
18. Who tears down the proud man's house, according to Proverbs?
19. What book of the Bible says that the Lord will "pay the proud back in full"?
20. In Jewish and Christian tradition, which angel was thrown out of heaven because of his pride?

THE PREENING OF THE PROUD (ANSWERS)

1. *Haughty (Proverbs 16:18)*

2. *Stiff. The idea is that the person is too proud to bow or kneel to God (2 Chronicles 30:8).*

3. *Ezekiel, who claimed that they made their jewelry into idols (Ezekiel 7:20)*

4. *The poor one (James 1:9)*

5. *He said nothing—or at least the Gospels do not record any words he uttered about pride. He did have plenty to say, however, about self-centeredness and vanity— all of it bad.*

6. *The heart*

7. *Quarrels (Proverbs 13:10)*

8. *The Beast (Revelation 13:5)*

9. *That he knows the Lord (Jeremiah 9:24)*

10. *King Uzziah (2 Chronicles 26:16)*

11. *Their deliverance from slavery in Egypt (Deuteronomy 8:14)*

12. *One of them was living in sin with his stepmother, which Paul chastised them for condoning (1 Corinthians 5:1-2).*

13. *Nebuchadnezzar (Daniel 4:37)*

14. *Ecclesiastes. Some modern translations have "meaningless" or "useless" instead of "vanity." However, in our modern world, the phrase "all is vanity" does seem to apply, doesn't it?*

15. *Love (1 Corinthians 13:4)*

16. *Lowly (Psalm 138:6)*

17. *Patience (Ecclesiastes 7:8)*

18. *The Lord (Proverbs 15:25)*

19. *Psalms (Psalm 31:23)*

20. *Lucifer, which (tradition says) was the name of Satan before he was expelled from heaven. Isaiah 14:12 speaks of a proud Lucifer, fallen from heaven; this has been interpreted to refer to Satan, the angel-turned-devil.*

UNCLEAN, AND NOT JUST ON THE SURFACE

Clean and *unclean* are words that crop up often in the Bible, particularly the Old Testament, with its code of kosher foods and other restrictions on small details of life. But the Bible's view of cleanliness goes way beyond those rules about food. In fact, much of what is taught about clean and unclean has nothing whatsoever to do with physical matters. *Unclean* generally meant "dirty on the inside"—spiritually polluted, you might say.

1. To whom did Jesus give power to cast out unclean spirits?
2. When Jesus said to his disciples, "You are not all clean," who was the unclean one?
3. Which apostle received a strange vision of a huge sheet filled with unclean animals?
4. According to the law of Moses, what is needed to cleanse the land of the blood of a murdered man?
5. According to Paul, what is the opposite of uncleanness?
6. According to Jesus, when an unclean spirit leaves a man, where does it go?
7. What, according to the New Testament, cleanses us from all sin?
8. According to the law of Moses, what could a man do with a wife in whom he had found some "uncleanness"?
9. What godly king cleansed Jerusalem by burning the bones of false priests on the altars?
10. What substance, according to Job, could wash a man's hands squeaky clean?
11. Which apostle said, "I know, and am persuaded by the Lord Jesus, that there is nothing unclean of itself"?
12. Who cleansed 10 lepers but received a thank-you from only one of them?
13. According to Psalms, what plant is used for cleansing a person?
14. Which prophet lamented that he was a man of unclean lips, living among an unclean people?
15. Which prophet predicted that the Israelites would eat unclean things in Assyrian exile?
16. Whom did Jesus criticize for being obsessive about cleaning their dishes but not their souls?
17. In the book of Revelation, what city is the habitation of every kind of unclean thing?

18. Where did Jesus send the unclean spirits who had possessed a man?
19. Who had a vision of unclean spirits shaped like frogs coming out of the mouth of a dragon?
20. What type of persons were forced to walk around in public crying out, "Unclean! Unclean!"?
21. Which prophet predicted a fountain in Jerusalem that would cleanse people from their sins?

UNCLEAN, AND NOT JUST ON THE SURFACE (ANSWERS)

1. The twelve disciples (Matthew 10:1)

2. Judas Iscariot (John 13:11)

3. Peter, who was being told by God that the clean (Jews) and unclean (Gentiles) are both loved by God (Acts 10)

4. The blood of the one who murdered him (Numbers 35:33)

5. Holiness (1 Thessalonians 4:7: "For God hath not called us unto uncleanness, but unto holiness.")

6. Into "dry places" (or "desert places" in some translations) (Matthew 12:43)

7. The blood of Jesus (1 John 1:7)

8. Divorce her (Deuteronomy 24:1)

9. Josiah (2 Chronicles 34:1-5)

10. Melted snow (Job 9:30)

11. Paul, who was commenting on dietary restrictions (Romans 14:14)

12. Jesus (Luke 17:14-18)

13. Hyssop (Psalm 51:7)

14. Isaiah, after his vision of the Lord in the Temple (Isaiah 6:5)

15. Hosea (Hosea 9:3)

16. The scribes and Pharisees (Matthew 23:25)

17. Babylon (Revelation 18:2)

18. Into a herd of pigs (Mark 5:13)

19. John (Revelation 16:13)

20. Lepers (Leviticus 13:45)

21. Zechariah (Zechariah 13:1)

A BUNDLE OF BACKSLIDERS

You might say that the Bible is the Book of Ingratitude, one story after another showing how people forget all the good things God has done for them. This shouldn't surprise us because we are chronically ungrateful to people (such as parents) who have been kind and generous. Time and time again, people in the Bible resolve to do better—then backslide once more. The great mystery is not human ingratitude and backsliding but the fact that God is always willing to forgive.

1. According to Joshua, what fate awaits those who forsake God and pursue false gods?
2. What book of the Bible laments that the people of Israel "remembered not the Lord their God," who had delivered them from enemies on every side?
3. Which prophet recorded God as saying, "Return unto me, and I will return unto you"?
4. Which prophet lamented that the ox and donkey knew their master, but the people of Israel did not know theirs?
5. Which Epistle states that a person who turns a sinner from his ways will "hide a multitude of sins"?
6. Which prophet records God as saying, "Return, backsliding Israel"?
7. What book of the Bible compares a backsliding fool to a vomiting dog?
8. Who lamented that Demas had forsaken him, "loving this present world"?
9. Which of Jesus' parables is concerned with people who embrace the faith but then turn from it?
10. What group of Christians did Paul lament had been "bewitched" away from the faith?
11. In which book of the Bible does Christ scold a group of believers who "left their first love" of the faith?
12. According to Paul, the love of _____ caused many people to wander from the faith.
13. In a famous saying of Jesus, whose wife was a symbol of people who "looked back" longingly on their sinful pasts?
14. Complete this verse from 1 Timothy: "Some have already turned aside after _____."
15. According to Isaiah, "They that forsake the Lord shall be _____."

16. Which prophet pronounced a curse on anyone "that departeth from the Lord"?
17. What New Testament man claimed he had to keep his body under control, "lest I myself should be a castaway"?
18. Complete this verse from 1 Timothy: "In the latter times some shall _____ from the faith, giving heed to seducing spirits."
19. Who warned that people of faith would betray each other and hate one another?
20. Complete this verse from 1 Chronicles 28: "If you forsake him, he will _____ you off forever."
21. In Acts, which Christian paid with his life for reminding the Jews of their constant backsliding?
22. Which Old Testament book warns against people who lead others astray by saying, "Let us follow other gods"?
23. Which prophet quotes the Lord as saying, "My people are bent to backslide from me"?
24. Complete this saying of Jesus: "No man, having put his hand to the _____ , and, looking back, is fit for the kingdom of God."
25. Complete this verse from Hosea: "I will heal their backsliding, I will _____ them freely."

A BUNDLE OF BACKSLIDERS (ANSWERS)

1. They will be "consumed" (Joshua 24:20).

2. Judges (8:34)

3. Malachi (Malachi 3:7)

4. Isaiah (Isaiah 1:3)

5. James (5:19-20)

6. Jeremiah (Jeremiah 3:12). The words are in Jeremiah, but the sentiment is found throughout the Bible.

7. Proverbs (26:11), which states that a fool returns to his folly the same way a dog returns to his vomit. Ugly, yes, but the words do stick in the mind, don't they?

8. Paul (2 Timothy 4:10). Apparently Demas had been a fellow Christian who lost his faith.

9. The parable of the sower, in which some of the "seeds" (people) look promising but fail to mature (Mark 4:7-19)

10. The Galatians (Galatians 3:1)—in the memorable phrase, "O foolish Galatians!"

11. Revelation (2:4)

12. Money—in the passage with the famous phrase, "the love of money is the root of all evil" (1 Timothy 6:10)

13. Lot's wife (Luke 17:32). In Genesis 19:26, Lot's wife is turned into a pillar of salt when she looks back on the burning city of Sodom.

14. Satan (1 Timothy 5:15)

15. Consumed (Isaiah 1:28)

16. Jeremiah (Jeremiah 17:5-6)

17. Paul (1 Corinthians 9:27)

18. Depart (1 Timothy 4:1)

19. Jesus (Matthew 24:10)

20. Cast (1 Chronicles 28:9)

21. Stephen, the first Christian martyr (Acts 7)

22. Deuteronomy (13:13)

23. Hosea (Hosea 11:7)

24. Plow (Luke 9:62)

25. Love (Hosea 14:4)

STUMBLING IN THE DARK

Darkness in the Bible refers to something spiritual more often than physical. God and his people are on the side of light, whereas Satan and all the wicked are on the side of darkness.

1. Which apostle told people to put on the "armor of light" and lay aside the works of darkness?
2. What Wisdom book says that wisdom excels over folly just as light excels over darkness?
3. Complete this verse from 2 Corinthians: "The _____ of this world has blinded the minds of unbelievers to keep them from seeing the light."
4. To what people was Paul sent to "open their eyes and turn them from darkness to light"?
5. What expectant father said that his son would be the prophet of the one who would "shine on those living in darkness"?

6. In Handel's *Messiah,* the words "the people that walked in darkness have seen a great light" are from which prophet?
7. Complete this verse from John: "The light shines in the darkness, but the darkness has never _____ it."
8. Which Epistle says that in a crooked and perverse world, believers should "shine like stars"?
9. What oppressive pagan nation experienced three full days of literal darkness?
10. Which Gospel says that light came into the world, but people preferred the darkness?
11. According to Paul, at what time would light shine upon all things now hidden in darkness?
12. Which apostle warned against being "unequally yoked" with unbelievers because light and darkness can have no fellowship?
13. In which Epistle does Paul refer to people who "became vain in their imaginations, and their foolish heart was darkened"?
14. According to 1 John, he who hates his _____ is in darkness.
15. To which prophet did God promise that he would "make darkness light before them, and crooked things straight"?

STUMBLING IN THE DARK (ANSWERS)

1. *Paul (Romans 13:12)*

2. *Ecclesiastes (2:13)*

3. *God—"god of this world" referring to Satan (2 Corinthians 4:4)*

4. *The Gentiles, that is, non-Jews (Acts 26:17-18)*

5. *Zechariah, the father-to-be of John the Baptist (Luke 1:67-79)*

6. *Isaiah (Isaiah 9). The words have been understood as a prophecy of Jesus (Matthew 4:16).*

7. *Understood—or overcome (John 1:5). The Greek word can mean either, which is why some versions have "mastered," a word that contains both meanings.*

8. *Philippians (2:15)*

9. *Egypt (Exodus 10:23), experiencing one of the 10 plagues*

10. *John (3:19)*

11. *Jesus' second coming (1 Corinthians 4:5)*

12. *Paul (2 Corinthians 6:14)*

13. *Romans (1:21)*

14. *Brother (1 John 2:11)*

15. *Isaiah (Isaiah 42:16)*

 ## SAY IT SLOWLY: DE-PRAV-I-TY

Are human beings basically good or basically evil? To answer that question, flip on the TV or pick up a newspaper. We've made a lot of technological progress over the centuries but not much moral and spiritual progress. This wouldn't have surprised the Bible authors at all, for they all believed humans were definitely inclined to be bad more often than good. The old word for man's evil tendency was *depravity*. The word may be out of style, but depravity isn't.

1. According to Genesis, what did God decide to do when he "saw that the wickedness of man was great in the earth"?
2. When the earth was full of violence and corruption, what one man stood out as righteous?
3. Complete this verse from Genesis: "The imagination of man's heart is evil from his _____."
4. In Christian tradition, all human beings inherit the sin of Adam and Eve. This is called the doctrine of _____ sin.
5. Who observed that "a bad tree bears bad fruit"?
6. Which Old Testament book says that "there is not a just man upon the earth that does good and sins not"?
7. What book of the Bible asks the question, "Who can bring a clean thing out of an unclean? No one"?
8. Complete this verse from Isaiah: "All we like _____ have gone astray, we have turned everyone to his own way."
9. According to Paul, "The _____ man receives not the things of the Spirit of God."
10. Complete this famous saying from Jeremiah: "Can the _____ change his skin, or the _____ his spots? Neither can you do good, who are accustomed to do evil."
11. What much-read Old Testament book states that "there is none that doeth good, no, not one"?
12. Who said that "this is the condemnation, that light is come into the world, and men loved darkness more than light"?

13. According to the book of Job, "Abominable and filthy is man, who drinks up _____ like water."
14. Paul told Christians that "the flesh lusteth against the _____, and the _____ against the flesh, and they are contrary to one another."
15. What short New Testament book says that "the whole world lieth in wickedness"?
16. Which prophet lamented that "the heart is deceitful above all things, and desperately wicked"?
17. Complete this verse from Proverbs: "Who can say, 'I have made my heart _____, I am _____ from my sin'?"
18. Which apostle lamented that with his mind he served the law of God, but with his flesh he served the law of sin?
19. According to 1 John, human beings are either the children of God or children of _____.
20. Which king was the author of these words: "Behold, I was shapen in inquity, and in sin did my mother conceive me"?

SAY IT SLOWLY: DE-PRAV-I-TY (ANSWERS)

1. Destroy the human race—except for a few—in a great flood (Genesis 6:5-7)

2. Noah (Genesis 6:8)

3. Youth (Genesis 8:21)

4. Original—in the sense of "from the origin"

5. Jesus (Matthew 7:17)

6. Ecclesiastes (7:20)

7. Job (14:4)

8. Sheep (Isaiah 53:6)

9. Natural (1 Corinthians 2:14)

10. Ethiopian, leopard (Jeremiah 13:23)

11. Psalms (Psalm 14:3)

12. Jesus (John 3:19)

13. Iniquity (Job 15:16)

14. Spirit, Spirit (Galatians 5:17)

15. 1 John (5:19)

16. Jeremiah (Jeremiah 17:9)

17. Clean, pure (Proverbs 20:9)

18. Paul (Romans 7:23)

19. *The devil (1 John 3:10)*
20. *David (Psalm 51:5)*

 ## A MORAL 180: REPENTANCE (SOMETIMES TEMPORARY)

Nothing is more satisfying than seeing a bad boy turn good. It so happens that the Bible has many such stories. Unfortunately, the repentance does not always "stick," and the sinner goes back to his old ways soon enough. Bad human beings can do a "moral 180-degree turn" to the good—but return to the bad.

1. Whose jealous brothers at long last were sorry they had sold him into slavery?
2. What wicked, idol-worshipping king of Israel repented—temporarily—after hearing a word of warning from the prophet Elijah?
3. What foreign leader would always "harden his heart" again after temporarily recognizing the power of Israel's God?
4. What pagan city's inhabitants repented of their sin after the preaching of Jonah?
5. Which king repented after being confronted by the prophet Nathan about his committing adultery and murder?
6. What idolatrous king of Judah repented after being carried away in chains to Babylon?
7. What pagan prophet repented after being confronted by God's angel—and by his talking donkey?
8. What plague from the Lord caused the Israelites to repent of their grumbling against Moses?
9. What book of the Bible records the repentance of the Jewish men for having married foreign wives?
10. Which Gospel records that the traitor Judas Iscariot changed his mind after delivering Jesus to the authorities?
11. Which leader heard the Israelites beg for a king, then repent of it after he explained the problems in having a king?
12. What famous parable of Jesus concerns a very forgiving father and a young man who squandered his money?

13. Whose preaching in the wilderness led many people to confess their sins and be baptized in the Jordan River?
14. What greedy (and short) tax collector turned his life around when Jesus visited his home?
15. What distraught king confessed to Samuel that he had broken the Lord's commandment?
16. What did the new Christians of Ephesus burn to show they had parted from their heathen ways?
17. Who lamented that many of the cities where he had worked miracles did not repent of their sins?
18. What converted magician was ordered to repent after he tried to purchase the power of the Holy Spirit?
19. What book of the Bible tells of people still refusing to repent of their evils even after several plagues had visited them?
20. Which disciple "went out and wept bitterly" after he had denied knowing Jesus?
21. What sin of David, which brought a plague on Israel, caused him to repent after much heartache?
22. Which of the psalms, supposed to have been written by David, is the classic "repentance psalm"?
23. Which prophet saw a vision of God in the Temple, and lamented that he was an unclean man living among unclean men?
24. What great apostle always grieved because in his earlier days he had persecuted Christians?
25. Complete this saying of Jesus: "I came not to call the _____, but sinners to repentance."
26. According to Psalms, "The Lord is near to those who are of a _____ heart."
27. What wayward king of Judah repented (temporarily) after the Egyptians plundered Jerusalem?
28. Complete this verse from Proverbs: "He that covers his sins shall not prosper, but whoever confesses and _____ them shall have mercy."
29. Which king of Judah promoted a religious revival after hearing the preaching of the prophet Azariah?
30. In the book of Isaiah, the Lord says, "I have blotted out, like a thick _____, your offenses and your sins."
31. In Acts, which apostle urged people to repent "so that times of refreshing may come from the Lord"?
32. Complete this verse from the Epistle of James: "Cleanse your hands, you sinners, and purify your _____, you double-minded."

33. What Israelite confessed that he had disobeyed God's command by keeping some of the treasures from the sacking of Ai?
34. Which king of Judah repented at the preaching of the prophet Micah?
35. What did a repentant woman do for Jesus while he dined in the home of a Pharisee?
36. In Acts 2, what gift did Peter promise those who repented?
37. What powerful Babylonian ruler turned to the Lord after going insane and living for a time like a beast?
38. Complete this verse from Psalms: "Depart from evil and do good; seek _____ and pursue it."
39. In what great pagan city did the people and even the livestock wear sackcloth as a sign of repentance?
40. Complete this verse from Isaiah: "Let the wicked forsake his way and the unrighteous man his _____."
41. Which scribe bowed in front of the Temple and confessed the sins of Israel while the people around him wept bitterly?
42. Who confessed the making of the golden calf to God?
43. Who confessed his sexual immorality with his daughter-in-law, Tamar?
44. Who confessed Israel's sins after he heard the walls of Jerusalem were in ruins?
45. Who was pardoned by David after confessing his sin and begging for mercy?

A MORAL 180: REPENTANCE (SOMETIMES TEMPORARY) (ANSWERS)

1. *Joseph's (Genesis 42:21; 45:14-15; 50:17-18)*

2. *Ahab (1 Kings 21:27-29)*

3. *The pharaoh at the time of Moses (Exodus 9:27-35; 10:16-20)*

4. *Nineveh's (Jonah 3:4-9)*

5. *David (2 Samuel 12:7-23)*

6. *Manasseh (2 Chronicles 33:10-17)*

7. *Balaam (Numbers 22:34)*

8. *The "fiery serpents" that caused many of them to die in the wilderness (Numbers 21:4-9)*

9. *Ezra (chapter 10)*

10. *Matthew (27:3-9)*

11. *Samuel (1 Samuel 12)*

12. *The Prodigal Son (Luke 15:11-32)*

13. *John the Baptist (Matthew 3:4-6)*

14. *Zacchaeus (Luke 19:6-8)*

15. *Saul (1 Samuel 15:24)*

16. *Their books of "magic arts" (Acts 19:17-19)*

17. *Jesus (Matthew 11:20)*

18. *Simon (Acts 8:9-24)*

19. *Revelation (9:20-21)*

20. *Peter (Matthew 26:75)*

21. *He took a census of the people, against the Lord's will (2 Samuel 24:10-17).*

22. *Psalm 51, beginning with "Have mercy upon me, O God"*

23. *Isaiah (Isaiah 6:1-5)*

24. *Paul (1 Corinthians 15:9)*

25. *Righteous (Luke 5:32)*

26. *Broken (Psalm 34:18)*

27. *Rehoboam, son of Solomon (2 Chronicles 12:9-12)*

28. *Forsakes (Proverbs 28:13)*

29. *Asa (2 Chronicles 15:1-16)*

30. *Cloud (Isaiah 44:22)*

31. *Peter (Acts 3:19)*

32. *Hearts (James 4:8)*

33. *Achan (Joshua 7:20-21)*

34. *Hezekiah (Jeremiah 26:18-19)*

35. *Anointed his feet with some expensive ointment (Luke 7:36-39)*

36. *The Holy Spirit (Acts 2:38)*

37. *Nebuchadnezzar (Daniel 4:28-37)*

38. *Peace (Psalm 34:14)*

39. *Nineveh (Jonah 3:8-9)*

40. *Thoughts (Isaiah 55:7)*

41. *Ezra (Ezra 10:1)*

42. *Moses (Exodus 32:31), who was confessing the Israelites' sin—not his own— because he had nothing to do with the calf idol*

43. *Judah (Genesis 38:26)*

44. *Nehemiah (Nehemiah 1:1-6)*

45. *Shimei (2 Samuel 19:18-23)*

 ## WITCHES, SORCERERS, AND OTHER OCCULT TYPES

Some things never change: Here we are in the 21st century, and people are still dabbling in witchcraft and the occult. (This includes, by the way, people we call "mediums" or "spiritualists"—that is, those who try to communicate with the dead.) Such practices have become almost respectable, with many educated (and supposedly intelligent) people openly declaring themselves to be pagans and Wiccans, not to mention the many TV shows centered around contacting the dead. Well, suffice it to say that the Bible takes a dim view of such practices, condemning all witchcraft as something utterly alien to a life of faith in an all-ruling God.

1. What Babylonian king had a bevy of magicians and psychics who could not interpret his strange dreams?
2. Which prophet called the city of Nineveh the "mistress of witchcrafts"?
3. In which city did Paul find many believers who had formerly dabbled in witchcraft?
4. Which queen of Israel practiced witchcraft?
5. Which prophet claimed that Edom, Moab, Ammon, and Tyre all had sorcerers?
6. Who called on magicians to duplicate the miracles of Moses?
7. Who was the sorcerer Paul encountered on the island of Paphos?
8. What medium was consulted by a king who had outlawed all mediums?
9. Who amazed the people of Samaria with his conjuring tricks?
10. What book of the Bible states, "Thou shalt not suffer a witch to live"?
11. What book of the Bible claims that witchcraft is an "abomination unto the Lord"?
12. Who told King Saul that rebellion was as bad as witchcraft?
13. Which Epistle mentions witchcraft as one of the works of the flesh?
14. Who called on magicians to interpret his dreams about cattle?

15. What names does the New Testament give to the magicians in Pharaoh's court in the time of Moses?
16. According to Revelation, what fate awaits those who dabble in witchcraft and magic?
17. Which prophet records God saying, "I will destroy your witchcraft"?
18. What book of the Bible connects divination and sorcery to the horrible practice of child sacrifice?
19. In Revelation, what wicked city leads the world astray with its magic?
20. What book of the Bible bluntly states, "Do not practice divination or sorcery"?

WITCHES, SORCERERS, AND OTHER OCCULT TYPES (ANSWERS)

1. *Nebuchadnezzar (Daniel 2:1-10)*

2. *Nahum (Nahum 3:4, 7)*

3. *Ephesus (Acts 19:17-19)*

4. *Jezebel (2 Kings 9:22)*

5. *Jeremiah (Jeremiah 27:3-10)*

6. *Pharaoh (Exodus 7:11-12)*

7. *Elymas (Acts 13:6-8)*

8. *The witch of Endor, who was visited by Saul (1 Samuel 28:7-25)*

9. *Simon the sorcerer (Acts 8:9)*

10. *Exodus (22:18)*

11. *Deuteronomy (18:9-12)*

12. *Samuel (1 Samuel 15:22-23)*

13. *Galatians (5:19-20)*

14. *Pharaoh (Genesis 41:8)*

15. *Jannes and Jambres (2 Timothy 3:8)*

16. *The lake of fire (Revelation 21:8)*

17. *Micah (Micah 5:12)*

18. *Deuteronomy (18:10). Alas, child sacrifice was common in the ancient world.*

19. *Babylon, the symbol of human pride and evil (Revelation 18:21-23)*

20. *Leviticus (19:26)*

"HOLIER THAN THOU": SELF-RIGHTEOUSNESS

One of the problems here in the 21st century is that we no longer believe in righteousness, so any person trying hard to be righteous strikes us as *self-righteous*. Well, there is a big difference. Simply put, righteousness is good, but self-righteousness is bad. People who are trying to do right are painfully aware that they are still far from perfect, so they don't allow themselves to put on airs and look down on others.

1. According to Proverbs, the way of a _____ is right in his own eyes.
2. In the time of Jesus, what Jewish group was often denounced by him as being self-righteous and hypocritical?
3. Which prophet stated, "We are all like an unclean thing, and all our righteousnesses are like filthy rags"?
4. In a saying of Jesus, the hypocrite who sees a speck in another man's eye has what in his own eye?
5. Who said that it is not he who commends himself that is approved, but him whom the Lord commends?
6. What kind of tombs did Jesus compare the Pharisees to?
7. Complete this verse from Proverbs: "There is a way that seems right to a man, but in the end it leads to _____."
8. In which of Paul's letters did he speak out against the man who "thinks himself to be something, when he is nothing"?
9. In Jesus' parable of the self-righteous Pharisee in the Temple, what other character is aware of his own sins?
10. Who told the Israelites they must never assume that the land of Canaan was a reward for their righteousness?
11. Finish this verse from Isaiah: "Woe unto them that are _____ in their own eyes, and _____ in their own sight."
12. Who predicted that on the Day of Judgment, many people who had prophesied and cast out demons in God's name would be rejected by God?
13. Which of Jesus' parables concerns two Jewish religious people who pass by a man wounded by the roadside?
14. What book of the Bible describes "a generation that is pure in their own eyes, and yet is not washed from their filthiness"?
15. What book is the source of the self-righteous phrase, "I am holier than thou"?

16. In Jesus' parable of the Prodigal Son, what very self-righteous character is not happy about the son's homecoming celebration?
17. Who said that salvation was the gift of God, not a result of human effort, so that no one could boast of being saved?
18. Which prophet told the Jews not to trust in the Jerusalem Temple to make them righteous?
19. What book of the Bible contains the words, "My doctrine is pure, and I am clean in God's eyes"?
20. Complete this verse from Proverbs: "Let another praise you, and not your own _____; a stranger, and not your own _____."

"HOLIER THAN THOU": SELF-RIGHTEOUSNESS (ANSWERS)

1. *Fool (Proverbs 12:15)*

2. *The Pharisees (Matthew 23:23)*

3. *Isaiah (Isaiah 64:6)*

4. *A plank (Matthew 7:3-5)*

5. *Paul (2 Corinthians 10:18)*

6. *Whitewashed—pretty on the outside but full of death on the inside (Matthew 23:27)*

7. *Death (Proverbs 14:12)*

8. *Galatians (6:3)*

9. *The tax collector (Luke 18:9-14)*

10. *Moses (Deuteronomy 9:4-6)*

11. *Wise, prudent (Isaiah 5:21)*

12. *Jesus (Matthew 7:22-23)*

13. *The parable of the Good Samaritan (Luke 10:25-37)*

14. *Proverbs (30:12)*

15. *Isaiah, who is quoting people who say, "Stand by yourself, come not near me, for I am holier than thou" (Isaiah 65:5)*

16. *The older brother, who had always behaved himself (Luke 15:11-32)*

17. *Paul (Ephesians 2:8-9)*

18. *Jeremiah (Jeremiah 7:4)*

19. *Job (11:4)*

20. *Mouth, lips (Proverbs 27:2)*

ABOMINATION STATION

The word *abomination* occurs often in the Bible and refers to something that (in the words of my neighbor's eight-year-old son) "makes God go *Ugh!*" Generally we find the word associated with idolatry, which is worshipping the created object rather than the Creator. But abomination went beyond simple idolatry, all the way to something . . . "ughy." In a few cases, there is great mystery about just what the abomination was, as you'll see below in questions 5 and 23.

1. What people considered it an abomination to eat with Hebrews?
2. Which Old Testament book declares that it is an abomination for a man to wear women's clothing (and vice versa)?
3. To which prophet did God say, "Your incense is an abomination unto me"?
4. In which Gospel does Jesus say, "That which is highly esteemed among men is abomination in the sight of God"?
5. What woman is "the mother of harlots and abominations of the earth"?
6. What city will not have any abomination within it?
7. Whose wages would be considered an abomination if offered to the Lord?
8. What loathsome god was "the abomination of the Ammonites"?
9. What sort of lips are an abomination to the Lord?
10. Whose sacrifice is an abomination to the Lord?
11. What innocent occupation was considered an abomination by the Egyptians?
12. What sort of seafood was an abomination?
13. What was the punishment for the abomination of homosexual intercourse?
14. King Ahaz of Judah committed what abomination with his own son?
15. What godly king expelled the sorcerers who were an abomination to the Lord?
16. What were the Israelites supposed to do with the idols of other nations?
17. What kind of animal was an abomination to sacrifice to the Lord?
18. Saul's military prowess made Israel an abomination to what people?

19. What kind of prostitutes—an abomination to the Lord—
    flourished under Solomon's son?
20. What wise king foolishly built pagan temples for his foreign wives?
21. What kind of scale is an abomination to the Lord?
22. What kind of heart is an abomination to the Lord?
23. Who talked about "the abomination of desolation" predicted by
    Daniel standing in the Jerusalem Temple?

ABOMINATION STATION (ANSWERS)

1. *The Egyptians (Genesis 43:32)*

2. *Deuteronomy (22:5)*

3. *Isaiah (Isaiah 1:13)*

4. *Luke (16:15)*

5. *Babylon, the scarlet woman (Revelation 17:5)*

6. *The new Jerusalem (Revelation 21:2, 27)*

7. *A prostitute's (Deuteronomy 23:18)*

8. *The god Milcom ("Molech" in some translations) (1 Kings 11:5)*

9. *Lying lips (Proverbs 12:22)*

10. *The sacrifice of the wicked (Proverbs 15:8)*

11. *Sheepherding (Genesis 46:34)*

12. *Anything without fins and scales (Leviticus 11:10)*

13. *Death (Leviticus 20:13)*

14. *Sacrificed him to a pagan god (2 Kings 16:3)*

15. *Josiah (2 Kings 23:24)*

16. *Burn them (Deuteronomy 7:25)*

17. *One with a blemish of any kind (Deuteronomy 17:1)*

18. *The Philistines (1 Samuel 13:4)*

19. *Male shrine prostitutes (1 Kings 14:24)*

20. *Solomon (1 Kings 11:1-8)*

21. *A false scale (Proverbs 11:1)*

22. *A proud heart (Proverbs 16:5)*

23. *Jesus (Matthew 24:15)*

"OUR NAME IS LEGION": DEMONS, EVIL SPIRITS, ETC.

In the 1970s, a book (and then a movie) titled *The Exorcist* had people shaking in their boots. Here was a story of a demon-possessed child saying and doing all sorts of horrible things and causing people to wonder, *Can this sort of thing still happen?* Well, the plain answer is yes, and the actions of demons as described in the Bible have been repeated throughout the centuries. (So, thankfully, have the works of God's people who drive out the demons.) Demons—also called evil spirits and unclean spirits—delight in tormenting human beings, as does their master, Satan.

1. In the Gospels, what name is given to the "prince of demons"?
2. What demon-possessed man ran around naked?
3. Which king of Israel was tormented by an evil spirit?
4. In the story of the demon-possessed boy healed by Jesus, what had the evil spirit been doing to the poor child?
5. What did the evil spirit do when Jesus cast him out of the man at Capernaum?
6. What was the affliction of the woman who had been possessed by an evil spirit for 18 years?
7. Which king had court prophets that were the agents of a lying spirit?
8. What woman had Jesus driven seven demons out of?
9. In Revelation, for what reason do the demons perform miracles?
10. According to Jesus, when an evil spirit returns to a person, how many companions does it bring with it?
11. When Jesus drove demons out of the two Gadarene men, where did the demons go?
12. When King Saul was bothered by an evil spirit, what would David do to soothe the king?
13. What people were given authority by Jesus to drive out demons?
14. In the famous story of the naked demon-possessed man, what did his demons say their name was?
15. In which Gospel do Jesus' enemies accuse him of being demon-possessed?
16. In Luke 10, what group of people happily reported to Jesus that they could drive out demons in his name?
17. In the book of Acts, which two apostles drove a demon out of a girl working as a psychic?

18. In which Epistle does Paul say that in the end times, people will follow the "doctrines of demons"?
19. In Revelation, the demon known as the "angel of the bottomless pit" has what names?
20. Which Epistle speaks of a type of wisdom that is "earthly, sensual, demonic"?
21. Who had seven sons who were overcome by the evil spirit they were trying to cast out of a man?
22. In Matthew 9, what had been the affliction of the demon-possessed man Jesus cured?
23. Which Gospel does not record Jesus driving out demons?
24. Complete this saying of Jesus: "If I drive out demons by the _____ of God, then the kingdom of God has come upon you."
25. Which prophet and kinsman of Jesus was called "demon-possessed" by his enemies?
26. Handkerchiefs touched by which apostle were said to have the power to drive out evil spirits?
27. In Paul's letter to the Ephesians, what does he say is protection against the "powers of this dark world"?
28. Complete this saying of Jesus: "Depart from me, you who are cursed, into the eternal _____ prepared for the devil and his angels."
29. When Jesus drove the demons out of the Gadarene demoniac, where did they beg him not to send them?
30. Which Epistle tells Christians to test the spirits to see whether they are from God?

"OUR NAME IS LEGION": DEMONS, EVIL SPIRITS, ETC. (ANSWERS)

1. Beelzebub, which is another name for Satan (Mark 3:22; Luke 11:15)

2. The Gadarene demoniac (Luke 8:26-27), who was healed by Jesus

3. Saul (1 Samuel 16:14-23)

4. Throwing him into the fire or water and making him foam at the mouth and grind his teeth (Mark 9:17-29)

5. Gave a loud scream (Mark 1:21-26)

6. She was bent and could not straighten up (Luke 13:11-16).

7. Ahab (1 Kings 22:19-22)

8. Mary Magdalene (Luke 8:2)

9. To bring the nations to war (Revelation 16:13-14)

10. *Seven (Matthew 12:45)*

11. *Into a herd of pigs, which ran off a cliff (Matthew 8:28-33)*

12. *Play his harp (1 Samuel 16:14-23)*

13. *His twelve disciples (Matthew 10:5-8)*

14. *Legion, as in, "My name is Legion, for we are many" (Mark 15:8-9)*

15. *John (7:20-21)*

16. *The Seventy, which apparently was a group of followers beyond the core group of twelve disciples (Luke 10:12-17)*

17. *Paul and Silas (Acts 16:16-18)*

18. *1 Timothy (4:1)*

19. *Abaddon in Hebrew and Apollyon in Greek (Revelation 9:11)*

20. *James (3:15)*

21. *Sceva (Acts 19:13-16)*

22. *He was mute (Matthew 9:32-33).*

23. *John's Gospel*

24. *Spirit (Matthew 12:28)*

25. *John the Baptist (Matthew 11:18)*

26. *Paul (Acts 19:11-12)*

27. *The "whole armor of God" (Ephesians 6:11-12)*

28. *Fire (Matthew 25:41)*

29. *The abyss—meaning (we think) hell (Luke 8:30-31)*

30. *1 John (4:1)*

 EAGER BEAVERS: TOO MUCH AMBITION

Ambition is usually considered a good thing. But is it? Not if it involves making oneself into one's own private god. The Bible is full of people who worshipped and served their own ambition instead of the true God. The Book takes a very realistic view of human striving and often compares human achievements to the works of the eternal God. Possessions and fame pass away, and we are left facing the more important matters of our relationships with God and our fellow man. So even though a person can be ambitious as well as good, most of the

Bible's eager beavers, hustlers, or whatever you care to call them fit into the Bad Guy category.

1. Which Old Testament book makes the observation that "wise men die, likewise the fool and senseless perish, and leave their wealth to others"?
2. What humble leader of Israel was falsely accused of trying to rule over them?
3. Who was tempted to possess "all the kingdoms of the world, and the glory of them"?
4. What two people were told they could "be like gods"?
5. What resulted when arrogant human beings tried to build a tower reaching all the way to heaven?
6. Complete this saying of Jesus: "What is a man profited if he shall gain the whole world, and lose his own _____?"
7. What overly ambitious man and woman made the Lord angry when they rebelled against their brother?
8. Which son of the judge Gideon (Jerubbaal) killed almost all his brothers and briefly managed to make himself king over Israel?
9. Which Old Testament book observes that "he that is greedy of gain troubles his own house"?
10. Complete this saying of Jesus: "Whoever will be great among you, let him be your _____."
11. What ambitious son of David rebelled against his father and tried to take over the kingdom?
12. In Jesus' parable of the rich man, what did the man build to accommodate his rising prosperity?
13. Which New Testament book warns against "the lust of the eyes and the pride of life"?
14. Which son of David tried to seize the throne during David's last years?
15. What Assyrian conqueror boasted he "cut down the cedars" of the nation of Judah?
16. What two ambitious disciples asked Jesus if they could sit by his side when he reigned in glory?
17. What book of the Bible observes that no matter how smart and talented people may be, "time and chance happen to them all"?
18. In Isaiah, who says, "I will ascend into heaven, I will exalt my throne above the stars of God"?
19. Complete this saying of Jesus: "Woe to you who are _____, for you have already received your consolation."

20. In which Epistle does Paul say that it is commendable for a man to want to be a bishop?
21. Which prophet condemned "those who add house to house, that lay field to field, till there be no places left"?
22. What short letter condemns a leader named Diotrephes, "who loved to have the preeminence"?
23. What ambitious (and Jew-hating) Persian official is the villain of the book of Esther?
24. To which prophet did God say, "Let him who glories glory in this, that he understands and knows me"?
25. Complete this verse from Proverbs: "Better to be of humble spirit with the lowly than to divide the spoil with the _____."
26. Who advised Christians, "Let nothing be done through ambition or vain conceit"?
27. In the book of Acts, what magician of Samaria boasted that he was someone great?
28. Who said, "That which is highly esteemed among men is abomination in the sight of God"?
29. Complete this saying of Jesus: "He that shall humble himself shall be _____."
30. Which Old Testament book says, "There are many devices in a man's heart; nevertheless, the counsel of the Lord, that shall stand"?

EAGER BEAVERS: TOO MUCH AMBITION (ANSWERS)

1. *Psalms (Psalm 49:10)*

2. *Moses (Numbers 16:13), who faced constant griping from the ungrateful Israelites*

3. *Jesus when Satan tempted him (Matthew 4:8)*

4. *Adam and Eve (Genesis 3:5-6)*

5. *God confused their languages so they could not communicate (Genesis 11:1-9).*

6. *Soul (Matthew 16:26)*

7. *Aaron and Miriam, whose brother was Moses (Numbers 12:2-10)*

8. *Abimelech, who came to a very bad end (Judges 9)*

9. *Proverbs (15:27)*

10. *Servant (Matthew 20:26)*

11. *Absalom (2 Samuel 15–18), who, like many ambitious men in the Bible, came to a violent end*

12. *Bigger barns to contain all his produce—but then he died suddenly (Luke 12:16-21)*

13. *1 John (2:16)*

14. *Adonijah (1 Kings 1)*

15. *Sennacherib (2 Kings 19:20-23)*

16. *James and John (Mark 10:35-37)*

17. *Ecclesiastes (9:11)*

18. *Lucifer, which is usually assumed to be another name for the proud Satan (Isaiah 14:12-13)*

19. *Rich (Luke 6:24)*

20. *1 Timothy (3:1). In those days, a bishop had a lot of work and no pay at all.*

21. *Isaiah (Isaiah 5:8)*

22. *3 John (1:9-10)*

23. *Haman (Esther)*

24. *Jeremiah (Jeremiah 9:24)*

25. *Proud (Proverbs 16:19)*

26. *Paul (Philippians 2:3)*

27. *Simon (Acts 8:9)*

28. *Jesus (Luke 16:15)*

29. *Exalted (Matthew 23:12)*

30. *Proverbs (19:21)*

 ## CRIMES OF THE HEART

Let's admit it: We know that the literal heart is an organ that pumps blood through the body, and it has nothing to do with affection, emotions, thought, or will. But we still *talk* the same way Bible folks did, referring to the good and bad things the heart is capable of. "He is good-hearted." "She is so coldhearted." "They are hard-hearted people." Thousands of years have passed, but our basic ideas about the heart haven't really changed. See what you know about the Bible's view of the human heart and the evil it was often the source of.

1. Who told his scheming mistress "all his heart" and lost his hair (and eyesight and freedom) as a result?

2. What evil Old Testament ruler had his heart repeatedly hardened by God?
3. When a man looks at a woman with lust in his heart, what sin has he committed?
4. Whose wife "despised him in her heart" because he was dancing merrily in the streets?
5. What handsome rebel prince "stole the hearts of the men of Israel"?
6. Who told the sinning Israelites to "circumcise the foreskins of their hearts"?
7. Which Old Testament book commands, "Thou shalt not hate thy brother in thy heart"?
8. What did God do when he perceived that man's heart was "only evil continually"?
9. According to Jesus, who takes away the Word sown in people's hearts?
10. According to Hosea, what two vices "take away the heart"?
11. What evil, pagan king lost his mind and had his heart changed from a man's to a beast's?
12. Who entered Judas's heart to urge him to betray Jesus?
13. Who says in his heart, "There is no God"?
14. What good man offered sacrifices because his children had possibly cursed God in their hearts?
15. What rebel was killed by three darts shot into his heart by Joab?
16. What book of the Bible says that the Lord's people have become as heartless as ostriches in the desert?
17. Who said that the Old Testament Law allowed divorce because of people's hardness of heart?
18. Which prophet claimed that "the heart is deceitful above all things and desperately wicked"?
19. Whom did Jesus ask, "Why do you entertain evil thoughts in your hearts"?
20. Which Old Testament book condemns people who speak cordially while harboring malice in their hearts?
21. What book of the Bible condemns the person who has an evil heart and fervent lips?
22. Who claimed that "out of the overflow of the heart the mouth speaks"?
23. Which king of Judah did evil "because he had not set his heart on seeking the Lord"?

CRIMES OF THE HEART (ANSWERS)

1. *Samson (Judges 16:17-22)*
2. *The pharaoh at the time of Moses (Exodus 7:3)*
3. *Adultery (Matthew 5:28)*
4. *David, whose wife Michal thought his dancing was undignified (2 Samuel 6:16)*
5. *David's son Absalom, who led a rebellion against his father (2 Samuel 15:6)*
6. *Moses (Deuteronomy 10:16), who was speaking figuratively, of course*
7. *Leviticus (19:17). This is a remarkable verse, because Leviticus is mostly concerned with offerings and sacrifices.*
8. *He decided to destroy the earth with a flood (Genesis 6:5-7).*
9. *Satan (Mark 4:15)*
10. *Whoredom and wine (Hosea 4:11)*
11. *Nebuchadnezzar of Babylon (Daniel 4:1-16)*
12. *Satan (John 13:2)*
13. *The fool (Psalm 14:1)*
14. *Job (Job 1:5)*
15. *Absalom, David's son (2 Samuel 18:14)*
16. *Lamentations (4:3)*
17. *Jesus (Matthew 19:8)*
18. *Jeremiah (Jeremiah 17:9)*
19. *The teachers of the law (Matthew 9:3-4)*
20. *Psalms (Psalm 28:3)*
21. *Proverbs (26:23)*
22. *Jesus (Matthew 12:34)*
23. *Rehoboam, Solomon's son (2 Chronicles 12:13-14)*

 ## FAKIN' IT: A HUDDLE OF HYPOCRITES

There's one place where the Bible and the modern world do fully agree: Hypocrisy is a bad thing. Basically, hypocrisy means "talkin' the talk" without "walkin' the walk." A hypocrite is one who tries to *seem* instead of *be* a certain type of person. Jesus had a lot to say about hypocrites as well as every other "wise" man of the Bible.

1. What two Jewish religious groups did Jesus often refer to as hypocrites?
2. Which New Testament book says that a "double-minded man is unstable in all his ways"?
3. Complete this verse from Job: "The triumphing of the wicked is short, and the _____ of the hypocrite is but for a moment."
4. Who condemned people who "profess that they know God, but in works they deny him"?
5. According to Jesus, where did hypocrites pray so they could be admired by others?
6. Which prophet quoted God as saying, "I hate, I despise your religious feasts, and I take no pleasure in your solemn assemblies"?
7. Complete this saying of Jesus: "Do not do as they do, for they do not _____ what they preach."
8. According to the Letter of James, we should "be _____ of the word, and not _____ only."
9. Jesus stated that the hypocritical Pharisees would "strain out a gnat but swallow a _____."
10. Which Epistle says that anyone who says he loves God and hates his brother is a liar?
11. Complete this saying of Jesus: "There is nothing _____ that shall not be _____, and nothing hid that shall not be known."
12. Which prophet lamented that "every one is a hypocrite and an evildoer, and every mouth speaks folly"?
13. According to Jesus, what object is found in the eye of the hypocrite?
14. Complete this verse from Isaiah: "These people draw near me with their mouth, but they have removed their _____ far from me."
15. In what wise Old Testament book do we learn that "he that works deceit shall not dwell" in God's house?
16. Jesus referred to the hypocrites as "you serpents, you generation of _____."
17. According to the Epistle of James, what must be "bridled" if our religion is sincere?
18. In a parable of Jesus, the smug Pharisee is contrasted with a man of what profession?
19. Who said that "if a man thinks himself to be something when he is nothing, he deceives himself"?
20. Which prophet claimed that "the heart is deceitful above all things, and desperately wicked"?

FAKIN' IT: A HUDDLE OF HYPOCRITES (ANSWERS)

1. The Pharisees and the scribes. (Some translations have "teachers of the law" or even "lawyers" instead of "scribes.")

2. James (1:8)

3. Joy (Job 20:5)

4. Paul (Titus 1:16)

5. On the street corners (Matthew 6:5)

6. Amos (Amos 5:21)

7. Practice (Matthew 23:3)

8. Doers, hearers (James 1:22)

9. Camel (Matthew 23:24)

10. 1 John (4:20)

11. Covered, revealed (Luke 12:2)

12. Isaiah (Isaiah 9:17)

13. A plank (in some translations, "board," or "beam"). The hypocrite sees the speck in someone else's eye, but not the plank in his own (Matthew 7:3-5).

14. Heart (Isaiah 29:13)

15. Psalms (Psalm 101:7)

16. Vipers (Matthew 23:33)

17. The tongue (James 1:26)

18. Tax collecting (Luke 18:9-14)

19. Paul (Galatians 6:3)

20. Jeremiah (Jeremiah 17:9)

IDOL MINDS

Is there just one God—or many? Just one, according to the Bible. All other gods are false, and images of them are only idols. Well, humanity is always eager to worship an idol instead of the real God. Idolatry was condemned by saintly people of the Bible, not because they were bigoted and intolerant, but because worship of these gods often involved such practices as sexual orgies, mass sacrifice of children, and other degenerate practices. The sad fact is, if you worship a cruel, bloodthirsty, promiscuous god, you probably won't be a very nice person.

1. The Ammonites' bloodthirsty god was widely known in Israel because of the horrible practice of child sacrifice. What was the name of this god?
2. This goddess of Canaan was associated with depraved worship practices. After Saul's death, his armor was placed in her temple by the Philistines. What was her name?
3. Solomon erected an altar for a god of the Moabites, but Josiah tore it down. What was this god called?
4. The people of Lystra were so dazzled by Paul and Barnabas that they called them by the name of two Greek gods. What were the names?
5. What fish-shaped god of the Philistines was disgraced when his statue was broken by the presence of the Ark of the Covenant?
6. This well-known Greek goddess had a magnificent temple in Ephesus, a city where Paul ran into trouble with some of her followers. Who was she?
7. This Babylonian god is mentioned by Jeremiah as being filled with terror after the downfall of Babylon. What was his name?
8. This false god of Canaan is mentioned more than any other foreign deity in the Bible. The prophet Elijah and later King Jehu of Israel worked hard to stamp out his cult. What was his name?
9. In Paul's speech to the men of Athens, he mentions the altar of a god. What was the altar's inscription?
10. After Gideon (Jerubbaal)'s death, what Canaanite god did the Israelites turn to?
11. Ezekiel saw women weeping for which god?
12. Which nation worshipped Succoth Benoth?
13. What gods did the Avites worship?
14. What was the god of Ekron, consulted by King Ahaziah?
15. What was Nehushtan?
16. To which gods did the Sepharvites sacrifice their children?
17. Which nation was Milcom the god of?
18. While in the wilderness, what Moabite god did the Israelites begin to worship?
19. Which god did Naaman the Syrian apologize to Elisha for worshipping?
20. What was the god of the men of Hamath?

21. Which god did Stephen (quoting Amos) say was symbolized by a star?
22. Who was King Sennacherib worshipping when his sons murdered him?
23. Who sailed on a ship that had figures of the Greek gods Castor and Pollux?
24. Who was the god of the men of Cuth?
25. Which nation was Bel a god of?
26. Which prophet mentions Nebo as one of the gods of Babylon?
27. Which New Testament Epistle ends with the words "Children, keep yourself from idols"?
28. In the book of Genesis, what woman stole her father's household idols?
29. In which Old Testament book does God say, "I will bring judgment on all the gods of Egypt"?
30. Who saved David from Saul's men by hiding an idol in the bed and pretending it was the sick David?
31. Which king of Israel allowed his foreign wives to "turn his heart after other gods"?
32. Who constructed a gold calf idol for the Israelites to worship while Moses was on the mountain with God?
33. In Genesis, what man ordered his household to bury all their idols under a tree?
34. According to Deuteronomy, what should you do to a relative or friend who tries to lead you into worshipping idols?
35. In what famous city was Paul when he was "distressed to see that the city was full of idols"?
36. What Babylonian king ordered his wise men executed because they could not determine the will of the gods?
37. Which prophet quoted his fellow Jews as saying, "It's no use, I love foreign gods, and I must go after them"?
38. What two groups of Greek philosophers thought Paul was "advocating foreign gods" when he preached the gospel?
39. What punishment was imposed on Shadrach, Meshach, and Abednego for refusing to worship the gods of Babylon?
40. Which king set up gold calf idols so his people would not have to visit the Lord's Temple in Jerusalem?
41. When Elijah challenged the priests of Baal, what were they sacrificing to their god?
42. Which idol, associated with Moses, was offered sacrifices by later generations?

43. What wicked king, a dabbler in sorcery, sacrificed his son in the fire?
44. What goddess did Jeremiah accuse the people of Judah of making sacrifices to?
45. What people burnt their children as an offering to the gods Adrammelech and Anammelech?
46. Which king despaired in the face of battle and offered his oldest son, the heir to the throne, as a sacrifice?
47. What wicked king of Judah built a Syrian-style altar and offered up his son as a sacrifice?
48. What was the name of the foreign god that many Israelites had sacrificed their children to?

IDOL MINDS (ANSWERS)

1. Molech (Leviticus 18:21; 2 Kings 23:10)

2. Ashtaroth (1 Samuel 31:10)

3. Chemosh (1 Kings 11:7; 2 Kings 23:11-13)

4. Jupiter and Mercury (or Zeus and Hermes in some Bible translations) (Acts 14:12)

5. Dagon (1 Samuel 5:1-5)

6. Artemis (called Diana in some translations) (Acts 19:23–20:1)

7. Marduk, or Merodach (Jeremiah 50:2)

8. Baal (1 Kings 18:40; 2 Kings 10:18-19)

9. "To an Unknown God" (Acts 17:22-23)

10. Baal-Berith (Judges 8:33)

11. Tammuz (Ezekiel 8:14)

12. Babylon (2 Kings 17:30)

13. Nibhaz and Tartak (2 Kings 17:31)

14. Baalzebub (2 Kings 1:2)

15. The brass serpent Moses had made, which the Israelites later worshipped as if it were a god (2 Kings 18:4)

16. Adrammelech and Anammelech (2 Kings 17:31)

17. Ammon (1 Kings 11:5)

18. Baal of Peor (Numbers 25:1-3)

19. Rimmon (2 Kings 5:9-18)

20. Ashima (2 Kings 17:30)

21. Rephan *(Amos 5:26; Acts 7:43)*

22. Nisroch *(2 Kings 19:36-37)*

23. Paul's *(Acts 28:11)*

24. Nergal *(2 Kings 17:30)*

25. Babylon *(Jeremiah 51:44)*

26. Isaiah *(Isaiah 46:1)*

27. 1 John *(5:21)*

28. Rachel, wife of Jacob and daughter of Laban *(Genesis 31:34)*

29. Exodus *(12:12)*

30. David's wife Michal *(1 Samuel 19:11-16)*

31. Solomon *(1 Kings 11:4)*

32. Aaron, his brother *(Exodus 32:1-6)*

33. Jacob *(Genesis 35:2-4)*

34. Stone him to death *(Deuteronomy 13:6-11)*

35. Athens, Greece *(Acts 17:16)*

36. Nebuchadnezzar *(Daniel 2:11-13)*

37. Jeremiah *(Jeremiah 2:25)*

38. The Epicureans and Stoics *(Acts 17:18)*

39. They were thrown into a fiery furnace, but God saved them *(Daniel 3)*.

40. Jeroboam *(1 Kings 12:26-28)*

41. A bull *(1 Kings 18:25)*

42. The brazen serpent *(2 Kings 18:4)*

43. Manasseh *(2 Kings 21:1-6)*

44. The queen of heaven *(Jeremiah 44:19)*

45. The Sepharvites *(2 Kings 17:31)*

46. The king of Moab *(2 Kings 3:26-27)*

47. Ahaz *(2 Chronicles 28:1-4, 23)*

48. Molech *(2 Kings 23:10)*

 ## A BEVY OF THE BLIND (SPIRITUALLY SPEAKING)

Because we've made great advances in medicine, there are far fewer blind people than in ancient times. But the Bible had a lot more to say about spiritual blindness than physical blindness, not because there is no sin in being physically blind, but because spiritual blindness is very serious. If the Bible authors were living today, would they think we had made much progress in curing spiritual blindness? Maybe not.

1. What respected group of Jewish leaders did Jesus refer to as "blind guides"?
2. What spiritually blind man was struck literally blind for three days before recovering his sight?
3. In one of Paul's epistles, who blinds the minds of unbelievers?
4. According to the New Testament, a man who hates his _____ is spiritually blind.
5. In Psalms, what sort of person says in his heart, "There is no God"?
6. Who coined the phrase "the blind leading the blind"?
7. What book of the Bible refers to a church that is "wretched, miserable, poor, blind and naked"?
8. In which Gospel does Jesus say, "O righteous Father, the world has not known you"?
9. According to Paul, God rescued us from the _____ of darkness.
10. Which prophet was told by God that Israel was a "rebellious house, who have eyes to see, and see not"?
11. Finish this verse from Proverbs: "The way of the _____ is like darkness."
12. According to Paul, what nation was deliberately blind to the gospel?
13. What man was blindfolded and slapped around by soldiers?
14. What book of the Bible says that people lacking in self-control and kindness are "blind and nearsighted"?
15. Complete this verse from Psalms: "They know not, neither will they understand; they walk on in _____."
16. What spiritually blind ruler said, "Who is the Lord, that I should obey his voice to let Israel go"?
17. Complete this verse from Micah: "They know not the thoughts of the Lord, neither _____ they his counsel."
18. What book of the Bible begs God to "pour out thy wrath upon the heathen that have not known thee"?
19. Which prophet stated that Israel's spiritual watchmen were both blind and mute?
20. Which apostle claimed that all human beings had some knowledge of God, if only from seeing the created world?

21. According to Jesus, what spirit can the world not receive because it is blind?
22. Complete this saying of Jesus: "O you _____, you can discern the face of the sky; but can you not discern the signs of the times"?
23. Which Gospel says that "the light shines in the darkness; and the darkness comprehended it not"?
24. According to the prophet Hosea, "The people that does not understand shall _____."
25. Complete this saying of Jesus: "You blind guides, who strain at a gnat, and swallow a _____."
26. Which prophet quoted God as saying, "Woe unto them that call evil, good, and good, evil; who that put darkness for light"?
27. According to 1 Corinthians, "The _____ man receiveth not the things of the Spirit of God."
28. Complete this saying of Paul: "They profess that they know God, but in _____ they deny him."
29. Who uttered the famous words, "Father, forgive them; for they know not what they do"?

A BEVY OF THE BLIND (SPIRITUALLY SPEAKING) (ANSWERS)

1. The Pharisees (Matthew 23:26)
2. Saul, later the great apostle Paul (Acts 9)
3. The "god of this age," meaning Satan (2 Corinthians 4:4)
4. Brother—meaning fellow human being (1 John 2:11)
5. The fool (Psalm 14:1)
6. Jesus (Matthew 15:14; Luke 6:39)
7. Revelation (3:17), referring to the church at Laodicea
8. John (17:25)
9. Power (Colossians 1:13)
10. Ezekiel (Ezekiel 12:2)
11. Wicked (Proverbs 4:19)
12. Israel—the Jews (Romans 11:25)
13. Jesus (Luke 22:64)
14. 2 Peter (1:9)
15. Darkness (Psalm 82:5)

16. *The pharaoh at the time of Moses (Exodus 5:2)*

17. *Understand (Micah 4:12)*

18. *Psalms (Psalm 79:6)*

19. *Isaiah (Isaiah 56:10)*

20. *Paul (Romans 1:19-20)*

21. *The Spirit of truth (John 14:17)*

22. *Hypocrites (Matthew 16:3)*

23. *John's (John 1:5)*

24. *Fall (Hosea 4:14)*

25. *Camel (Matthew 23:24)*

26. *Isaiah (5:20)*

27. *Natural (1 Corinthians 2:14)*

28. *Works (Titus 1:16)*

29. *Jesus on the cross (Luke 23:34)*

PART 9

WATCH YOUR TONGUE

CURSE YOU!

Say the word *cursing* and people think you are referring to profanity. In the Bible, however, cursing meant literally putting a curse on someone or something. In Bible times, calling down a curse on someone was serious business, not just a matter of tossing around idle swear words. As you read the questions, note that not all curses are evil. God himself placed curses when they were deserved. In fact, the Bible's bad guys were often the recipients of divine curses.

1. What was the only animal to be cursed by God?
2. What pagan prophet was told by the king of Moab to put a curse on Israel?
3. Which grandson of Noah was cursed for his father's sins?
4. Who cursed a fig tree for not bearing fruit?
5. Who put a curse on Cain and made him a wanderer?
6. Which son of Josiah was cursed by God?
7. In which story did Jesus place a curse on the unrighteous?
8. According to Paul, what was put under a curse because of man's sin?
9. What nation did God say would have its towns and fields cursed because of disobedience?
10. What happened to the ground as a result of God's curse?
11. In which book of the Bible do people curse God because of great plagues?
12. According to Galatians, what people remain under a curse?
13. Who said that people who taught a false gospel would be cursed?
14. According to Paul, who was made a curse for our sins?
15. According to the Law, what sort of handicapped people should we not curse?
16. Who was told by his wife to curse God and die?
17. Which prophet ended his book with God's threat to come and strike the land with a curse?
18. Which Epistle says that blessing and cursing should not come out of the same mouth?
19. Who had enemies that bound themselves under a curse because they were so determined to kill him?
20. Who told God that Job would curse him to his face?
21. What book of the Bible says that kings should not be cursed because little birds will tell on the cursing person?

22. According to Exodus, what punishment is mandated for one who curses his father or mother?
23. What wicked queen was referred to as "that cursed woman"?
24. What suffering man cursed the day of his birth?
25. What book of the Bible compares an "undeserved curse" to a "fluttering sparrow"?
26. Which prophet said, "Cursed is the one who trusts in man"?
27. Which of Jesus' disciples called down curses on himself?
28. Which apostle stated, "When we are cursed, we bless"?
29. Who lamented that the same mouth produced both blessing and cursing?
30. What sad prophet said, "Cursed be the day I was born!"?
31. Who received a promise from God that all persons who cursed him would be cursed themselves?
32. What book of the Bible promises a future time when "there shall be no more curse"?

CURSE YOU! (ANSWERS)

1. The serpent (Genesis 3:14-15)

2. Balaam (Numbers 22:1-41)

3. Canaan (Genesis 9:25)

4. Jesus (Mark 11:13-14)

5. God (Genesis 4:11)

6. Jehoiakim (Jeremiah 22:18-19; 36:29-30)

7. The story of the sheep and the goats (Matthew 25:31-41)

8. Nature (Romans 8:19-22)

9. Israel (Deuteronomy 28:15-16)

10. It brought forth thorns and weeds (Genesis 3:17-18).

11. Revelation (16:9-11)

12. Those who attempt to remain under the Law (Galatians 3:10)

13. Paul (Galatians 1:8)

14. Christ (Galatians 3:13)

15. The blind and the deaf (Leviticus 19:14)

16. Job (Job 2:9)

17. Malachi (Malachi 4:6)

18. James (3:10)

19. *Paul (Acts 23:12)*

20. *Satan (Job 1:11; 2:5)*

21. *Ecclesiastes (10:20)*

22. *Death (Exodus 21:17)*

23. *Jezebel (2 Kings 9:34)*

24. *Job (Job 3:1)*

25. *Proverbs (26:2). Because the curse is undeserved, it doesn't "rest" on the person just as a fluttering sparrow doesn't light anywhere.*

26. *Jeremiah (Jeremiah 17:5)*

27. *Peter (Matthew 26:74), when he was denying he knew Jesus*

28. *Paul (1 Corinthians 4:12)*

29. *James (James 3:9-10)*

30. *Jeremiah (Jeremiah 20:14)*

31. *Abraham (Genesis 12:3)*

32. *Revelation, appropriately enough (22:3)*

QUOTABLE BAD FOLKS

If you're the type who likes to underline or highlight verses in the Bible, most of what you highlight are phrases spoken by good people, such as Jesus, Paul, and Moses. When people think of famous Bible quotations, these passages come to mind. But let's admit that the bad folks of the Bible did manage to come up with a quotable phrase now and then. If they didn't possess morals, at least they did (on occasion) possess a way with words. Try to guess the bad guys who are quoted here.

1. "If thou be the Son of God, cast thyself down."
2. "Hath the Lord indeed spoken only by Moses? Hath he not spoken also by us?" (Hint: family)
3. "I . . . saw a dream which made me afraid, and the thoughts upon my bed and the visions of my head troubled me." (Hint: a king)
4. "This is John the Baptist; he is risen from the dead; and therefore mighty works do show forth themselves in him."
5. "My father made your yoke heavy, and I will add to your yoke." (Hint: a king)

6. "Who is the Lord, that I should obey his voice to let Israel go?"
7. "Treason! Treason!" (Hint: a woman)
8. "Behold, thou hast mocked me, and told me lies; now tell me, I pray thee, wherewith thou mightest be bound." (Hint: a mistress)
9. "Why are ye come out to set your battle in array? Am I not a Philistine, and ye servants to Saul?"
10. "Skin for skin, yea, all that a man hath will he give for his life."
11. "Dost thou still retain thine integrity? Curse God, and die."
12. "Why was not this ointment sold for 300 pence, and given to the poor?"
13. "The serpent beguiled me, and I did eat."
14. "Had Zimri peace, who slew his master?" (Hint: a queen)
15. "I heard thy voice in the garden, and I was afraid."
16. "Get thee from me, take heed to thyself, see my face no more; for in that day thou seest my face thou shalt die."
17. "My punishment is greater than I can bear."
18. "My father also chastised you with whips, but I will chastise you with scorpions."
19. "Am I a dog, that thou comest to me with staves?"
20. "I find no fault in this man."

QUOTABLE BAD FOLKS (ANSWERS)

1. Satan (Matthew 4:6)
2. Miriam and Aaron (Numbers 12:2)
3. Nebuchadnezzar (Daniel 4:5)
4. Herod (Matthew 14:2)
5. Rehoboam (1 Kings 12:14)
6. Pharaoh (Exodus 5:2)
7. Athaliah (2 Kings 11:14)
8. Delilah (Judges 16:10)
9. Goliath (1 Samuel 17:8)
10. Satan (Job 2:4)
11. Job's wife (Job 2:9)
12. Judas Iscariot (John 12:5)
13. Eve (Genesis 3:13)
14. Jezebel (2 Kings 9:31)

15. *Adam (Genesis 3:10)*
16. *Pharaoh (Exodus 10:28)*
17. *Cain (Genesis 4:13)*
18. *Rehoboam (1 Kings 12:14)*
19. *Goliath (1 Samuel 17:43)*
20. *Pilate (Luke 23:4)*

 ## WHOLE LOT O' LYIN' GOIN' ON ON

No, you won't actually find the words *Thou shalt not lie* in the Bible, and it seems that on a few (and very rare) occasions, good people did lie. Still, the Bible is definitely antideception (or, to put it more positively, pro-honesty). It has harsh words to say against deceit of all kinds, especially when the liars are those who are servants of God.

1. Who was the first person to lie to God about a murder?
2. Who was probably the most deceptive future father-in-law in the Bible?
3. What doting mother lied to procure a blessing for her favorite son?
4. What frustrated Egyptian wife claimed her husband's Hebrew servant had tried to seduce her?
5. What lying prophet put Jeremiah in the stocks and was later told by Jeremiah that he and his whole household would die in exile?
6. Who was turned into a leper for lying to the prophet Elisha?
7. What owner of a vineyard was executed by Ahab because lying witnesses claimed he had blasphemed against God and the king?
8. Which king of Israel claimed to be a devout worshipper of Baal in order to gather together Baal-worshippers and butcher them?
9. Who died after lying to Peter about the value of the possessions they had sold?
10. What godly prophet lied to Ahab about the outcome of a battle?
11. What two men—father and son—claimed at different times that their wives were actually their sisters?

12. What suffering man accused his three friends of being "physicians of no value" who smeared him with lies?
13. What woman lied to God about her laughing?
14. What woman did a strongman lie to several times before finally telling her the truth?
15. According to Psalms, what type of person tells lies from the time he is born?
16. Who, according to Jesus, is "a liar and the father of it"?
17. In which Epistle would you find the words, "Let God be true, and every man a liar"?
18. In Revelation, what is the final fate of liars?
19. In which book of the Bible would you find the words "All men are liars"?
20. In the Epistle to Titus, what group of people are referred to as liars, brutes, and gluttons?
21. According to 1 John, a liar is a person who denies what Christian doctrine?
22. Which Old Testament book states that "a poor man is better than a liar"?
23. What two brave Hebrew women lied to the mighty Egyptian pharaoh?

WHOLE LOT O' LYIN' GOIN' ON ON (ANSWERS)

1. Cain (Genesis 4:8-9)

2. Laban, father-in-law of Jacob (Genesis 29)

3. Rebekah, mother of Jacob and Esau (Genesis 27)

4. The wife of Potiphar, Joseph's master (Genesis 39)

5. Pashhur (Jeremiah 20:1-3, 6)

6. His servant, Gehazi (2 Kings 5:20-27)

7. Naboth (1 Kings 21)

8. Jehu (2 Kings 10)

9. Ananias and Sapphira (Acts 5:1-10)

10. Micaiah (1 Kings 22)

11. Abraham (Genesis 12:11-13) and Isaac (26:6-7)

12. Job (Job 13:4)

13. Sarah, Abraham's wife (Genesis 18:15)

14. *Delilah, who finally did wheedle from Samson the secret of his great strength (Judges 16)*

15. *The wicked (Psalm 58:3)*

16. *The devil (John 8:44)*

17. *Romans (3:4)*

18. *The lake of fire and brimstone (Revelation 21:8)*

19. *Psalms (Psalm 116:11)*

20. *Cretians (Titus 1:12)—that is, the people of Crete, where Titus was a pastor. In his letter to Titus, Paul was quoting an old proverb about the Cretians.*

21. *That Jesus is the Christ (1 John 2:22)*

22. *Proverbs (19:22)*

23. *The two Hebrew midwives, Shiphrah and Puah (Exodus 1:15-19), who had been ordered to kill the male babies of the Hebrews*

THE ULTIMATE VERBAL SIN: BLASPHEMY

Deliberately insulting, slandering, or dishonoring God is referred to as blasphemy, and the Bible takes it very seriously. Humans have a habit of saying cruel, malicious things about one another—and even worse, about the God who made them.

1. Which of the Ten Commandments prohibits blasphemy?
2. In Revelation, who "opened his mouth in blasphemy against God"?
3. According to Jesus, what form of blasphemy cannot be forgiven?
4. Which apostle admitted he had been a blasphemer in his pre-Christian days?
5. In Leviticus, what punishment is given to a blasphemer?
6. Which official tore his robe because he believed Jesus was a blasphemer?
7. What Christian martyr was accused of blaspheming God and the laws of Moses?
8. Who was denounced as a blasphemer because he claimed the power to forgive sins?
9. In Acts 19, Paul was accused of blaspheming against what pagan goddess?

10. In which Gospel did the Jews wish to stone Jesus for claiming to be God's Son?
11. In 2 Peter, what people speak evil of the things they do not understand?
12. Complete this verse from Jeremiah: "Because of _____ the land mourneth."
13. In which book of the Bible do people suffering from plagues blaspheme the name of God?
14. Who told Christians to put "filthy communication out of your mouth"?
15. Complete this verse from Psalms: "They set their _____ against the heavens."
16. Which prophet quoted the Lord as saying, "Your words have been stout against me"?
17. Which Christian lamented that "out of the same mouth proceedeth blessing and cursing"?
18. In Revelation, what creature was "full of names of blasphemy"?
19. What notorious sin of King David gave Israel's enemies a reason to blaspheme God?
20. Which New Testament Epistle refers to a "man of sin" who blasphemes?
21. Who lamented that in his younger days he had tried to get Christians to blaspheme?
22. In Numbers, what did God send as punishment for the Israelites who were cursing him and Moses?
23. Complete this verse from Psalms: "O Lord . . . the _____ people have blasphemed thy name."
24. Who referred to the two Christians Hymenaeus and Alexander, who had been "delivered unto Satan, that they may learn not to blaspheme"?

THE ULTIMATE VERBAL SIN: BLASPHEMY (ANSWERS)

1. The third—not taking the name of God in vain (Exodus 20:7)

2. The Beast (Revelation 13:6)

3. Blaspheming against the Holy Spirit (Matthew 12:31-32)

4. Paul (1 Timothy 1:13). He regarded his former persecution of Christians as a form of blasphemy.

5. Death by stoning (Leviticus 24:16, 23)

6. The Jewish high priest (Matthew 26:65). Tearing one's robe was a sign of intense rage.

7. Stephen (Acts 6:11). As prescribed in Leviticus 24, he was given the legal punishment for blasphemy—stoning.

8. Jesus (Mark 2:7)

9. Artemis, or Diana (Acts 19:23-24)

10. John (10:33-36)

11. False teachers (2 Peter 2:12)

12. Swearing (Jeremiah 23:10)

13. Revelation (16:9)

14. Paul (Colossians 3:8)

15. Mouth (Psalm 73:9)

16. Malachi (Malachi 3:13)

17. James (James 3:10)

18. The "scarlet-colored beast" (Revelation 17:3)

19. His adultery with Bathsheba (2 Samuel 12:14)

20. 2 Thessalonians (2:3-4)

21. Paul, in his pre-Christian days (Acts 26:11)

22. Venomous snakes (Numbers 21:5-6)

23. Foolish (Psalm 74:18)

24. Paul (1 Timothy 1:20)

 ## GRAB BAG OF BRAGGARTS

Try saying the chapter title three times fast, and you'll have something to brag about! Seriously, boasting is a human habit that none of us likes, yet we endure it. Maybe it's a matter of "I'll tolerate your loud ego if you'll tolerate mine." But the fact that it irritates us tells us a lot. Somehow we know instinctively that if we asked certain people, "Who do you think you are—God?" they might honestly answer, "Yes!" The Bible has its share of shameless braggarts—including some big names in the world's history books. It has a lot to say—totally negative—about boastful folks.

1. What Philistine giant boasted to the boy David that he would give his flesh "unto the fowls of the air and to the beasts of the field"?

2. What arrogant king of Israel foolishly boasted that his little finger was thicker than his father's thighs?
3. Who was Moses referring to when he said, "The enemy said, 'I will pursue, I will overtake, I will divide the spoil; my lust shall be satisfied upon them'"?
4. Complete this verse from Proverbs: "Boast not thyself of _____; for thou knowest not what a day may bring forth."
5. What wicked Persian official boasted about his wealth and his many sons?
6. According to 1 Corinthians, what wonderful thing is not boastful?
7. In the book of Acts, what magician boasted that he was someone great?
8. Which prophet said, "Let not the wise man glory in his wisdom, neither let the strongman glory in his might, let not the rich man glory in his riches"?
9. Complete this verse from Proverbs: "Whoso boasteth himself of a false _____ is like clouds and wind without rain."
10. What braggart king of Syria sent a threatening message to King Ahab of Israel?
11. Which prophet had a strange vision of a horn that spoke boastfully?
12. What immoral act were the Corinthian Christians actually boasting about?
13. In Revelation, what wicked city falls after boasting, "I sit a queen, . . . and shall see no sorrow"?
14. Complete this verse from Psalms: "Why boasteth thou thyself in mischief, O _____ man?"
15. Whose army did the Lord reduce so men would give credit for victory to God instead of boasting?
16. Complete this verse from Jeremiah: "Let him that glorieth, glory in this, that he understandeth and knoweth me, that I am the _____."
17. Which New Testament Epistle says that all such boasting is evil?
18. Complete this verse from Psalms: "The wicked boasteth of his heart's _____, and blesseth the covetous, whom the Lord abhorreth."
19. In the Gospels, what group of people boasted that they had power of demons?
20. Which New Testament Epistle says that people are saved by faith, not by works, so that no one can boast?
21. Which prophet spoke out against the Edomites for boasting about the misfortunes of Judah?

22. Complete this verse from Psalms: "The Lord shall cut off all flattering lips, and the _____ that speaketh proud things."

23. Who claimed that he boasted about nothing except the cross of Jesus Christ?

24. Which Epistle says that in the end times, "Men will be lovers of their own selves, covetous, boasters, proud, blasphemous, disobedient to parents, unthankful, unholy"?

25. Complete this verse from Psalms: "Confounded be all those who serve images, who boast themselves of _____."

26. Which New Testament Epistle talks about the dangerous boasting of the tongue?

27. Which prophet lamented, "Woe unto them who are wise in their own eyes, and prudent in their own sight"?

28. In what famous parable of Jesus does a character pray, "God, I thank thee, that I am not as other men are"?

29. Complete this verse from Romans: "Professing themselves to be wise, they became _____."

30. What book of the Bible advises, "Cease from thine own wisdom"?

GRAB BAG OF BRAGGARTS (ANSWERS)

1. Goliath, of course (1 Samuel 17:44). He was proved wrong.

2. Rehoboam, Solomon's son (1 Kings 12:10). He was speaking figuratively, but his arrogance led to a split in the kingdom.

3. The Egyptian soldiers, who drowned in the sea (Exodus 15:9)

4. Tomorrow (Proverbs 27:1)

5. Haman (Esther 5:11)

6. Love (1 Corinthians 13:4)

7. Simon (Acts 8:9)

8. Jeremiah (Jeremiah 9:23)

9. Gift (Proverbs 25:14)

10. Ben-hadad (1 Kings 20:10)

11. Daniel (Daniel 7:8-11)

12. A man was having relations with his stepmother (1 Corinthians 5:1-6).

13. Babylon (Revelation 18:7)

14. Mighty (Psalm 52:1)

15. Gideon (Jerubbaal)'s (Judges 7:2)

16. *Lord (Jeremiah 9:24)*

17. *James (4:16)*

18. *Desire (Psalm 10:3)*

19. *The disciples known as the Seventy (Luke 10:17-20)*

20. *Ephesians (2:8-9)*

21. *Obadiah (Obadiah 1:12)*

22. *Tongue (Psalm 12:3)*

23. *Paul (Galatians 6:14)*

24. *2 Timothy (3:2)*

25. *Idols (Psalm 97:7)*

26. *James (3:5)*

27. *Isaiah (Isaiah 5:21)*

28. *The parable of the Pharisee and the tax collector (Luke 18:11). It is the smug Pharisee who praises himself.*

29. *Fools (Romans 1:22)*

30. *Proverbs (23:4)*

MOCKERS, SCOFFERS, AND OTHER SNEERY FOLKS

You probably won't find the words *cynic* or *smart-aleck* in your Bible, but such folks existed in Bible times, and the Bible uses words like *mockers, scoffers,* and *the scornful.* You know the type—lots of attitude, sneering at the world, accentuating the negative, and doing their best to eliminate the positive. They may not seem as harmful as murderers and thieves, but they don't exactly make the world a better place, and the Bible is pretty harsh toward them.

1. What much-read book of the Old Testament opens with a blessing on those who do not sit in the "seat of the scornful"?
2. What saintly king's messengers were "laughed to scorn" and mocked when they asked the people of Israel to repent and return to God?
3. When the apostles were filled with the Holy Spirit at Pentecost, what did the scoffers say?
4. What book of the Bible states that God "scoffeth at the scoffers"?

5. According to 2 Chronicles, Judah fell under God's wrath because of its mocking of what people?
6. What new mother was mocked by the son of her servant?
7. What seductive woman complained to a strongman that he had mocked her by telling her lies?
8. What lying woman said that her husband's Hebrew servant had "mocked" her by trying to seduce her?
9. What irritated prophet believed that his donkey was mocking him?
10. Which prophet of the Lord was mocked by some children for his bald head?
11. According to Proverbs, what kind of people "make a mock of sin"?
12. What men did King Herod believe had mocked him by making a fool of him?
13. What righteous prophet mocked 450 false prophets when their god failed to appear?
14. Where was Paul when some snobbish philosophers mocked his preaching of the gospel?
15. Who foretold that he would be mocked and killed by the Gentiles?
16. According to Proverbs, what kind of drink is a "mocker" that deceives men?
17. Who mocked the Jews who were attempting to rebuild the walls of Jerusalem?
18. Complete this verse from Proverbs: "Whoever mocks the _____ reproaches his Maker."
19. Who was mocked with the words "He saved others; himself he cannot save"?
20. Which city's scoffing rulers did Isaiah say had hidden themselves under falsehood?
21. Which prophet uses the word *aha* several times to refer to the pagans mocking the Jews?
22. What cynical ruler mocked Jesus after failing to make him perform a miracle?
23. What suffering man said, "I am as one mocked by his neighbor" and my friends scorn me"?
24. What Assyrian conqueror did the Lord say had been "laughed to scorn"?
25. Who was mocked for saying, "The maid is not dead, but sleepeth"?
26. Which apostle warned that scoffers would poke fun at Christians for believing in the second coming of Jesus?

MOCKERS, SCOFFERS, AND OTHER SNEERY FOLKS (ANSWERS)

1. Psalms (Psalm 1:1)

2. Hezekiah's (2 Chronicles 30:1-10)

3. "These men are full of new wine" (Acts 2:13).

4. Proverbs (3:34)

5. God's prophets (2 Chronicles 36:16)

6. Sarah, wife of Abraham, who was mocked by Ishmael, son of her husband and her maid, Hagar (Genesis 21:9)

7. Delilah, who finally wheedled out of Samson the secret of his strength (Judges 16)

8. Potiphar's wife, who had tried but failed to seduce Joseph (Genesis 39:17)

9. Balaam (Numbers 22:29)

10. Elisha (2 Kings 2:23)

11. Fools (Proverbs 14:9)

12. The wise men, who did not tell him where they had found the baby Jesus (Matthew 2:16)

13. Elijah (1 Kings 18:27)

14. Athens, Greece (Acts 17:16-32)

15. Jesus (Matthew 20:19)

16. Wine (Proverbs 20:1)

17. Sanballat (Nehemiah 4:1)

18. Poor (Proverbs 17:5)

19. Jesus, while he was on the cross (Matthew 27:42)

20. Jerusalem (Isaiah 28:14)

21. Ezekiel (Ezekiel 25:3; 26:2; 36:2)

22. Herod (Luke 23:11)

23. Job (Job 12:4; 16:20)

24. Sennacherib (2 Kings 19:21)

25. Jesus (Matthew 9:24), who brought back to life a girl who had just died

26. Peter (2 Peter 3:3-4)

SPEAKING OF TONGUES

Words can hurt and words can heal. Alas, people seem to take more pleasure in hurting others than in healing them. The Bible has some harsh words to say about sinning with the tongue.

1. Which prophet compared the tongue to a bow that shoots arrows?
2. Which king (and poet) compared the deceitful tongue to a sharp razor?
3. Which New Testament Epistle talks about the importance of "bridling" the tongue?
4. According to Psalm 140, what animal's tongue does an evil man's tongue resemble?
5. Who called the tongue "a fire, a world of iniquity"?
6. Following Paul's advice to Timothy, what type of men should not be "double-tongued"?
7. According to the book of Job, the wicked man will be slain by what animal's tongue?
8. What New Testament man was made temporarily tongue-tied because he doubted the words of an angel?
9. Which parable of Jesus features a rich man in hell, begging for someone to cool his tongue with a drop of water?
10. At what place did the "confusion of tongues" occur?
11. Which of the Ten Commandments is concerned with speaking truthfully?
12. What little-read Old Testament book commands people, "You shall not go up and down as a talebearer among your people"?
13. Complete this verse from Psalms: "Keep your tongue from evil and your lips from speaking _____."
14. Who asked, "O generation of vipers, how can you, being evil, speak good things"?
15. Which apostle advised, "He that will love life, and see good days, let him refrain his tongue from evil"?
16. What book of the Bible states that "in the multitude of words there is no lack of sin, but he who controls his lips is wise"?
17. Complete this saying of Jesus: "Blessed are you when men shall _____ you and and persecute you."

18. Which prophet told people to "fear not the reproach of men, neither be afraid of their revelings"?

19. Who said, "Whatever you do in word or deed, do all in the name of the Lord Jesus"?

20. According to Jesus, "What you have spoken in the ear in private shall be proclaimed upon the _____."

21. What kind of answer, according to Proverbs, "turns away wrath"?

22. Which apostle told Christians to lay aside "all malice, and all guile, and hypocrisies, and envies, and all evil speakings"?

23. According to Proverbs, what does a perverse man sow?

24. Complete this verse from Psalms: "The words of the [wicked] man's mouth were smoother than _____, but war was in his heart."

25. What young pastor did Paul advise to "shun profane and vain babblings"?

26. What book of the Bible states that evil people have swords "in their lips"?

27. Who said that what defiled a man was not what went into his mouth but what came out of it?

28. Who ordered Christians to "speak not evil one of another"?

29. According to Proverbs, the words of a talebearer are as dainty _____.

30. Complete this verse from Psalms: "Whoever secretly _____ his neighbor, him will I cut off."

31. Which Epistle says that "if you are reproached for the name of Christ, happy are you"?

32. Who said, "Judge not, and you shall not be judged; condemn not, and you shall not be condemned"?

33. What book of the Bible says that "the north wind driveth rain away; so doth an angry countenance a backbiting tongue"?

34. Which Epistle says that the tongue is "an unruly evil, full of deadly poison"?

35. According to Revelation, what is the final fate of liars?

36. Complete this verse from Ephesians: "Wherefore, putting away lying, speak every man truth with his _____; for we are members one of another."

37. According to Psalms, everyone speaks vanity with his neighbor. "With flattering lips and with a _____ heart do they speak."

38. According to the Lord's words to Isaiah, "This people draw near me with their mouth . . . but [they] have removed their _____ far from me."

39. Which Epistle condemns the person who says he knows God but does not keep his commandments?

40. Complete this verse from Psalms: "They bless with their mouth, but they _____ inwardly."

SPEAKING OF TONGUES (ANSWERS)

1. *Jeremiah (Jeremiah 9:8)*

2. *David (Psalm 52:2)*

3. *James (1:26)*

4. *A serpent's (Psalm 140:3)*

5. *James (James 3:6)*

6. *Deacons (1 Timothy 3:8). For that matter, no Christian should be double-tongued.*

7. *A viper's (Job 20:16)*

8. *Zechariah, father of John the Baptist (Luke 1)*

9. *The parable of the rich man and Lazarus the beggar (Luke 16:24)*

10. *At Babel (Genesis 11). Until that time, men had all spoken one common language. Because of human pride and arrogance in building the tower, God "confused the tongues" of men.*

11. *"You shall not bear false witness against your neighbor" (Exodus 20:16).*

12. *Leviticus (19:16)*

13. *Guile (Psalm 34:13)*

14. *Jesus (Matthew 12:34)*

15. *Peter (1 Peter 3:10)*

16. *Proverbs (10:19)*

17. *Revile (Matthew 5:11)*

18. *Isaiah (Isaiah 51:7)*

19. *Paul (Colossians 3:17)*

20. *Housetops (Luke 12:3)*

21. *Soft (Proverbs 15:1)*

22. *Peter (1 Peter 2:1)*

23. *Strife (Proverbs 16:28)*

24. *Butter (Psalm 55:21)*

25. *Timothy (2 Timothy 2:16)*

26. *Psalms (Psalm 59:7)*

27. *Jesus (Matthew 15:18-20)*
28. *James (James 4:11)*
29. *Morsels (Proverbs 18:8)*
30. *Slanders (Psalm 101:5)*
31. *1 Peter (4:14)*
32. *Jesus (Luke 6:37)*
33. *Proverbs (25:23)*
34. *James (3:8)*
35. *The lake of fire and brimstone (Revelation 21:8)*
36. *Neighbor (Ephesians 4:25)*
37. *Double (Psalm 12:2)*
38. *Heart (Isaiah 29:13)*
39. *1 John (2:4)*
40. *Curse (Psalm 62:4)*

 ## MORE QUOTABLE BAD FOLKS

Once again, here are some juicy quotes from some of the Bible's baddest. And again, a reminder: Not all the folks quoted here were villains through and through. Some were (like all of us) doing bad and saying bad at the moment they were speaking.

1. "Am I my brother's keeper?"
2. "Lie with me." (Hint: in Egypt)
3. "As the Lord liveth, the man who hath done this thing shall surely die."
4. "I have sinned this time; the Lord is righteous, and I and my people are wicked." (Hint: a pagan king)
5. "Give me thy vineyard, that I may have it for a garden of herbs, because it is near unto my house, and I will give thee for it a better vineyard."
6. "All these things will I give thee, if thou wilt fall down and worship me."
7. "What is truth?"

8. "Dost thou now govern the kingdom of Israel? Arise, and eat bread, and let thine heart be merry. I will give thee the vineyard of Naboth."
9. "Entreat the Lord, that he may take away the frogs from me, and from my people."
10. "Except I shall see in his hands the print of the nails, and put my finger into the print of the nails, and thrust my hand into his side, I will not believe."
11. "The Philistines are upon thee, Samson."
12. "The Lord watch between me and thee, when we are absent one from another."
13. "Go and search diligently for the young child; and when ye have found him, bring me word again, that I may come and worship him also." (Hint: a scheming king)
14. "Behold, this dreamer cometh. Come now, therefore, and let us slay him, and cast him into some pit."
15. "Behold, the people of the children of Israel are more and mightier than we."
16. "There is a certain people scattered abroad and dispersed among the people in all the provinces of thy kingdom, and their laws are diverse from all people; neither keep they the king's laws." (Hint: a Persian)
17. "Great is Diana of the Ephesians."
18. "Woman, I know him not."
19. "Let not Hezekiah deceive you; for he shall not be able to deliver you out of his hand." (Hint: a Babylonian official)
20. "Give me here the head of John the Baptist on a charger."
21. "He hath brought in a Hebrew unto us to mock us; he came in unto me to lie with me, and I cried with a loud voice."
22. "If thou be the Christ, save thyself and us."
23. "He hath spoken blasphemy! What further need have we of witnesses?"
24. "The woman whom thou gavest to be with me, she gave me of the tree, and I did eat."
25. "My punishment is greater than I can bear." (Hint: brothers)
26. "Pray ye to the Lord for me, that none of these things which ye have spoken come upon me." (Hint: a magician)
27. "Whomsoever I shall kiss, that same is he; hold him fast."
28. "There is no god."

MORE QUOTABLE BAD FOLKS (ANSWERS)

1. Cain (Genesis 4:9)

2. Potiphar's wife (Genesis 39:7). The words were addressed to Joseph.

3. David (2 Samuel 12:5). Ironically, David was referring to himself, having just committed adultery with Bathsheba and having had her husband killed.

4. Pharaoh (Exodus 9:27)

5. Ahab (1 Kings 21:2)

6. The devil (Matthew 4:9)

7. Pilate (John 18:38)

8. Jezebel (1 Kings 21:7)

9. Pharaoh (Exodus 8:8)

10. Thomas (John 20:25)

11. Delilah (Judges 16:20)

12. Laban (Genesis 31:49), Jacob's tricky father-in-law

13. Herod (Matthew 2:8)

14. Joseph's brothers (Genesis 37:19-20)

15. Pharaoh (Exodus 1:9)

16. Haman (Esther 3:8)

17. The people of Ephesus (Acts 19:34)

18. Peter, denying that he knew Jesus (Luke 22:57)

19. Rabshakeh (2 Kings 18:29)

20. The daughter of Herodias (Matthew 14:8)

21. Potiphar's wife (Genesis 39:14)

22. One of the two thieves crucified with Jesus (Luke 23:39)

23. Caiaphas, the high priest who condemned Jesus (Matthew 26:65)

24. Adam (Genesis 3:12)

25. Cain (Genesis 4:13)

26. Simon the sorcerer (Acts 8:24)

27. Judas Iscariot (Matthew 26:48)

28. The fool (Psalm 14:1; 53:1)

PART 10

SINFUL SITES

SIN CENTRAL: WICKED OLD SODOM

"The men of Sodom were wicked and great sinners before the Lord."
So says Genesis 13:13, giving the first hint that this wicked city was
going to meet a bad end. The memory of Sodom, its sins, and its
destruction stuck in the memory of the Bible writers, so this sin pit is
mentioned again and again in the Bible, usually as a warning about
divine wrath.

1. What righteous man argued with God about destroying Sodom?
2. Which relative of the man in question 1 had settled in Sodom?
3. In what form did the Lord visit Sodom?
4. Where did the visitors propose to stay until Lot dissuaded them?
5. Why did the men of Sodom surround Lot's house on that fateful
   night?
6. What did Lot propose as an alternative for the men of Sodom
   instead of forcing themselves on his male visitors?
7. What divine punishment was inflicted on the men of Sodom for
   their many evils and for trying to force their way into Lot's house?
8. What two people would not listen to Lot's pleading to leave
   Sodom before it was destroyed?
9. How many people fled the doomed city?
10. What command of the two angels did Lot's wife famously disobey?
11. What was Lot's wife's punishment for disobeying?
12. What did God use to destroy the wicked city when dawn came?
13. What nearby city was destroyed along with Sodom?
14. Who went and observed the destroyed cities, seeing the smoke rise
    like "the smoke of a furnace"?
15. Which Old Testament book warned the Israelites that if they were
    unfaithful, their own land could be destroyed like Sodom and
    Gomorrah, "which the Lord overthrew in his anger"?
16. What major city did Isaiah prophesy would be overthrown by God
    as Sodom and Gomorrah were?
17. Which brief New Testament Epistle states that Sodom and
    Gomorrah were punished for their sexual perversion?
18. Who said that on the Day of Judgment, the towns of Galilee would
    suffer worse punishment than Sodom?
19. Which Epistle says that the rescue of Lot from Sodom is an
    example of the Lord who rescues his people from evil?

20. What city did Isaiah condemn for parading its sin the way Sodom did?
21. Which prophet lamented that his city had been overthrown by the Lord as Sodom was?
22. What book of the Bible refers to some unnamed city "which is spiritually called Sodom and Egypt"?
23. Who said, "Remember Lot's wife"?
24. Which prophet said that the sins of wicked Sodom were "pride, fullness of bread, and abundance of idleness"?
25. The perversion and destruction of Sodom is depicted in what popular 1966 movie?
26. Where do archaeologists believe the remains of the wicked city may now be?
27. What British actor played Lot in the 1963 movie *Sodom and Gomorrah*?
28. Which Old Testament book refers to the "vine of Sodom," which yields grapes filled with poison?

SIN CENTRAL: WICKED OLD SODOM (ANSWERS)

1. Abraham, who asked, "Will you indeed sweep away the righteous with the wicked?" (Genesis 18:22-33). Apparently there were not enough righteous people in Sodom to justify saving it.

2. His nephew, Lot (Genesis 13:12)

3. Two angels in the form of men (Genesis 19:1)

4. In the town square. Lot persuaded them that his home was safe (which proved to be wrong) (Genesis 19:2-3).

5. They wanted the two visitors to be brought out so they could have sex with them (Genesis 19:4-6).

6. Sex with his two virgin daughters (Genesis 19:8)

7. The two angels struck them with blindness (Genesis 19:11).

8. His daughters' husbands, who thought he was jesting (Genesis 19:14)

9. Four—Lot, his wife, and their two daughters (Genesis 19:16)

10. They told the family not to look back on the city. The wife disobeyed (Genesis 19:17, 26).

11. She was turned into a pillar of salt (Genesis 19:26).

12. Fire and brimstone, which may possibly be referring to a volcano (Genesis 19:24).

13. Gomorrah (Genesis 19:24)

14. *Abraham (Genesis 19:28)*

15. *Deuteronomy (29:23)*

16. *Babylon (Isaiah 13:19)*

17. *Jude (1:7)*

18. *Jesus (Matthew 10:15), who was condemning the cities for rejecting the gospel*

19. *2 Peter (2:6)*

20. *Jerusalem (Isaiah 3:9)*

21. *Jeremiah, who (tradition says) was the author of Lamentations (4:6)*

22. *Revelation (11:8). Sodom was a symbol of immorality, whereas Egypt symbolized oppression and slavery.*

23. *Jesus (Luke 17:32). He was using her as a warning not to look back.*

24. *Ezekiel (Ezekiel 16:49)*

25. *The Bible . . . In the Beginning*

26. *Under the waters of the Dead Sea*

27. *Stewart Granger*

28. *Deuteronomy (32:32)*

 ## PHARAOH-LAND: EGYPT

Of Israel's many neighboring nations, none is more intriguing than Egypt. From the early chapters of Genesis on through the New Testament, this mighty pagan nation was never far from the thoughts of the Bible authors. Test your knowledge of the mighty empire of Egypt, keeping in mind that things haven't changed much—just look at your daily newspaper to see how the hostilities continue.

1. Who was the first Hebrew to leave his famine-struck country to seek sustenance in Egypt?
2. The pharaoh bestowed the name *Zaphenath-paneah* on what Hebrew leader?
3. In the book of Revelation, which city is "spiritually called Sodom and Egypt"?
4. Who told Joseph to take Mary and the newborn Jesus to Egypt?
5. What Hebrew name is Egypt also known by in the Old Testament?
6. Which servant of Abraham and Sarah was an Egyptian?
7. According to Proverbs, what sort of fine cloth comes from Egypt?

8. Which pharaoh killed Israel's good king Josiah in battle?
9. What was the name of the Hebrew slaves' ghetto in Egypt?
10. Which king of Israel married a daughter of the pharaoh?
11. What villainous king caused Joseph, Mary, and the baby Jesus to flee to Egypt?
12. Who was the son of Abraham and his Egyptian maidservant?
13. What Hebrew liberator killed an Egyptian and buried his body in the sand?
14. Which apostle was accused of being an Egyptian terrorist?
15. Whose heart was hardened by God?
16. Which author of a large section of the Bible never once mentions Egypt?
17. Which king extended the boundary of Israel all the way to Egypt?
18. What New Testament martyr gave a long account of Israel and Egypt before he was stoned to death?
19. Whom did Moses say good-bye to before he went back to Egypt?
20. What Israelite king had wisdom that excelled "all the wisdom of Egypt"?
21. What Old Testament prophet predicted that "Egypt shall be a desolation"?
22. The great river of Egypt is never named in the Bible but merely referred to as "the stream." What is the name of the river?
23. What famous peninsula lies between Egypt and Israel?
24. The Egyptian city of Noph (its name in the Bible) is also known by another name (which happens to be a large city in Tennessee). What is it?
25. What Hebrew leader married the daughter of the priest of the Egyptian city of On?
26. Whose wife was considered gorgeous by the men of Egypt?
27. What tribe of people sold Joseph as a slave to the Egyptians?
28. What four pharaohs are mentioned by name in the Bible?
29. Who interpreted Pharaoh's strange dreams?
30. Egypt was noted for its many gods. Which ones are mentioned by name in the Bible?
31. The "river of Egypt" was the boundary between which two regions?
32. Which prophet uttered the surprising words, "Blessed be Egypt, my people"?
33. Which prophet was carried off to Egypt after Jerusalem was captured by Babylonians?
34. What Egyptian wife made passes at her Hebrew slave?

35. Which official of Solomon's fled to Egypt and later became king of Israel?
36. Which pharaoh stripped Jerusalem of its Temple treasures?
37. What book of the Bible refers to the practice of mummification?
38. Which form of pagan worship did the Hebrews carry with them out of Egypt?
39. Who was the slave of an Egyptian named Potiphar?
40. Who told the Egyptians that his beautiful wife was in fact his sister?
41. Who was given land "from the river of Egypt unto the great river, the river Euphrates"?
42. Which prophet accused the Jews of committing "fornication with the Egyptians, thy neighbors"?
43. Which is the only Gospel to mention the land of Egypt?
44. Which king established calf worship in Israel after living for a while among the pagan Egyptians?
45. Which pharaoh probably has the shortest royal name in the Bible?
46. According to the Epistle to the Hebrews, who esteemed "the reproach of Christ greater riches than the treasures in Egypt"?
47. What sea did God dry up so the Israelites could cross it?
48. What two servants of Pharaoh had their mysterious dreams interpreted by Joseph?
49. What modern musical play is based on the adventures of Joseph in Egypt?
50. Which king made a fatal attempt to stop the Egyptian forces at Megiddo?
51. What thirty-year-old Hebrew supervised a food storage program in Egypt?
52. Were there Egyptians present when the Holy Spirit descended at Pentecost?
53. What book of the Bible opens by telling of "a new king over Egypt, who knew not Joseph"?
54. What great composer of choral music wrote *Israel in Egypt* with words taken from the book of Exodus?
55. What was the important occupation of the two Hebrew women named Puah and Shiphrah?
56. What wealthy king of Israel purchased horses from Egypt?
57. Which prophet quotes God as saying, "When Israel was a child, then I loved him, and called my son out of Egypt"?
58. What Hebrew baby was hidden in a basket in a river to protect him from an Egyptian decree?

59. Which king of Judah was carried off to Egypt and died there?
60. To whom did God say, "I have surely seen the affliction of my people who are in Egypt"?
61. Which king took away Egypt's possessions in Palestine?
62. What was the first plague God sent against the Egyptians?
63. In the book of Judges, who led the Israelites against the Egyptians?
64. Who was embalmed in Egypt after dying at the age of 110?
65. What was the last plague God sent against the Egyptians?
66. From which direction did God send the wind that parted the Red Sea?
67. When the Hebrews left Egypt, whose bones did they carry with them?
68. Who sent 10 of his sons to find food in Egypt?
69. Which king received a wedding present of a Canaanite city whose inhabitants had been slaughtered by the pharaoh?
70. What two sons (whose names were two of the tribes of Israel) were sons of Joseph and his Egyptian wife?
71. Which prophet predicted that Egyptians would slaughter one another?
72. How many years did the Hebrews wander in the wilderness after leaving Egypt?
73. Who fled to Egypt to escape the wrath of Solomon?
74. What objects did the Egyptians force the Hebrews to create without straw?
75. Which of Aaron's miracles were the Egyptian magicians able to duplicate?
76. What did Moses toss into the air to create the plague of boils on the Egyptians?
77. What caused Jeroboam to leave Egypt and return to Israel, where he became a king?
78. From which son of Noah were the Egyptians descended?
79. When hail fell on Egypt, what was the only region not affected?
80. What pagan king taunted the Israelites for believing the Egyptians would aid them?

PHARAOH-LAND: EGYPT (ANSWERS)

1. *Abraham (Genesis 12:10)*

2. *Joseph (Genesis 41:45)*

3. *Jerusalem (Revelation 11:8)*

4. An angel (Matthew 2:13)

5. Mizraim (Genesis 10:6). Mizraim was one of the sons of Ham, Noah's son.

6. Hagar, the mother of Ishmael (Genesis 16:1)

7. Linen (Proverbs 7:16)

8. Pharaoh-nechoh (2 Kings 23)

9. Goshen (Exodus 9:26)

10. Solomon (1 Kings 3:1)

11. Herod (Matthew 2:15)

12. Ishmael (Genesis 16), whose mother was Hagar

13. Moses (Exodus 2:12)

14. Paul, who was confused with an Egyptian agitator (Acts 21:38)

15. The pharaoh's (Exodus 4:21)

16. Paul. Egypt is mentioned constantly in the Old Testament and the Gospels, but not in Paul's letters.

17. Solomon (1 Kings 4:21)

18. Stephen (Acts 7)

19. His Midianite father-in-law, Jethro (Exodus 4:18)

20. Solomon (1 Kings 4:30)

21. Joel (Joel 3:19)

22. The Nile, of course. It is probably not named because it is the main river of Egypt.

23. The Sinai Peninsula

24. Memphis

25. Joseph (Genesis 41:45)

26. Abraham's (Genesis 12:14)

27. The Midianites (Genesis 37:36)

28. Shishak (1 Kings 11:40), So (2 Kings 17:4), Neco (2 Kings 23:29-35), and Hophra (Jeremiah 44:30). Curiously, the very important pharaohs of Joseph's and Moses' times are never named.

29. Joseph (Genesis 41)

30. None are. This is curious, because the Bible mentions the false gods of most of the other surrounding nations.

31. Canaan and Egypt (Genesis 15:18)

32. Isaiah (Isaiah 19:25)

33. Jeremiah (Jeremiah 43)

34. *The wife of Potiphar, who made amorous advances to Joseph (Genesis 39)*

35. *Jeroboam (1 Kings 11–12)*

36. *Shishak (1 Kings 14)*

37. *Genesis, which mentions the embalming of Joseph (50:3)*

38. *Calf worship (Exodus 32)*

39. *Joseph, Jacob's son (Genesis 39)*

40. *Abraham, husband of Sarah (Genesis 12)*

41. *Abraham (Genesis 15:18)*

42. *Ezekiel (Ezekiel 16:26)*

43. *Matthew. This is the only Gospel that tells of Joseph, Mary, and Jesus fleeing to Egypt.*

44. *Jeroboam (1 Kings 12:28)*

45. *So (2 Kings 17:4)*

46. *Moses (Hebrews 11:26)*

47. *The Red Sea (Exodus 13)*

48. *The butler and the baker (Genesis 40)*

49. Joseph and the Amazing Technicolor Dreamcoat

50. *Josiah (2 Kings 23)*

51. *Joseph (Genesis 41)*

52. *Yes (Acts 2:10)*

53. *Exodus*

54. *George Frideric Handel, more famous for his* Messiah

55. *They were the midwives who delivered the Hebrew babies in the land of Egypt (Exodus 1).*

56. *Solomon (1 Kings 10:28)*

57. *Hosea (Hosea 11:1)*

58. *Moses (Exodus 1)*

59. *Jehoahaz, son of Josiah (2 Kings 23:34)*

60. *Moses (Exodus 3:7)*

61. *The king of Babylon (2 Kings 24:7)*

62. *Turning the river to blood (Exodus 7:14-24)*

63. *No one. This was one period of Israel's history when the Egyptians were not invading Israel.*

64. *Joseph (Genesis 50:26)*

65. *Killing the firstborn in every family (Exodus 11)*

66. *The east (Exodus 14:21)*

67. *Joseph's (Exodus 13:19)*

68. *Jacob (Genesis 42)*

69. *Solomon, who married Pharaoh's daughter (1 Kings 9)*

70. *Ephraim and Manasseh (Genesis 46:20)*

71. *Isaiah (Isaiah 19:2)*

72. *Forty (Joshua 5:6)*

73. *Jeroboam (1 Kings 11:40)*

74. *Bricks (Exodus 5:7)*

75. *Turning a staff into a snake (Exodus 7)*

76. *Ashes (Exodus 9:10)*

77. *The death of Solomon (1 Kings 11:40)*

78. *Ham (Genesis 10:6)*

79. *Goshen, the district where the Hebrew slaves lived (Exodus 9:26)*

80. *Sennacherib, king of Assyria (2 Kings 18:21)*

DOING AS THE ROMANS DO

Christianity began and spread when the Roman Empire ruled much of Europe, the Middle East, and North Africa. Although the Romans boasted about their many achivements—a fine system of roads, magnificent buildings, a fairly humane set of laws—the empire was notoriously cruel and immoral, basing its magnificence and power on heavy taxation and military oppression. Its emperors and ruling classes seemed to delight in finding new ways to be decadent and depraved. Borrowing a phrase from a former U.S. president, it was an "evil empire"— pretty much like every empire that has ever existed. Test your knowledge of Rome and its important place in the New Testament.

1. According to tradition, what Roman emperor was responsible for executing both Paul and Peter?
2. Which Gospel is the only one to mention Roman emperors by name?
3. What noted Jerusalem landmark was renovated and enlarged by King Herod?

4. Who had the apostle James executed by the sword?
5. Who followed Pontius Pilate as Roman governor in Palestine?
6. What Roman ruler ordered a census of the empire?
7. What was the name of the Jewish agitators who wanted to revolt against Roman rule?
8. When Jesus said, "Render unto Caesar what is Caesar's," which Roman ruler was he referring to?
9. What paranoid king, appointed to his post by the Romans, ordered the massacre of babies in Bethlehem?
10. This Jewish princess, mentioned in Acts 25 and present at Paul's trial, was noted for being the mistress of the Roman general Titus, who later became emperor. Who was she?
11. What Roman ruler expelled the Jews from Rome?
12. What Rome-appointed ruler was called "that fox" by Jesus?
13. According to tradition, the cruel Roman emperor Domitian had which apostle exiled on the island of Patmos?
14. What Roman governor hoped to receive a bribe from the apostle Paul?
15. Whom did the Roman soldiers force to carry Jesus' cross?
16. Which Christian was the empire's director of public works in the city of Corinth?
17. Which apostle was a flunky for the Roman government?
18. What "wee little man" was a dishonest tax collector for the Romans before his conversion?
19. What demon had a Roman military name?
20. What early Christian convert was a Roman centurion?
21. What part of the Roman military diet was offered to Jesus when he was on the cross?
22. Which Gospel tells of a compassionate Roman centurion who asked Jesus to heal a favorite slave?
23. Which New Testament Epistle was sent to the owner of a runaway slave?
24. What were former slaves called in the Roman Empire?
25. In which Epistle did Paul urge Christians to pray for the Roman rulers?
26. In which city with a Roman name did Peter proclaim that Jesus was the Messiah?
27. What Roman-appointed governor was struck down by a fatal illness in the middle of a speech?
28. What Roman construction was admired by Jesus' disciples?
29. What Christian leaders were Roman citizens?

30. What Roman governor tried to make himself popular with the Jews by persecuting the Christians?
31. Which of Jesus' disciples was a Zealot, an agitator against Roman rule?
32. At the time of Jesus' trial, who was in prison for being a notorious political agitator?
33. In the book of Revelation, what "code name" is used to refer to the persecuting Roman Empire? (Hint: It's the name of an ancient empire.)
34. The book of Revelation also mentions the number of hills Rome was built on. How many?
35. What Roman gods are mentioned in the New Testament?
36. When Paul preached in Athens, his audience included people who followed two popular philosophies in the Roman Empire. What were the two?
37. Who was emperor while Paul languished in prison in Caesarea for two years?
38. Which apostle was chained to a Praetorian guard?
39. Although the New Testament was written in Greek, what was the basic language used throughout the Roman Empire?
40. Who spoke of "twelve legions of angels"?
41. In which Epistle does Paul describe the "whole armor of God," modeling it after the Roman soldier's equipment?
42. Which Epistle mentions that some of the early Christians were in fact slaves?
43. In which city did Paul face an angry mob in a Roman theater?
44. The Parthian empire was the long-standing enemy of the Roman Empire. Which New Testament book mentions the Parthians?
45. What sort of woman does the book of Revelation compare Rome to?
46. The Roman general Titus destroyed the Temple in AD 70. Who predicted this?
47. Which Epistle mentions the presence of saints in Caesar's household?
48. What Jewish group expressed fear that Jesus' miracles would result in Rome destroying the Temple and the entire Jewish religion?
49. What two men were thrown into prison for advocating practices against Roman customs?
50. What cruel punishment was about to be inflicted on Paul before he announced that he was a Roman citizen?

DOING AS THE ROMANS DO (ANSWERS)

1. Nero, who was assassinated in AD 68
2. Luke's. He mentions Augustus (2:1) and Tiberius (3:1).
3. The Temple
4. Herod Agrippa, grandson of Herod the Great (Acts 12:1)
5. Felix (Acts 24)
6. Caesar Augustus (Luke 2)
7. The Zealots
8. Emperor Tiberius
9. Herod, known throughout history as "Herod the Great" (Matthew 2:13-18)
10. Bernice. Titus had to abandon her after he became emperor.
11. Claudius (Acts 18:2)
12. Herod Antipas, son of Herod the Great
13. John, author of Revelation
14. Felix (Acts 24:26)
15. Simon of Cyrene (Matthew 27:32)
16. Erastus (Romans 16:23)
17. Matthew, the tax collector (Matthew 9:9)
18. Zacchaeus of Jericho (Luke 19:2)
19. Legion (Mark 5:9)
20. Cornelius (Acts 10)
21. Vinegar, or sour wine (Matthew 27:48)
22. Luke (7:2)
23. Philemon, who was the owner of Onesimus
24. Freedmen (Acts 6:9)
25. 1 Timothy (2:1-3)
26. Caesarea Philippi (Mark 8:29)
27. Agrippa (Acts 12:21-23)
28. The renovated Temple in Jerusalem (Mark 13)
29. Paul and Silas (Acts 16:38)
30. Herod Agrippa (Acts 12:1)
31. Simon (Luke 6:15)
32. Barabbas (Matthew 27:15-17)

33. *Babylon (Revelation 14–18)*

34. *Seven*

35. *Jupiter and Mercury (Acts 14:12) and Diana (Acts 19:24). (These are the Roman names. Some translations of the Bible use the Greek names for these gods: Zeus, Hermes, and Artemis.)*

36. *Stoics and Epicureans (Acts 17:18)*

37. *Claudius*

38. *Paul (Acts 28:16, 20)*

39. *Latin*

40. *Jesus (Matthew 26:53)*

41. *Ephesians (6:13-18)*

42. *Philippians (4:22)*

43. *Ephesus (Acts 19:29)*

44. *Acts (2:9). There were Parthians in Jerusalem on the Day of Pentecost.*

45. *A prostitute (Revelation 17)*

46. *Jesus (Luke 21)*

47. *Philippians (4:22)*

48. *The Sanhedrin (John 11:48)*

49. *Paul and Silas (Acts 16:21)*

50. *Scourging ("flogging" in some translations) (Acts 22:25)*

MOABITES, EDOMITES, AND OTHER "-ITES": ISRAEL'S NASTY NEIGHBORS

Israel's occupation of the land of Canaan has never gone uncontested. From the book of Genesis to the present day, other groups have vied with the Chosen People for the Promised Land. Test your knowledge of Israel's neighbors—more accurately, Israel's *enemies*—in Bible times. And be aware that some of those enemy neighbors—notably the Philistines—had names that don't quite fit the "-ite" category. (Note: We've devoted separate sections to Israel's big neighbors—Egypt, Babylon, Assyria, and the Roman Empire—so none of the questions here will deal with them.)

1. What people worshipped the grisly god Molech, sacrificing children to him?

2. What warlike people occupied the coastal plain near Israel and were always referred to as "the uncircumcised"?
3. What nation was so wealthy that its camels had gold chains around their necks?
4. From what Old Testament people do today's Arabs trace their descent?
5. The people of what fierce nation threatened to gouge out the right eyes of all the inhabitants of Jabesh-gilead?
6. What woman was given as a wife after her future husband brought her father 200 Philistine foreskins as a dowry?
7. What people were noted for wearing gold earrings?
8. Uriah, the first husband of King David's wife Bathsheba, was from what nation?
9. What tribe occupied the site of Jerusalem before the Israelites took over?
10. What country did Moses live in when he fled Egypt the first time?
11. King Balak called upon his prophet Balaam to curse the Israelites, but Balaam ended up blessing them. What nation were Balak and Balaam from?
12. The judge Jephthah led the Israelites against what nation?
13. Samson was captured and blinded by what pagan people?
14. When David was in trouble with King Saul, where did he take his father and mother to protect them?
15. What warlike people often attacked Israel and were notable because "they had no fear of God"?
16. The man who killed King Saul was from what tribe?
17. The book of Obadiah is directed against what violent neighbor nation?
18. What pagan nation had a fish-shaped god named Dagon?
19. What neighboring country of Israel traced its descent from Jacob's hairy twin brother, Esau?
20. Milcom is the god of which nation?
21. The god Chemosh had child sacrifice as part of his worship. Solomon erected an altar for him, but Josiah tore it down. What nation worshipped Chemosh?
22. What pagan people captured the Ark of the Covenant from Israel?
23. Abraham's son by his wife Keturah was the founder of what nomadic people?
24. In what country did Moses die?
25. Joshua, with God's help, defeated five kings of what people?
26. What people did Joseph's brothers sell Joseph to?

27. Which king of Israel had Ammonite women in his large harem?
28. Which king of the Amalekites was spared death by Saul, only to be executed later by Samuel?
29. What overweight king of Moab oppressed the Israelites for 18 years?
30. Moses' wife, Zipporah, was from what country?
31. What tribe was descended from "a wild man"?
32. Who grieved his Hebrew parents by marrying two Hittite women?
33. What country had a road called "the King's Highway"?
34. What brutal method did Phinehas, Aaron's grandson, use to kill an Israelite man and his Midianite lover?
35. By what other name is the Mediterranean Sea known in the Old Testament?
36. What people were noted for riding camels into battle?
37. When Joshua and his armies conquered Canaan, what tribe did Jerusalem belong to?
38. The cities of Ashdod, Gaza, and Gath belonged to what pagan nation?
39. Nahash, a pagan friend of King David, was king of what country?
40. Ahimelech, a friend of David in his outlaw days, was what nationality?
41. What group of people destroyed the Lord's shrine at Shiloh?
42. What people worshipped a fly god named Baalzebub?
43. What Old Testament patriarch was described as "a wandering Aramean"?
44. What group of people told Abraham that they would not refuse him burial in their tombs?
45. Who was Jerusalem's first ruler?
46. What wise king of Israel received gifts and money from "all the kings of Arabia"?
47. What country controlled the distribution of iron and prevented Israel from having any really useful weapons?
48. Mesha, a pagan king who was a sheep breeder, gave a gift of 100,000 sheep to Israel. What country did he rule?
49. Caphtor, an island in the Mediterranean Sea, was the original home of what pagan people (thorns in Israel's side)?

MOABITES, EDOMITES, AND OTHER "-ITES": ISRAEL'S NASTY NEIGHBORS (ANSWERS)

1. The Ammonites (Leviticus 18:21; 1 Kings 11:7). Apparently an idol of Molech was heated, and the bodies of the slain children were placed in its arms.

2. The Philistines (Judges 14:3; 1 Samuel 14:6). Israel and most of its neighbors circumcised male children, but the Philistines were noted for not doing so.

3. Midian (Judges 8:26)

4. The Ishmaelites, descendants of Abraham's son Ishmael (Genesis 16; 21). The Arabs base their belief on a proclamation of Muhammad.

5. Ammon (1 Samuel 11:2)

6. Michal, daughter of King Saul (1 Samuel 18:27)

7. The Ishmaelites (Judges 8:24)

8. The Hittites (2 Samuel 11:3). Apparently there were many Hittite soldiers in Israel's armies.

9. The Jebusites (2 Samuel 5:69). The original name of Jerusalem was Jebus.

10. Midian (Exodus 2:15)

11. Moab (Numbers 22-24)

12. Ammon (Judges 11)

13. The Philistines (Judges 14–16)

14. Moab (1 Samuel 22:3-4)

15. The Amalekites (Deuteronomy 25:18)

16. The Amalekites (2 Samuel 1:8-10)

17. Edom. The country had invaded and plundered Israel many times, and Obadiah announced God's judgment against them.

18. Philistia (1 Samuel 5:2)

19. Edom (Genesis 25:30; 36:1). Edom was another name for Esau, just as Jacob's other name was Israel.

20. Ammon (1 Kings 11:5)

21. Moab (Numbers 21:29; 1 Kings 11:7; 2 Kings 23:13)

22. The Philistines (1 Samuel 5)

23. The Midianites—the son was named Midian (Genesis 25)

24. Moab (Deuteronomy 34:5). He was not allowed to enter the Promised Land.

25. The Amorites (Joshua 10–11)

26. The Ishmaelites (Genesis 37:25-28)

27. *Solomon (1 Kings 11)*

28. *Agag (1 Samuel 15)*

29. *Eglon (Judges 3), who was assassinated by the Israelite leader Ehud*

30. *Midian (Exodus 2:21)*

31. *The Ishmaelites (Genesis 16:12), descendants of Abraham's son Ishmael*

32. *Esau, son of Isaac and Rebekah (Genesis 26:34-35)*

33. *Moab (Judges 11:17)*

34. *He drove a spear through the two of them when he caught them in the act (Numbers 25:7-8). He did this because many of the Israelite men were being led into pagan worship by the Midianite and Moabite women.*

35. *The Sea of the Philistines (Exodus 23:31)*

36. *The Midianites*

37. *The Amorites (Joshua 10)*

38. *Philistia (Joshua 13:2-3)*

39. *Ammon (2 Samuel 10)*

40. *He was a Hittite (1 Samuel 26:6).*

41. *The Philistines (1 Samuel 4)*

42. *The Philistine people of Ekron (2 Kings 1:2). The name Baalzebub means "lord of the flies."*

43. *Jacob (Deuteronomy 26:5)*

44. *The Hittites (Genesis 23:5-6)*

45. *Adoni-zedek, a Jebusite (Joshua 10:1)*

46. *Solomon (1 Kings 10:15)*

47. *Philistia. The Philistines were skilled in metalworking (1 Samuel 13:19-22).*

48. *Moab (2 Kings 3:4)*

49. *The Philistines (Amos 9:7; Jeremiah 47:4). Archaeologists believe that Caphtor may be the ancient name for the Greek island of Crete in the Mediterranean.*

 ## GENTILE ON MY MIND

Depending on the translation you use, your Bible refers many times to *the Gentiles, the heathen, the nations,* etc. All these terms refer to non-Jews, and for the most part, the Bible takes a harsh view of such people because it was assumed they were worshippers of false gods, and thus immoral, cruel, and oppressive. And they very often were. Keep in mind, though, that the Bible's harshest words are not directed against the Gentiles but against the Jews, who had God's law and special care but behaved badly anyway.

1. Who told his followers that when they pray, they should not babble as the pagans did?
2. Which apostle lamented that the gospel was "foolishness" to the Gentiles?
3. What book of the Bible predicts that at the end times, Gentiles will trample on the Holy City for 42 months?
4. Which apostle told Christians to live such moral lives that the pagans would eventually glorify God?
5. What two missionaries took the gospel to the Gentiles after the Jews rejected it?
6. Complete this verse from Psalms: "Why do the heathen _____, and the peoples imagine a vain thing."
7. Which prophet lamented that the Jews had "done after the manners of the heathen that are round about you"?
8. Who observed that the Gentiles like to lord it over one another?
9. Who lamented that some Christians were practicing sexual immorality that was even worse than that of the pagans?
10. According to Psalms, "The idols of the heathen are _____ and _____, the work of men's hands."
11. Which of Paul's letters says that the Gentiles "are a law unto themselves"?
12. Which prophet observed that the Gentiles, who dabbled in astrology, were "dismayed at the signs of heaven"?
13. Which king of Judah sacrificed his own son in the fire, "according to the abominations of the heathen"?
14. According to Paul, the sacrifices of the pagans were not offered up to God but to whom?
15. Who told people not to fret over things like food and clothing because that was how pagans behaved?
16. In which book of the Bible would you find this verse: "The Lord is King forever and ever; the heathen are perished out of his land"?
17. What evil king of Judah made his country "do worse than the heathen"?
18. In Acts, Jewish Christians were amazed that the Gentile Christians had received what gift?
19. Which of Paul's letters advises Christians not to give themselves up to passionate lust like the heathen?

20. Complete this verse from Psalms: "The heathen are sunk down in the _____ that they made."
21. Who predicted that he would be handed over to the Gentiles to be mocked, spit on, and killed?
22. In Acts, who told the Gentiles that in times past, God had allowed them to "walk in their own ways"?
23. Which Old Testament book says that the Israelites could have Gentile slaves but not Israelite slaves?
24. In which Epistle does Paul counsel Christians to no longer walk as the Gentiles do, "in the vanity of their mind"?
25. Who prophesied that "Jerusalem will be trodden down by the Gentiles, until the times of the Gentiles be fulfilled"?

GENTILE ON MY MIND (ANSWERS)

1. Jesus (Matthew 6:7)

2. Paul (1 Corinthians 1:23)

3. Revelation (11:2)

4. Peter (1 Peter 2:12)

5. Paul and Barnabas (Acts 13:46)

6. Rage (Psalm 2:1)

7. Ezekiel (Ezekiel 11:12)

8. Jesus (Mark 10:42)

9. Paul (1 Corinthians 5:1)

10. Silver, gold (Psalm 135:15)

11. Romans (2:14)

12. Jeremiah (Jeremiah 10:2)

13. Ahaz (2 Kings 16:3)

14. Demons (1 Corinthians 10:20)

15. Jesus (Matthew 6:31-33)

16. Psalms (Psalm 10:16)

17. Manasseh (2 Chronicles 33:9)

18. The Holy Spirit (Acts 10:45)

19. 1 Thessalonians (4:5)

20. Pit (Psalm 9:15)

21. *Jesus (Luke 18:32)*
22. *Paul (Acts 14:16)*
23. *Leviticus (25:44)*
24. *Ephesians (4:17)*
25. *Jesus (Luke 21:24)*

 ## MAMMOTH EMPIRES: ASSYRIA, BABYLONIA, PERSIA

Due to its location, the Holy Land in Bible times had numerous dealings (mostly unpleasant) with the two great empires to the east (Assyria and Babylon) and later, with a slightly more humane empire even farther east, Persia. Israel, the small kingdom in a strategic location, had some colorful (and often violent) run-ins with these three imperial giants. Test your knowledge of these empires in the Bible, keeping in mind that things haven't really changed—after all, Assyria, Babylon, and Persia occupied the land that is now Iraq and Iran.

1. Which Old Testament book is set in the capital city of Persia?
2. What renowned king of Assyria was murdered by his two sons while he was worshipping?
3. What renowned Babylonian ruler went insane while walking on the roof of his palace?
4. This Babylonian god is mentioned by Jeremiah as being utterly disgraced after the fall of Babylon. What was his name?
5. What nation saw 185,000 of its soldiers slaughtered by an angel of the Lord?
6. What Persian king was considered to be God's anointed one?
7. Which king of Babylon burned Jerusalem?
8. What book of the Bible speaks of dashing the babies of Babylon against stones?
9. Who held the first "world's fair"?
10. Who built ancient Babylon?
11. Which king of Judah was blinded and imprisoned because he defied Babylonian authority?
12. The ancient city of Ur lay in which country?
13. What Babylonian king, prominent in the Bible, built the impressive Hanging Gardens of Babylon, one of the Seven Wonders of the World?

14. Who had enemies that wrote smear letters about him to the Persian king?
15. Which king of Babylon, driven from his palace, lived in the wilderness and let his hair grow long and shaggy?
16. Which king was criticized by the prophet Isaiah for showing Judah's treasure to Babylonian ambassadors?
17. Where was the first beauty contest in the Bible, and who won?
18. Who rebuilt Babylon on a grand scale?
19. What evil king of Israel rode into battle in a chariot but was fatally wounded by an Assyrian arrow?
20. Who knelt toward Jerusalem and prayed looking out of his eastern window in Babylon?
21. When the Assyrians deported the people of Israel, how many of the 12 original tribes were left?
22. What Persian queen upset the king and his aides by refusing to appear for them at their drunken banquet?
23. What nation had Nebo as one of its gods?
24. Which king issued an edict ending the exile of the Jews?
25. What Babylonian king had a dream of a tree in which every bird found shelter?
26. Who scandalized the godly by having an Assyrian-style altar made for the Jerusalem Temple?
27. What nation's ambassadors were taken on a tour of the palace by King Hezekiah?
28. What army was defeated when an angel of the Lord struck down 185,000 soldiers?
29. Which king of Israel was imprisoned for defying Assyrian authority?
30. Who served as a cupbearer in Persia's royal palace?
31. Which king of Israel had much of his territory taken away by the Assyrian king?
32. What great city did Isaiah predict would become like a helpless widow?
33. Who taxed the Israelites in order to pay off Pul, the king of Assyria?
34. After the death of the sinister Persian prime minister Haman, who received the Persian king's signet ring?
35. Which king of Assyria sent foreigners to settle in Israel after the Israelites had been taken away to exile?
36. What city in Revelation was seen as a place that would never again hear the voices of brides and grooms?

37. What Assyrian king brought about the fall of Samaria and the deportation of the Israelites to other countries?
38. What Jewish girl married a Persian emperor and helped save her exiled people from extermination?
39. What Assyrian field commander tried to intimidate King Hezekiah by speaking propaganda to the people of Jerusalem?
40. When the Jews were allowed to defend themselves against the Persians, how many Persians were killed?
41. Who plotted to have the entire Hebrew nation completely exterminated?
42. Which king of Judah was blinded and taken away in chains to Babylon?
43. Nehemiah waited until this Persian king was softened up with wine before he asked the king to let the Jews return to their homeland. Who was the king?
44. What four faithful young men refused to eat the rich foods provided by the king of Babylon?
45. Which festival was to be a memorial of the Jews' salvation from the wicked Persian Haman?
46. Which king of Israel paid tribute money to King Shalmaneser of Assyria?
47. What Hebrew patriarch was originally from Babylon?
48. Who prophesied that Assyria would become a desolate roosting place for all sorts of strange night birds?
49. What evil king of Judah was humbled and repentant after being taken to Babylon in chains?
50. Which king removed the gold from the doors of the Temple and gave it to the king of Assyria?
51. Which king of Persia issued the decree that the people of Judah could rebuild their Temple?
52. Which apostle, according to tradition, preached in Assyria and Persia and died a martyr in Persia?
53. What upright young man was made ruler over the whole province of Babylon?
54. What Babylonian king caused famine in Jerusalem?
55. Which prophet advised building a signal fire as a sign of the coming invasion of Babylon?
56. What Assyrian king attacked the Philistines and Egyptians, after which Isaiah walked around naked for three years?
57. Which prophet in Babylon wore sackcloth while seeking the Lord?
58. Who laid a tax on the whole Persian Empire?

59. The city of Babylon is located on what great river of the Middle East?
60. Which prophet, famous for his vision of the dry bones, was with the exiles in Babylon?
61. What was another name in ancient times for the Babylonian Empire?
62. In what country were the Jews when they fasted after learning of an executive order to have them all killed?
63. The arrogant Babylonian king Belshazzar, drunk at his feast, committed an outrage when he asked for new drinking cups to be brought in. What were these cups that led to so much trouble for the king?
64. Where, according to tradition, did the three wise men in the Christmas story come from?
65. What Persian gods are mentioned in the Bible?
66. What Hebrew prophet was sent by God to preach to the Assyrians?
67. What Persian king conquered the Babylonian Empire?
68. The city of Susa was the capital of which empire?
69. Who was sent by the Persian king to reorganize the Temple services in Jerusalem?
70. In the New Testament period, which empire occupied the area formerly called Persia?
71. Which apostle visited the church at Babylon?
72. What Assyrian king received 38 tons of silver as tribute money from Menahem of Israel?
73. The Persian king Xerxes is called by what name in the Bible?
74. What book of prophecy opens with the prophet standing by a river in Babylon?
75. Which Old Testament historical book opens with a reading of a decree from the Persian king Cyrus?
76. What great river of the Middle East did Nineveh, the capital of Assyria, lie on?

MAMMOTH EMPIRES: ASSYRIA, BABYLONIA, PERSIA (ANSWERS)

1. *Esther, which takes place at the royal court at Susa*

2. *Sennacherib (2 Kings 19:37)*

3. *Nebuchadnezzar (Daniel 4:28-33)*

4. *Marduk—or Merodach (Jeremiah 50:2)*

5. *Assyria (2 Kings 19:35)*

6. *Cyrus (Isaiah 45:1). Presumably, he was called this because he allowed the Jews to return from Persia to Palestine.*

7. *Nebuchadnezzar (2 Kings 25:9)*

8. *Psalms (Psalm 137:8-9)*

9. *King Ahasuerus of Persia. Esther 1:4 states that he "showed the riches of his glorious kingdom and the honor of his excellent majesty many days, even an hundred and fourscore days." That's 180 days of display.*

10. *Nimrod (Genesis 10:8-10)*

11. *Zedekiah (2 Kings 25:6-7)*

12. *Babylon. It was Abraham's home before he moved to Canaan. The city has been excavated by archaeologists.*

13. *Nebuchadnezzar. The acclaimed gardens are not mentioned in the Bible, but they were famous throughout the ancient world.*

14. *Zerubbabel (Ezra 4:6-16)*

15. *Nebuchadnezzar (Daniel 4:33)*

16. *Hezekiah (2 Kings 20:12-18)*

17. *The one at the court of Persian ruler Ahasuerus. The winner was Esther (Esther 2).*

18. *Nebuchadnezzar (Daniel 4:30)*

19. *Ahab (1 Kings 22:34-38)*

20. *Daniel (Daniel 6:10)*

21. *One—Judah (2 Kings 17:18)*

22. *Vashti, wife of King Ahasuerus (Esther 1)*

23. *Babylon (Isaiah 46:1)*

24. *Cyrus of Persia (2 Chronicles 36:22-23)*

25. *Nebuchadnezzar (Daniel 4:12)*

26. *King Ahaz (2 Kings 16:10-17)*

27. *Babylon's (2 Kings 20:16-18)*

28. *Assyria's (2 Kings 19:35)*

29. *Hoshea (2 Kings 17:4)*

30. *Nehemiah (Nehemiah 1:1; 2:1)*

31. *Pekah (2 Kings 15:29)*

32. *Babylon (Isaiah 47:8)*

33. *King Menahem (2 Kings 15:19-20)*

34. *Mordecai, Esther's kinsman (Esther 8:2-13)*

35. *Esarhaddon (Ezra 4:2)*

36. *Babylon (Revelation 18:23)*

37. *Shalmaneser (2 Kings 17:3-6)*

38. *Esther, who married King Ahasuerus and saved the Jews from the plot of the wicked Haman*

39. *Rabshakeh (2 Kings 18:17-37)*

40. *Seventy-five thousand (Esther 9:15-16)*

41. *Haman, minister of Persia (Esther 3:5-6)*

42. *Zedekiah (2 Kings 25:7)*

43. *Artaxerxes (Nehemiah 2:1)*

44. *Daniel, Shadrach, Meshach, and Abednego (Daniel 1:3-16)*

45. *Purim (Esther 9:28), which is still a major holiday for Jews*

46. *Hoshea (2 Kings 17:3-4)*

47. *Abraham, who was from Ur of the Chaldees (Genesis 11:28). Ur was in the area that was considered to be a part of the Babylonian Empire.*

48. *Zephaniah (Zephaniah 2:13-14)*

49. *Manasseh (2 Chronicles 33:10-13)*

50. *Hezekiah (2 Kings 18:16)*

51. *Cyrus (Ezra 1:1-4)*

52. *Jude. Nothing in the Bible indicates this, but the tradition arose fairly early.*

53. *Daniel (Daniel 2:48)*

54. *Nebuchadnezzar (2 Kings 25:1-3)*

55. *Jeremiah (Jeremiah 6:1)*

56. *Sargon (Isaiah 20). Isaiah's action was supposed to be a sign to the Israelites not to trust in the power of Egypt and Ethiopia to defend Israel from Assyria.*

57. *Daniel (Daniel 9:3)*

58. *King Ahasuerus (Esther 10:1)*

59. *The Euphrates*

60. *Ezekiel*

61. *Chaldea, a name that occurs a few times in the Bible. Abraham was originally from Ur of the Chaldees (Genesis 11:28).*

62. *Persia (Esther 4:1-3, 15-16)*

63. The sacred gold and silver cups that his predecessor, Nebuchadnezzar, stole from the Temple of Jerusalem (Daniel 5:1-5)

64. From Persia. Although Matthew's Gospel refers to them only as "wise men from the east" (Matthew 2:1), in the original Greek text the word used is magi, which refers to a class of priests or magicians from Persia.

65. None are. The Persians worshipped several gods, including Ahura-Mazda and Mithra, but none are mentioned in the Bible.

66. Jonah, who convinced the people of Nineveh, the Assyrian capital, to repent

67. Darius (Daniel 5)

68. Persia (Daniel 8:2; Nehemiah 1:1)

69. Ezra (Ezra 7:12)

70. Parthia, which is mentioned only in Acts 2:9 (there were Parthians in Jerusalem on the Day of Pentecost). In spite of the Bible's relative silence about the Parthian Empire, it was an important political empire in New Testament days, a power that the Roman Empire feared.

71. Peter (1 Peter 5:13). (It is possible that Babylon may actually be a sort of code name for Rome, and that Peter never actually visited Babylon itself.)

72. Tiglath-pileser (2 Kings 16:7-8)

73. Ahasuerus (the book of Esther), which is his name in Hebrew. Some modern translations of the Bible refer to him as Xerxes, but the King James Version has Ahasuerus.

74. Ezekiel (1:1), where the prophet is standing by the river (or canal) Kebar

75. Ezra

76. The Tigris

 # WORLDLY WISE (AND THAT'S NO COMPLIMENT)

As you browse through the Bible, you get the distinct impression that the world—marred by human sin and the work of Satan—is a not-so-nice place. In fact, the saints are very *unworldly* people, taking their marching orders from God and not from sinful human beings. You can't read far in the New Testament without realizing that the world is very much opposed to God and his people.

1. According to Revelation, who deceives the whole world?
2. Which apostle wrote that believers are "strangers and pilgrims" in this world?

3. Complete this saying of Jesus: "If the world _____ you, you know that it _____ me before it hated you."
4. According to 1 John, what sort of person "overcomes the world"?
5. Paul stated that believers "have received not the _____ of the world, but the _____ who is of God."
6. John stated that though "the world and its desires pass away," a certain type of person lives forever. What type?
7. Who stated that friendship with the world is hatred toward God?
8. What people is the Epistle to the Hebrews referring to when it says "the world was not worthy" of them?
9. According to Galatians, unsaved people are enslaved to the basic _____ of the world.
10. Which Epistle states that "greater is he that is in you, than he that is in the world"?
11. Who stated, "We brought nothing into the world, and it is certain we can carry nothing out"?
12. The devil tempted Jesus by taking him to a high mountain, showing him all the _____ of the world, and promising to give them to him.
13. John the Baptist announced that Jesus was "the _____ of God, who taketh away the sin of the world."
14. Who wrote that Christians were treated as "the filth of the world," like everybody's trash?
15. Complete this saying of Jesus: "Light has come into the world, and men loved darkness rather than light, because their _____ were evil."
16. Complete this statement of Paul: "This world _____ away."

WORLDLY WISE (AND THAT'S NO COMPLIMENT) (ANSWERS)

1. *Satan, of course (Revelation 12:9)*

2. *Peter (1 Peter 2:11)*

3. *Hates, hated (John 15:18)*

4. *Anyone who believes that Jesus is the Son of God (1 John 5:5)*

5. *spirit, Spirit (1 Corinthians 2:12)*

6. *One who does the will of God (1 John 2:17)*

7. *James (James 4:4)*

8. *People of faith (Hebrews 11:38)*

9. *Principles (Galatians 4:3)*

10. *1 John (4:4)*

11. *Paul (1 Timothy 6:7)*

12. *Kingdoms (Matthew 4:8-9). Jesus resisted the temptation.*

13. *Lamb (John 1:29)*

14. *Paul (1 Corinthians 4:13)*

15. *Deeds (John 3:19)*

16. *Passeth (1 Corinthians 7:31)*

 ## THE CITIES (NOT!) OF GOD

It's an old cliche, but one with a lot of truth in it: Country folk tend to behave better than city folk. Cities are big enough to provide ample opportunities for evil, and for that reason cities don't come off looking very good in the Bible. Large imperial cities like Babylon, Nineveh, and Rome were notorious for their immorality, but even some of the cities of Israel had a reputation for ungodly behavior. The prophets were constantly predicting that the cities would fall under the judgment of God, and history proved the prophets right. Incidentally, it is due to the Bible that we still use the city name *Babylon* to refer to any place of great wickedness.

1. What domineering man built ancient Babylon?
2. What murderer built a city called Enoch east of Eden?
3. Who built the Egyptian treasure cities of Pithom and Raamses?
4. Who rebuilt Gezer, which had been given as a wedding gift to his Egyptian wife by her father?
5. Who built Nineveh?
6. What evil city is mentioned numerous times in the book of Revelation?
7. Which of Paul's epistles were addressed to a Greek city notorious for its immorality?
8. What city did Jesus refer to as the one that "kills the prophets"?
9. What evil king of Israel built the nation's new capital at Samaria?
10. Which prophet preached a long sermon against the prosperous (and immoral) port city of Tyre?
11. What city in Genesis, with a famous tower, was a symbol of human pride and arrogance?
12. Who rebuilt Babylon on a grand scale?

13. What two immoral cities of Genesis have become proverbial names for sin and wickedness?
14. What large and wicked pagan city repented (temporarily) after the prophet Jonah preached in it?
15. What Roman emperor expelled all the Jews from the city of Rome?
16. Which prophet predicted that God would overthrow "Babylon, the glory of kingdoms," as he had overthrown Sodom and Gomorrah?
17. Which New Testament Epistle was written in Babylon?
18. Which prophet's book is a long rant against the wicked city of Nineveh?
19. What city was Isaiah referring to with the words "How the faithful city [has] become a harlot!"?
20. In what pagan city was there a long, loud anti-Christian riot in praise of the goddess Diana?
21. Which king foolishly displayed his treasures to ambassadors from Babylon?
22. According to Jesus, the cities he visited had even less faith than what two wicked cities of the past?
23. What book of the Bible states that a city is destroyed "by the mouth of the wicked"?
24. What evil Philistine city had its city gates carried off by the strongman Samson?
25. What two cities did King Jeroboam establish as rival worship centers of Jerusalem?
26. What city's rebuilding was accompanied by child sacrifice?
27. According to Proverbs, what type of people stir up a city?
28. The prophet Ezekiel referred many times to the "city of bloodshed." Which city did he mean?
29. Which prophet said, "Woe to him who buildeth a town with blood, and establisheth a city by iniquity"?
30. What famous city of Greece disturbed the apostle Paul because of its many idols?
31. What book reports the men of Gibeah trying to rape a male visitor to the city?
32. Which prophet lamented a wicked city that was "stained with footprints of blood"?
33. What heathen city on the Euphrates did Abram leave?
34. What Canaanite city, destroyed by the Israelites, had a name that meant "ruin"?
35. In which city did Paul encounter cynical, skeptical philosophers?

36. What Philistine city was home to the giant Goliath?
37. What city was said by the book of Revelation to have "Satan's seat"?
38. What Philistine city did Amos curse for its slave trade with Edom?
39. In Revelation, what city was said to have Christians who were neither hot nor cold?
40. In what idolatrous city was Paul mistaken for the god Hermes (Mercury)?
41. What city was punished by Gideon for refusing to feed his hungry troops?
42. Where were the bodies of Saul and Jonathan nailed to a wall?
43. Where were a number of men slain for looking into the Ark of the Covenant?
44. What Philistine city worshipped the god Baalzebub?
45. Where was the witch that Saul consulted?
46. What Phoenician city was home to evil Queen Jezebel?

THE CITIES (NOT!) OF GOD (ANSWERS)

1. *Nimrod (Genesis 10:8-10)*

2. *Cain (Genesis 4:17)*

3. *The enslaved Israelites (Exodus 1:11)*

4. *Solomon (1 Kings 9:15-17), who slipped into idolatry thanks to his many foreign wives*

5. *Nimrod (Genesis 10:11)*

6. *Babylon, which may simply be a symbol for all wicked cities or of human wickedness in general*

7. *1 and 2 Corinthians, which explains why these two letters have so many warnings against immorality. Corinth had such a bad reputation in those days that Corinthian meant "prostitute."*

8. *Jerusalem (Matthew 23:37; Luke 13:34)*

9. *Omri (1 Kings 16:23-24)*

10. *Ezekiel (Ezekiel 26–28)*

11. *Babel, which was supposed to have a tower that reached to heaven (Genesis 11:4-9)*

12. *Nebuchadnezzar (Daniel 4:30)*

13. *Sodom and Gomorrah, both destroyed by God for their immorality (Genesis 18–19)*

14. *Nineveh (Jonah 3)*

15. *Claudius (Acts 18:2)*

16. *Isaiah (Isaiah 13:19)*

17. *1 Peter, although the reference to Babylon in 5:13 is probably a reference to Rome*

18. *Nahum*

19. *Jerusalem (Isaiah 1:21)*

20. *Ephesus (Acts 19), which was home to a world-famous temple of Diana.*

21. *Hezekiah (2 Kings 20). Years later, the Babylonians would conquer Jerusalem and steal all those treasures.*

22. *Tyre and Sidon (Matthew 11:21)*

23. *Proverbs (11:11)*

24. *Gaza (Judges 16:1-3)*

25. *Bethel and Dan (1 Kings 12:29)*

26. *Jericho, rebuilt by Hiel, who sacrificed his own sons (1 Kings 16:34)*

27. *Mockers (Proverbs 29:8)*

28. *Jerusalem*

29. *Habakkuk (Habakkuk 2:12)*

30. *Athens (Acts 17:16)*

31. *Judges (19:22)*

32. *Hosea (Hosea 6:8)*

33. *Ur (Genesis 15:7)*

34. *Ai (Joshua 8:3-29)*

35. *Athens (Acts 17)*

36. *Gath (1 Samuel 17:4)*

37. *Pergamos (Revelation 2:13)*

38. *Gaza (Amos 1:6-7)*

39. *Laodicea (Revelation 3:14-19)*

40. *Lystra (Acts 14:6-20)*

41. *Succoth (Judges 8:5-16)*

42. *Beth-shan (1 Samuel 31:8-10)*

43. *Beth-shemesh (1 Samuel 6:19-21)*

44. *Ekron (2 Kings 1:2)*

45. *Endor (1 Samuel 28:7-25)*

46. *Sidon (1 Kings 16:31-33)*

MORE DOING AS THE ROMANS DO

If you made it through the first set of questions about the Roman Empire, give yourself a pat on the back. Also, remind yourself that the Roman Empire, for all its many faults, proved to be a blessing for Christianity because the Roman roads and the relative peace in the empire made it easier to spread the gospel.

1. Who told Paul that he would bear witness to the Lord in Rome?
2. What Roman soldier admitted that he had used money to buy his Roman citizenship?
3. What Roman governor had a Jewish wife named Drusilla?
4. Who uttered the famous words "I appeal unto Caesar"?
5. What Roman governor accused Paul of being insane?
6. Publius was the chief ruler of what island in the Mediterranean (famous because Paul was shipwrecked there)?
7. Besides Rome, what three Italian cities are mentioned in the Bible?
8. When the book of Acts ends, how many years had Paul been in Rome?
9. Did Paul write the Epistle to the Romans before or after he came to Rome?
10. What Christian woman did Paul ask the Roman Christians to receive warmly?
11. What Greek city was known throughout the empire as a den of sin?
12. Which New Testament book never mentions Rome but is very clearly anti-Roman?
13. Were there Romans in Jerusalem on the Day of Pentecost?
14. What Roman governor planned to execute the apostle Peter?
15. What city (with a very Roman name) witnessed the conversion of the Roman soldier Cornelius?
16. What was the name of the Roman province in which Jesus lived?
17. What Roman province was the first European territory visited by Paul?
18. The area we now call Greece was known in the New Testament by its Roman name. What was it?
19. What Roman territory mentioned in the Bible was farthest from Palestine?
20. Cilicia was the home province of what New Testament leader?
21. The Roman province of Asia, mentioned often in the New Testament, lies in what modern country?

22. Which Epistle of Paul's was sent to a province instead of to a particular city or individual?
23. The book of Revelation is addressed to the "seven churches" in which Roman province?
24. What Roman province, mentioned often in the New Testament, has the same name as a nation in the Middle East today?
25. The Egyptian city of Alexandria was the great intellectual center of the Roman Empire. What Christian leader was a native of Alexandria?
26. What Roman official became a Christian under Paul's influence?
27. Who said to Pilate, "We have no king but Caesar"?
28. The empire's official language, Latin, is mentioned only once in the Bible in connection with a famous sign. What did the sign say?
29. Who ordered a guard posted at Jesus' tomb?
30. Who bribed the Roman guards at Jesus' tomb, paying them to say that Jesus' body had been stolen?
31. At what Jewish feast did the Roman governor customarily release a prisoner?
32. What was the name of the governor's palace in Jerusalem?
33. Which Gospel mentions that Pilate and Herod became friends after they met Jesus?
34. What was the name of the imperial bodyguard?
35. What New Testament book bears the same name as a Roman emperor?
36. What Roman emperor ruled in the New Testament period but is not mentioned in the Bible at all?
37. Which island has a St. Paul's Bay, commemorating Paul's being shipwrecked there on his way to Rome?
38. Which Epistle is addressed to Christians in the Roman provinces of Pontus, Galatia, Cappadocia, Asia, and Bithynia?
39. When Paul "appealed to Caesar," which caesar (emperor) was he appealing to?
40. Who was the first apostle to witness to a Roman official?
41. A famine during the reign of the emperor Claudius had been predicted by what Christian prophet?
42. In the Roman division of Jewish land, what territory lay between Judea and Galilee?
43. What famous body of water, called Our Sea by the Romans, is never mentioned in the Bible?
44. Cyrene, the homeland of the man who carried Jesus' cross, was a Roman province on which continent?
45. What type of Roman flunky was widely considered to be dishonest and corrupt?

46. What is the only Roman coin mentioned in the Bible?
47. When Paul was in Rome, could he possibly have seen the famous Colosseum?
48. Augustus, the Roman ruler who ordered the census at the time of Jesus' birth, was what relation to the famous Julius Caesar?
49. Cyrenius, the Roman governor of Syria, is mentioned in which Gospel?
50. Luke's Gospel mentions something important happening "in the fifteenth year of the reign of Tiberius Caesar." What happened?

MORE DOING AS THE ROMANS DO (ANSWERS)

1. The Lord (Acts 23:11)

2. A chief captain (Acts 22:28)

3. Felix (Acts 24:24)

4. Paul (Acts 25:11). It was a Roman citizen's right to be tried before the emperor.

5. Festus (Acts 26:24)

6. Melita (Acts 28:1-7)

7. Syracuse, Rhegium, and Puteoli (Acts 28:12-13)

8. Two (Acts 28:30)

9. Before

10. Phebe (Romans 16:1)

11. Corinth

12. The book of Revelation, which was probably written to encourage Christians who were being persecuted by the Romans

13. Yes (Acts 2:10)

14. Agrippa (Acts 12)

15. Caesarea (Acts 10)

16. Judea

17. Macedonia (Acts 16)

18. Achaia (Acts 19:21)

19. Spain (Romans 15:24)

20. Paul. Its chief city was Tarsus, Paul's hometown.

21. Turkey

22. Galatians

23. Asia

24. Syria

25. Apollos (Acts 18:24)

26. Sergius Paulus, governor of Cyprus (Acts 13:1-12)

27. The chief priests (John 19:15)

28. "Jesus of Nazareth, King of the Jews" (John 19:19)

29. Pilate (Matthew 27:65)

30. The chief priests (Matthew 28:13-15)

31. Passover

32. The Praetorium (Mark 15:16)

33. Luke (23:12)

34. The Praetorian guard. In the New Testament, the guards were not necessarily the emperor's private guard but any guards associated with the empire's officials.

35. Titus

36. The mad emperor Caligula, who reigned after Tiberius and before Claudius

37. Melita

38. 1 Peter

39. Nero, who is not actually mentioned by name in the New Testament

40. Peter, who preached to the Roman centurion Cornelius (Acts 10)

41. Agabus (Acts 11:27-28)

42. Samaria

43. The Mediterranean. Though mentioned often as "the sea," it is never called by any particular name.

44. Africa

45. Tax collector (also called a publican)

46. The denarius, mentioned many times, although many translations use the word penny.

47. No. It wasn't built until several years after his stay in Rome.

48. His nephew—actually, his adopted nephew

49. Luke (2:2)

50. John the Baptist began preaching (Luke 3).

MORE MOABITES, EDOMITES, AND OTHER "-ITES"

Can you handle more "-ites" questions? Give these a try, and remember that the category also includes some of Israel's neighbor nations—the Philistines, for example—that weren't called by an "-ite" name.

1. In which land did Moses see a burning bush that was not consumed?
2. What did the Israelite leader Ehud use to kill fat King Eglon of Moab?
3. Whose ill-fated daughter came out dancing after his victory over the Ammonites?
4. What strongman was ordained before birth to deliver Israel from the Philistines?
5. What barley farmer married a Moabite woman and became an ancestor of David?
6. Whose daughters became the mothers of the Moabites and the Ammonites?
7. Who was commissioned by an angel to save Israel from the Midianites?
8. Who sold out Samson for the price of 1,100 pieces of silver from each of the Philistine chieftains?
9. One of Gideon's soldiers dreamed of a Midianite tent being overturned by an unlikely object. What was it?
10. Which warriors were so wealthy that even their camels wore necklaces?
11. Which prophet claimed that Edom, Moab, Ammon, and Tyre all had sorcerers?
12. Which prophet of Moab had a talking donkey?
13. Which king sacrificed his son on the city wall when the Moabites were losing the battle to Israel?
14. In the time of Saul's reign an earthquake occurred during the attack on the Philistines at Michmash. Who led the attack?
15. What wicked king of Judah built a Syrian-style altar and offered up his son as a sacrifice?
16. In the time of the judges, what tribe did the Israelites hide from in caves?
17. What Israelite woman lived in Moab but returned to Israel after her husband's death?

18. Which judge from Gilead was called to be a commander against the Ammonites?
19. This goddess of Canaan was associated with depraved worship practices. After Saul's death, his armor was placed in her temple by the Philistines. What was her name?
20. In Saul's time, what marauding people drove the Israelites into caves?
21. What Israelite leader met his future wife at a well in Midian?
22. What boy (and future king) entered the Philistine camp to confront their best warrior?
23. Which judge of Israel gave up his Philistine wife to his friend?
24. What Syrian king was getting drunk at a time when he was supposed to be making war on the Samaritans?
25. Which judge and his men killed 120,000 Midianites?
26. Which tribe was descended from Ben-ammi, the son of Lot?
27. What strongman burned the Philistines' crops by tying torches to the tails of foxes and turning them loose in the fields?
28. Which king was critically wounded by Philistine arrows?
29. Which judge confused the Midianite army by having his men blow their rams horns and break the jars they were using as lanterns?
30. What two animals owned by the Philistines carried the Ark of the Covenant back to Israel?
31. What woman with a cumbersome name was the Hivite wife of Esau?
32. What Syrian king fled when 100,000 of his soldiers were killed in one day by the Israelites?
33. What beautiful woman of Israel was married to a Hittite warrior?
34. Who killed 600 Philistines with an ox goad?
35. From what oppressive nation did the judge Gideon (Jerubbaal) deliver Israel?
36. Which king of Israel had an Ammonite mother?
37. Which king of Israel headed up the slaying of 47,000 Syrians?
38. What Israelite king's body was fastened to the wall of Beth-shan by the Philistines?
39. What happened to the Syrian soldiers when Elisha prayed?
40. Who asked his Midianite brother-in-law to be the Israelites' guide through the wilderness?
41. What man of Bethlehem migrated to Moab to escape a famine?
42. What camel-riding raiders did Saul and David fight against?
43. What godly king of Judah tore down the idols devoted to the gods of the Moabites and Ammonites?
44. Rabbah was the capital city of what enemy nation of Israel?

45. What neighbor nation was noted as having kings as rulers long before the Israelites had a king?
46. What people were descended from the 12 sons of Isaac's son by his Egyptian maid?
47. Which king of Judah watched while an invading army of Edomites, Ammonites, and Moabites all destroyed one another (instead of destroying Israel)?
48. What Syrian king besieged Samaria, causing a great famine that led to cannibalism?
49. What nation south of Egypt invaded Israel but was fought off by King Asa's army?

MORE MOABITES, EDOMITES, AND OTHER "-ITES" (ANSWERS)

1. *Midian (Exodus 3:2)*
2. *A two-edged dagger (Judges 3:16-21). Eglon was so obese that Ehud's dagger got completely lost in the fat.*
3. *The Israelite judge Jephthah's (Judges 11:30-34). Jephthah had made a vow to sacrifice her.*
4. *Samson (Judges 13:2-5)*
5. *Boaz, who married Ruth (Ruth 1:22–2:3)*
6. *Lot's (Genesis 19:30-38)*
7. *Gideon (Jerubbaal) (Judges 6:11-23)*
8. *Delilah (Judges 16:5)*
9. *A cake of barley bread (Judges 7:13)*
10. *The Midianites (Judges 8:24-26)*
11. *Jeremiah (Jeremiah 27:3-10)*
12. *Balaam (Numbers 22:21-33)*
13. *Mesha, king of Moab (2 Kings 3:27)*
14. *Saul's son Jonathan (1 Samuel 14:1-15)*
15. *Ahaz (2 Chronicles 28:1-4, 23)*
16. *The Midianites (Judges 6:2)*
17. *Naomi, Ruth's mother-in-law (Ruth 1)*
18. *Jephthah (Judges 11:6)*
19. *Ashtaroth, or Ashtoreth (1 Samuel 7:3; 31:10; 1 Kings 11:33)*
20. *The Philistines (1 Samuel 13:5-7)*

21. *Moses (Exodus 2:15-21)*

22. *David (1 Samuel 17:48-49)*

23. *Samson (Judges 14:20)*

24. *Ben-hadad (1 Kings 20:12-19)*

25. *Gideon (Jerubbaal) (Judges 8:10)*

26. *The Ammonites (Genesis 19:38)*

27. *Samson (Judges 15:4-5)*

28. *Saul (1 Samuel 31:3)*

29. *Gideon (Jerubbaal) (Judges 7:16-21)*

30. *Two cows (1 Samuel 6:7-12)*

31. *Aholibamah (Genesis 36:2)*

32. *Ben-hadad (1 Kings 20:29)*

33. *Bathsheba, wife of Uriah, and later wife of David (2 Samuel 11:3)*

34. *The Israelite judge Shamgar (Judges 3:31)*

35. *Midian (Judges 6–9)*

36. *Rehoboam, Solomon's son, whose mother was one of Solomon's many wives (1 Kings 14:21)*

37. *David (1 Chronicles 19:18)*

38. *Saul's (1 Samuel 31:10)*

39. *They were struck blind (2 Kings 6:18).*

40. *Moses, whose brother-in-law Hobab was asked to be the "eyes" in the desert (Numbers 10:29-32)*

41. *Elimelech, whose sons married the Moabite women Ruth and Orpah (Ruth 1:1-2)*

42. *The Amalekites (1 Samuel 15:3; 27:9; 30:17)*

43. *Josiah (2 Kings 23:13)*

44. *Ammon (2 Samuel 12:26)*

45. *Edom. The Edomites were the descendants of Jacob's brother, Esau (Genesis 36:31-39).*

46. *The Ishmaelites, descended from Ishmael, son of Abraham and concubine Hagar (Genesis 16:16)*

47. *Jehoshaphat (2 Chronicles 20)*

48. *Ben-hadad (2 Kings 6:24-30)*

49. *Ethiopia. It roughly corresponds to the modern nation of Sudan (2 Chronicles 14:9-12).*

PART 11

BAD BOYS AT LARGE
IN THE CULTURE

WORDS, WORDS:
OUR BIBLE-SATURATED LANGUAGE

Is our culture becoming biblically illiterate? Perhaps. But then again, it would take the English language a long, long time to get rid of all words and names that are rooted in the Bible. These terms crop up in the strangest places—houses, gardens, wine cellars, and ordinary conversation. Many of these happen to be connected with some of the Bible's bad boys and girls.

1. What wicked Old Testament queen's name now means "an evil and shameless woman"?
2. What Philistine giant's name is often applied to any oversized person or thing?
3. Which part of the human body is named for a man in the book of Genesis?
4. What group of people, often criticized by Jesus, had a name that now means "legalistic hypocrites, especially the religious kind"?
5. What pagan people, mentioned often in the Old Testament, had a name that has come to mean "crude, uncultured folk"?
6. What sinful city in the book of Genesis has given its name to sexual sins in general, and one sexual sin in particular?
7. Any traitor is liable to be referred to by the name of which of Jesus' disciples?
8. What do we call a comforter who is more prone to criticize than to provide real consolation?
9. What Old Testament conqueror's name now means "hunter," particularly an overbearing one?
10. What city visited by Paul lends it name to a wild, pleasure-loving person?
11. What do we call a scheming, beautiful, seductive woman, particularly one that leads a man to ruin?
12. What pagan empire's name now means a place devoted to sensuous pleasure and materialism?
13. What do we call the practice of buying or selling a church office?
14. Which disciple of Jesus has a tree named for him?
15. What burial ground for paupers is named for the place purchased by Judas' betrayal money?
16. A tyrant is often called what (after a famous king in the Old Testament)?

17. What wicked man's name occurs in a phrase that is a polite way of saying, "Raising hell"?
18. The word *diabolical* is connected with what nasty character of the Bible?
19. What name from the Old Testament sometimes refers to a man whose wife is cheating on him?

WORDS, WORDS: OUR BIBLE-SATURATED LANGUAGE (ANSWERS)

1. Jezebel's (1 and 2 Kings), the pagan wife of Israel's King Ahab

2. Goliath's, the giant slain by the shepherd boy (and later king) David

3. The Adam's apple, of course. The bulge in the neck is, according to legend, the piece of the forbidden fruit that stuck forever in the throat of the sinning Adam.

4. The Pharisees, whom Jesus criticized not only for their hypocrisy but also for their obsessive attention to unimportant details

5. The Philistines. Not that they were particularly uncultured, but for some reason the English author Matthew Arnold (writing in the 1800s) used the name Philistine and gave it this new meaning.

6. Sodom

7. Judas, referring to the betrayer, Judas Iscariot

8. A Job's comforter, named for Job's three so-called friends who, as Job himself said, were "miserable comforters."

9. Nimrod's, who was a "mighty hunter before the Lord" (Genesis 10)

10. Corinth. A Corinthian (then and now) was one known for high living and low morals. In fact, the word goes back even farther than Paul's day, for Corinth had a long pre-Paul reputation as a sinful city.

11. A Delilah, named for the Philistine mistress of Samson. She wormed out of him the secret of his strength, resulting in his capture and blinding by the Philistines (Judges 16).

12. Babylon's, noted in the Old Testament for its luxury and idolatry

13. Simony, named for Simon the magician who wanted to buy spiritual power from Peter (Acts 8). Simony was widely practiced years ago when the church was state supported and high-ranking church leaders were well paid.

14. The worst disciple, Judas. The Judas tree is cultivated for its showy red flowers. The name stems from the belief that when Judas hung himself on a tree of this kind, the flowers, once white, turned red. The redbud tree of the eastern United States is often called a Judas tree.

15. *It's called a potter's field (Matthew 27:7). At that time it was intended to be a place for burying foreigners, but later the term was extended to include burial for paupers, criminals, and anyone else outside mainstream society.*

16. *A pharaoh, based on the oppressive pharaoh in the book of Exodus*

17. *Cain, as in "raising Cain." Since Cain, the first murderer, was presumably in hell, "raising Cain" became an acceptable substitute for "raising hell."*

18. *Satan, or the devil. In the original Greek New Testament, he is the* diabolos.

19. *Potiphar, the Egyptian official who thought highly of his Hebrew slave Joseph—until, that is, Joseph was accused of trying to seduce Potiphar's wife. In fact, the randy wife had tried to seduce Joseph and did not take kindly to being rejected. So a potiphar is a man with a promiscuous wife.*

 ## BIBLE BAD BOYS ON-SCREEN

The Bible can still make a splash at the box office, as was proven by *The Passion of the Christ.* Although we live in a secular (even anti-Christian) world, the ancient stories of the Bible still strike a chord with people. Some of Hollywood's classics have been based on the Bible, giving us not only some admirable heroes (such as the classic Moses played by Charlton Heston), but some of the more vile, hissable villains as well.

1. What famous bald actor played the wicked Pharaoh Ramses in the 1956 classic *The Ten Commandments*?
2. What vamp from the soap opera *Dynasty* had the role as the crude wife of Potiphar in the PBS production of *Joseph and the Amazing Technicolor Dreamcoat*?
3. Pop singer Carl Anderson played the role of Judas in what 1973 movie?
4. What murderous role did actor Richard Harris play in the 1966 movie *The Bible . . . In the Beginning*?
5. What gorgeous actress played the wicked Delilah in the 1949 Cecil B. DeMille movie *Samson and Delilah*?
6. What 1953 film starred Charles Laughton as a lecherous Herod and Rita Hayworth as the wicked title character?
7. Actor Sam Neill played what evil character in *The Final Conflict*?
8. This gaudy 1951 film was based on a popular novel by Polish author Henryk Sienkiewicz. It told the story of the early Christians

and their persecution under Nero, played by Peter Ustinov. What was the film?

9. What actor, familiar to audiences for his portrayals of gangsters, played the troublemaking Dathan in *The Ten Commandments*?

10. Actor Rip Torn played the role of Judas in what popular 1961 biography of Jesus?

11. In the all-star Jesus movie *The Greatest Story Ever Told,* Martin Landau played what nasty character who played a role in Jesus' death?

12. What very wicked cities were the subjects of a 1963 movie starring Stewart Granger?

13. What criminal from the Gospels was the subject of a 1962 movie starring Anthony Quinn?

14. What 1932 film showed the declining Roman Empire and the growth of the church and featured Charles Laughton as the despised Emperor Nero?

15. What blond British actor played Judas Iscariot in *The Greatest Story Ever Told*?

16. Noted actor Edward Woodward played the unhappy, bitter, and jealous King Saul in what 1985 Richard Gere movie?

17. What mean (but funny) role did chubby Joshua Mostel play in *Jesus Christ Superstar*?

18. What recent animated movie featured two of the sinister magicians in the court of Pharaoh?

19. What classic silent movie directed by D. W. Griffith shows Jesus being persecuted by both the Jews and the Romans?

20. In the 1951 movie *David and Bathsheba,* what attractive actor and actress played the adulterous couple?

21. What popular 2004 movie caused a great controversy because it was accused of being anti-Semitic?

22. What controversial movie of the 1980s featured actor Harvey Keitel in the role of Judas Iscariot?

23. What actress (and former wife of Charlie Chaplin) played wicked queen Jezebel in a 1954 movie?

BIBLE BAD BOYS ON-SCREEN (ANSWERS)

1. *Yul Brynner*

2. *Joan Collins, who tries unsuccessfully to seduce the virtuous Joseph, played by Donny Osmond*

3. Jesus Christ Superstar

4. *Cain*

5. *Hedy Lamarr. Victor Mature was the not-so-long-haired Samson.*

6. *Salome. Hayworth played the woman who demanded (and got) John the Baptist's head on a platter.*

7. *The Antichrist, named Damien Thorn. This was the third and last of The Omen trilogy.*

8. Quo Vadis

9. *Edward G. Robinson*

10. King of Kings

11. *Caiaphas, the high priest*

12. *Sodom and Gomorrah*

13. *Barabbas, with Quinn playing the criminal who was released in place of Jesus. Based on a novel by Swedish author Pär Lagerkvist, it shows Barabbas as finally turning out good.*

14. The Sign of the Cross

15. *David McCallum, perhaps best remembered as one of the stars of* The Man from U.N.C.L.E.

16. King David, *in which Gere played David*

17. *King Herod, with his cynical invitation to Jesus to "walk across my swimming pool"*

18. *The Prince of Egypt, which tells the story of Moses and the Exodus*

19. Intolerance

20. *Gregory Peck and Susan Hayward*

21. The Passion of the Christ, *which, being based on the Gospels, did (naturally) depict the Jewish leaders in a bad light. The movie did not make the Romans look good, either.*

22. The Last Temptation of Christ

23. *Paulette Goddard, in* The Sins of Jezebel. *Considering Goddard's rather immoral life, she was well cast.*

BACK TO THE BOOKS:
BIBLE BAD BOYS IN LITERATURE

The Bible has had an enormous effect on the world's literature, not only in its morality, but in lending plots and titles to innumerable novels, stories, and poems. Test your knowledge of the Bible's bad guys and their presence in the world of literature.

1. What noted American author wrote the novel *East of Eden* (which took its title from the Bible)?

2. In the famous medieval poem *The Divine Comedy* by Dante, what is the name of the region where people are punished for their sins before entering heaven?

3. Science fiction author Ray Bradbury wrote a novel titled *Something Wicked This Way Comes* about an evil character named Mr. Dark visiting a small town. What bad boy of the Bible is he?

4. *Lord of the Flies*—a much-read 1955 novel by Nobel Prize–winner William Golding—took its title from what pagan god mentioned in the Bible?

5. What noted French author wrote *The End of Satan,* in which the proud Satan realizes that his rebellion has led to eternal separation from God?

6. Russian author Fyodor Dostoyevsky's novel *The Possessed* is a story of political terrorists, but he took the name for the title from a character in the Gospels. Which character?

7. English poet Matthew Arnold, writing in the 1800s, borrowed the name of what Old Testament nation and used it to refer to people who are uncultured and crude?

8. English poet Lord Byron, who led a scandalous life, wrote a famous poem about the Lord destroying an Assyrian king's army. Which king?

9. Mississippi novelist William Faulkner's novel *Absalom! Absalom!* was named for the wayward son of which king of Israel?

10. English poet John Masefield wrote a long poetic drama titled *A King's Daughter*. What notorious Old Testament woman is the main character?

11. English poet John Milton's great 1671 poem *Paradise Regained* is based on what key event in Jesus' life?

12. American novelist Winston Churchill wrote *The Inside of the Cup,* which took its title from Jesus' criticism of which group of people?

13. American novelist Albion Tourgee wrote many novels about the

Reconstruction era in the South. One of the novels, *Bricks without Straw,* took its title from which Old Testament book?

14. The demented ship captain who is the chief character in *Moby Dick* has what biblical name?

15. John Bunyan's famous allegory *Pilgrim's Progress* has a New Testament demon as a character. Who is he?

16. English poet Lord Byron wrote a long poem about what violent character from the book of Genesis?

17. Novelist Taylor Caldwell wrote popular novels on the lives of Paul and Luke. She also wrote one about what villain of the Bible?

18. Modern French novelist Marcel Proust published the novel titled (in English) *Cities of the Plain.* What two immoral Old Testament cities does the title refer to?

19. What great English poet wrote the masterpiece *Paradise Lost,* based on the sin of Adam and Eve?

20. *Quo Vadis,* the great novel about the persecution of Christians under evil Emperor Nero, features what two apostles as key characters?

21. Pär Lagerkvist, a Nobel Prize–winning Swedish novelist, wrote a short novel about what criminal character in the life of Jesus?

22. In the great medieval poem *The Divine Comedy* by Dante, what evil character is in the lowest region of hell?

23. Which of Jesus' disciples is with him?

24. Louis Bromfield's 1924 novel *The Green Bay Tree* took its title from the Psalms' description of a certain type of man. What type?

25. In John Milton's poem about Eden, *Paradise Lost,* Satan is the leader of the fallen angels. What biblical demon is his second-in-command?

26. Gloomy American poet Robinson Jeffers published a book of poems named for a scandalous Old Testament woman. Whom?

27. Samuel Sewall, an author in colonial America, wrote an antislavery tract in 1700 titled *The Selling of ——.* What Old Testament character, sold into slavery, is named in the title?

28. American novelist Winston Churchill's 1915 novel *A Far Country* took its title from what famous parable of Jesus?

29. *The Wanderings of Cain* is by an English poet, famous for *Kubla Khan* and *The Rime of the Ancient Mariner.* Who was he?

30. What two biblical characters are the only humans in John Milton's epic poem *Paradise Lost*?

31. The novelist Carlo Maria Franzero wrote a novel about a famous

Roman in Jesus' life. The novel is *The Autobiography of* ——.
What man is named in the title?

32. English poet John Dryden wrote a long, humorous poem about a famous rebellion in the Old Testament. The rebellion was against King David, but the poem was named for the two instigators. Who were they?

33. Archibald MacLeish wrote *Songs for* ——, glorifying the sin of a certain Old Testament woman. What woman?

34. French novelist Anatole France wrote a novel titled *The Procurator of Judea*. What man from the Gospels is its main character?

35. John Milton, the great English poet, wrote a masterpiece about what Old Testament man being betrayed by a woman?

36. In C. S. Lewis's popular book *Screwtape Letters*, the book's letters are written by what sort of beings?

37. What noted American humorist wrote *The Diary of Adam and Eve*?

38. American novelist Elmer Davis's 1928 novel *Giant Killer* is about what Old Testament character?

39. One of the best-selling books in colonial America was *The Day of Doom*, a long poem by Michael Wigglesworth. What biblical event is it concerned with?

40. Contemporary American novelist Howard Fast wrote a novel titled *Prince of Egypt*. What Old Testament character is the lead character?

41. Germany's Nobel Prize–winning author Thomas Mann wrote four long novels dealing with a dysfunctional family in the book of Genesis. Who were the main characters?

BACK TO THE BOOKS: BIBLE BAD BOYS IN LITERATURE (ANSWERS)

1. *John Steinbeck, also famous for his* Grapes of Wrath. East of Eden *refers to the land where Cain lived after he murdered Abel.*

2. *Purgatory. Dante was reflecting the traditional Catholic teaching that humans must be cleansed—purged—before entering the presence of God in heaven.*

3. *Satan, naturally*

4. *Baalzebub (see 2 Kings 1:2 and Matthew 12:24). The name Baalzebub literally translates as "lord of the flies."*

5. *Victor Hugo, famous for his novels* Les Misérables *and* The Hunchback of Notre Dame

6. *The demoniac who was healed by Jesus. The demoniac was possessed by a legion of demons. Dostoyevsky believed the political agitators were similarly possessed.*

7. *The Philistines. The term is still often used as Arnold used it.*

8. *Sennacherib. The poem is titled "The Destruction of Sennacherib" and is based on 2 Kings 19.*

9. *David. The title comes from David's lament for the dead Absalom (2 Samuel 18:33), who had rebelled against his father and tried to seize the throne. The plot of Faulkner's book does have some parallels to the David-Absalom story in the Bible.*

10. *Jezebel, Ahab's wife*

11. *His temptation by Satan*

12. *The Pharisees. Jesus said, "Woe unto you, scribes and Pharisees, hypocrites! For ye make clean the outside of the cup and the platter, but within they are full of extortion and excess. Thou blind Pharisee, first cleanse the inside of the cup" (Matthew 23:25). By the way, this Winston Churchill is not the same as the British prime minister.*

13. *Exodus. It refers to the Hebrews being forced by the wicked Egyptian pharaoh to make bricks without straw (Exodus 5).*

14. *Ahab, the name of one of the most wicked kings in the Old Testament*

15. *Apollyon, mentioned in Revelation 9:11*

16. *Cain, which is also the title of the poem. Byron, always a rebel in society, apparently found Cain an appealing character.*

17. *Judas Iscariot, in the novel* I, Judas

18. *Sodom and Gomorrah*

19. *John Milton. The poem was published in 1674 and has been a classic ever since.*

20. *Paul and Peter*

21. *Barabbas, in which the very bad man finally finds salvation. The novel was made into a movie starring Anthony Quinn.*

22. *Satan, of course*

23. *Judas Iscariot*

24. *The wicked. "I have seen the wicked in great power, spreading himself like a green bay tree" (Psalm 37:35).*

25. *Beelzebub, whom Jesus mentions as the "prince of demons" (Matthew 12:24)*

26. *Tamar, the daughter-in-law of Judah. The book of poems is* Tamar and Other Poems.

27. *Joseph, who was sold by his jealous, scheming brothers to be a slave in Egypt*

28. *The Prodigal Son. Jesus said "The younger son gathered all together, and took his journey into a far country, and there wasted his substance with riotous living" (Luke 15:13).*

29. *Samuel Taylor Coleridge*

30. *Adam and Eve, who start out innocent and good but, sadly, sin and are expelled from Eden.*

31. *Pilate. The book's full title is* The Autobiography of G. Pontius Pilate.

32. *Absalom and Achitophel. The poem (written in 1681) was meant to compare Absalom's rebellion against David with the recent rebellion of England's Duke of Monmouth against his father, King Charles II.*

33. *Eve. MacLeish's collection is* Songs for Eve.

34. *Pontius Pilate. In the novel, Pilate, years after Jesus' crucifixion, is unable to remember the event at all.*

35. *Samson. Milton's poem, published in 1672, is* Samson Agonistes, *and it deals with Samson's imprisonment by the Philistines. In the poem, the wicked Delilah—Milton spelled it Dalila—is not Samson's mistress but his wife, making her treachery even worse.*

36. *Demons*

37. *Mark Twain, who interpreted the old story in his usual irreverent way*

38. *David. The giant of the title is, of course, the Philistine warrior Goliath.*

39. *Judgment Day—a happy day for the saints, a sad day for the sinners*

40. *Moses. Naturally the wicked pharaoh is one of its main characters.*

41. *Jacob's 12 sons. Mann's work, finished in 1943, was collectively titled* Joseph and His Brothers. *As in Genesis, the brothers who sold Joseph into slavery start out as villains, but all ends happily.*

 ## HISS TIME: BIBLE VILLAINS ONSTAGE

Because the Bible has some very wicked and very well-known villains, it is inevitable that some of these bad boys would appear as characters on the stage. Satan has, of course, been a favorite—sometimes under his own name, sometimes under an alias. The questions below deal with the human bad boys (and girls) that have been seen onstage, sometimes in very popular plays.

1. What controversial rock opera features Judas as a bad but somehow sympathetic character?

2. *It Should Happen to a Dog* is the title of Wolf Mankowitz's play about what reluctant Old Testament prophet?

3. What rock opera, popular on Broadway in the 1980s, deals with Jacob and his 12 sons?

4. American prizewinning poet Archibald MacLeish wrote the 1926 play *Nobodaddy*. What noted characters from the book of Genesis are the subjects of this unusual play?

5. Oscar Wilde was noted for his witty comedies, but his one tragic play concerns the imprisonment and death of John the Baptist. What is the play's title?

6. Twentieth-century English author Christopher Fry's play *The Firstborn* deals with what prominent Old Testament character? (Hint: It isn't Adam.)

7. Norman Nicholson's 1946 play *The Old Man of the Mountains* deals with a fiery prophet and a wicked king from the Old Testament. Who are they?

8. The great French author Jean Racine wrote a tragedy about what villainous Old Testament queen?

9. Archibald MacLeish wrote an unusual stage play published in 1958, *J. B.* What Old Testament character is this based on? (Hint: The character's name sounds a lot like J. B.)

10. What biblical couple is the subject of a still-popular opera by Camille Saint-Saëns?

11. American poet Robinson Jeffers wrote a play that tries to enhance the reputation of a particular disciple of Jesus. Which disciple?

12. The poet Howard Nemerov, at one time Poet Laureate of the United States, wrote the play *Endor*. What pitiable Old Testament king is its subject?

13. George Frideric Handel, famed for his oratorio *Messiah*, also wrote an oratorio about what wicked queen of the Old Testament?

14. Laurence Housman wrote a play titled *The Kingmaker,* which concerns an Old Testament prophet and his dealings with two important kings. Who was he?

15. One of Shakespeare's contemporaries wrote a play about King David's adulterous involvement with a voluptuous woman. Who was she?

16. Laurence Housman's play *The Burden of Nineveh* concerns which Old Testament prophet?

17. In *Jesus Christ Superstar,* what wicked, worldly king plays a comic role?

18. The James Forsyth comedy *Screwtape,* dealing with demons tempting human beings, is based on a book by what noted English author?

19. One of Shakespeare's plays refers to the treachery of the New Testament king Herod by using the phrase "It out-Herods Herod." What play contains that line?

20. In what famous Richard Strauss opera does the daughter of Herodias kiss the mouth of the decapitated John the Baptist?

21. What popular oratorio by Felix Mendelssohn is concerned with a great prophet and his confrontation with the false prophets of Baal?

22. French playwright Edmond Rostand, author of the popular *Cyrano de Bergerac*, also wrote a play about an immoral woman whose life was deeply changed by meeting Jesus. Who was she?

23. French composer Etienne Mehul wrote an opera about what young man with some very treacherous brothers?

24. Which oratorio by George Frideric Handel is concerned with God's people being oppressed as slaves?

25. What famous Italian composer wrote *Nabuco* about the Jews' captivity under King Nebuchadnezzar of Babylon?

26. What noted American author wrote the 1972 play *The Creation of the World and Other Business* featuring Lucifer as a character?

27. What 17th-century play about a scholar who sells his soul includes Lucifer among its characters?

HISS TIME: BIBLE VILLAINS ONSTAGE (ANSWERS)

1. Jesus Christ Superstar *by Andrew Lloyd Webber and Tim Rice*

2. Jonah. *Mankowitz's play is an amazingly comical view of poor Jonah.*

3. Joseph and the Amazing Technicolor Dreamcoat. *Joseph's jealous, scheming brothers turn out to be good men in the end, of course.*

4. *Adam, Eve, Cain, and Abel*

5. *Salome, named for the daughter of Herodias who asks for (and gets) John's head on a platter*

6. Moses. *In the play, the wicked pharaoh of Egypt is a prominent character.*

7. *Elijah and Ahab*

8. Athaliah. *Racine wrote the play (Athalie in French) in 1691.*

9. Job. *In the play, as in the book of Job, the main character's three friends would qualify as bad boys, as would the Satan character (named Nickles), but in the play, God (named Zuss in the play) doesn't seem very nice either.*

10. *Samson and Delilah*

11. *Judas. The play is* Dear Judas.

12. *Saul. The title refers to the witch of Endor, whom Saul ordered to summon up the ghost of Samuel.*

13. *Athaliah*

14. *Samuel. The play concerns his relations with Saul and David, and it takes a very critical view of Samuel, portraying him as vain and devious.*

15. *Bathsheba. The play is* David and Bathsheba, *by George Peele, written in 1598. Curiously, Bible characters were seldom presented onstage in those days.*

16. *Jonah. Notice that Jonah has, for some odd reason, been a subject of some interest to playwrights.*

17. *Herod. In the comical "Herod's Song," he taunts Jesus, trying to get him to perform a miracle.*

18. *C. S. Lewis. The play is based on his very popular book* The Screwtape Letters.

19. Hamlet *(Act III, scene ii, if you care to look it up)*

20. Salome, *which was based on Oscar Wilde's play (mentioned in question 5)*

21. Elijah

22. *The woman of Samaria, also known as the woman at the well. The play gives her name as Photine, and it opens with the ghosts of Abraham, Isaac, and Jacob at the well where Photine later meets Jesus.*

23. *Joseph—the Joseph in the book of Genesis, that is*

24. Israel in Egypt. *Like his* Messiah, *its words are taken directly from the Bible.*

25. *Giuseppe Verdi*

26. *Arthur Miller, renowned for his play* Death of a Salesman—*and for being one of Marilyn Monroe's husbands. However,* The Creation of the World, *a spoof of the Adam and Eve story, was a resounding failure.*

27. Doctor Faustus, *by Christopher Marlowe. This is only one of many plays about the knowledge-seeking man who, at the play's end, is dragged into hell.*

PART 12

SOME JUICY LEFTOVERS

THIRTY REALLY JUICY QUOTES ABOUT SIN

The word *sin* occurs in almost every book of the Bible, and certainly the idea occurs in all 66 books. Such a topic sometimes led the Bible authors to inspired (and inspiring) words. See if you can fill in the blanks in the quotes below. Some will be very familiar, others less so. If you are really a Bible whiz, maybe you can provide the book (perhaps even chapter and verse) as well as the missing words.

1. "Be sure your sin will _____ you out."
2. "The soul that sinneth, it shall _____."
3. "All have sinned, and come short of the _____ of God."
4. "If we say that we have no sin, we _____ ourselves, and the truth is not in us."
5. "Behold the _____ of God, who taketh away the sin of the world."
6. "Though your sins be as _____, they shall be as white as snow."
7. "I came not to call the _____, but sinners to repentance."
8. "There is not a just man upon earth, that doeth _____ and sinneth not."
9. "God, be _____ to me a sinner."
10. "The wages of sin is _____, but the gift of God is eternal life."
11. "Whoever committeth sin is the _____ of sin."
12. "Where sin abounded, _____ did much more abound."
13. "If thou doest not well, sin is _____ at the door."
14. "God commendeth his love toward us in that, while we were yet sinners, Christ _____ for us."
15. "God was in Christ _____ the world unto himself, not imputing their trespasses unto them."
16. "Above all things, have fervent love among yourselves; for love shall cover a _____ of sins."
17. "Come out of her, my people, that you be not _____ of her sins."
18. "If we _____ our sins, he is faithful and just to forgive us our sins and, cleanse us from all unrighteousness."
19. "Wash me, and I shall be whiter than _____."
20. "All we like _____ have gone astray; we have turned everyone to his own way."
21. "The _____ is deceitful above all things, and desperately wicked—who can know it?"
22. "If you _____ men when they sin against you, your heavenly Father will also _____ you."

23. "Some men's sins are open beforehand, going before to _____ ."
24. "The ungodly shall not stand in the judgment, nor sinners in the _____ of the righteous."
25. "Righteousness exalteth a _____, but sin is a reproach to any people."
26. "You only have I known of all the _____ of the earth; therefore I will punish you for all your iniquities."
27. "Blessed is he whose transgression is forgiven, whose sin is _____."
28. "He that covereth his sins shall not _____, but whosoever confesseth and forsaketh them shall have mercy."
29. "Thy _____ have I hidden in mine heart, that I might not sin against thee."
30. "God is come to test you, [so] that his _____ may be before your faces, that ye sin not."

THIRTY REALLY JUICY QUOTES ABOUT SIN (ANSWERS)

1. *Find (Numbers 32:23)*
2. *Die (Ezekiel 18:4)*
3. *Glory (Romans 3:23)*
4. *Deceive (1 John 1:8)*
5. *Lamb (John 1:29)*
6. *Scarlet (Isaiah 1:18)*
7. *Righteous (Mark 2:17)*
8. *Good (Ecclesiastes 7:20)*
9. *Merciful (Luke 18:13)*
10. *Death (Romans 6:23)*
11. *Servant (John 8:34)*
12. *Grace (Romans 5:20)*
13. *Crouching (Genesis 4:7)*
14. *Died (Romans 5:8)*
15. *Reconciling (2 Corinthians 5:19)*
16. *Multitude (1 Peter 4:8)*
17. *Partakers (Revelation 18:4)*
18. *Confess (1 John 1:9)*
19. *Snow (Psalm 51:7)*

20. *Sheep (Isaiah 53:6)*

21. *Heart (Jeremiah 17:9)*

22. *Forgive, forgive (Matthew 6:14)*

23. *Judgment (1 Timothy 5:24)*

24. *Congregation (Psalm 1:5)*

25. *Nation (Proverbs 14:34)*

26. *Families (Amos 3:2)*

27. *Covered (Psalm 32:1)*

28. *Prosper (Proverbs 28:13)*

29. *Word (Psalm 119:11)*

30. *Fear (Exodus 20:20)*

 ## SCHOOL OF FOOLS

A fool in the Bible isn't just someone lacking in intelligence. A fool is also someone lacking *moral* sense, someone who won't observe the difference between right and wrong, who won't keep in mind that God is watching that person's every move. Needless to say, there are plenty of such folks around, and there were in Bible times as well. The Bible's main message to such people is not just "Be smart!" but "Behave!"

1. Complete this famous verse from Psalms: "The fool hath said in his heart, 'There is no _____.'"
2. According to Proverbs, "_____ shall be the promotion of fools."
3. Which parable of Jesus concerns a fool dying and going to hell?
4. What smart wife of David had been married to a foolish man whose name literally meant "fool"?
5. In one of Jesus' parables, a foolish man built his house upon what kind of foundation?
6. According to Jesus, when a man says, "You fool!" to someone, what is he in danger of?
7. According to Paul, what people found the message of the gospel to be "foolishness"?
8. Complete this verse from Proverbs: "A _____ is for the back of him that is void of understanding."
9. Jesus told a famous parable of 10 _____, five who were wise and five who were foolish.

10. Who admitted to Moses that he had behaved foolishly by rebelling against him?
11. Complete this verse from Romans: "Professing themselves to be _____, they became fools."
12. Which prophet looked forward to a future time when the fool would no longer "be called noble [nor the] scoundrel said to be bountiful"?
13. What group of Christians heard this question from Paul: "O foolish _____, who hath bewitched you"?
14. Who said, "O fools, and slow of heart to believe all that the prophets have spoken"?
15. According to Isaiah, wicked fools will not be allowed to travel on the way of _____.
16. Complete this verse from Ephesians: "Be ye not unwise, but understanding what the _____ of the Lord's is."
17. According to Proverbs, use a whip for the horse, a bridle for the donkey, and a _____ for the fool's back.
18. Who asked, "Hath not God made foolish the wisdom of this world"?
19. According to Ecclesiastes, what rests in the bosom of fools?
20. Isaiah claims that the fool speaks folly, "and his heart will work _____."
21. According to Paul, believers "are fools for _____ sake."
22. What, according to Proverbs, is the sport of fools?
23. What man accused his wife of talking like a foolish woman?

SCHOOL OF FOOLS (ANSWERS)

1. *God (Psalm 14:1)*

2. *Shame (Proverbs 3:35)*

3. *The parable of the rich fool, who heaps up possessions and then dies suddenly, ending up in hell (Luke 12:16-20)*

4. *Abigail, wife of the deceased (and foolish) Nabal, whose name did indeed mean "fool" (1 Samuel 25). He was "churlish and evil in his doings."*

5. *Sand—so his house didn't survive a great storm (Matthew 7:26-27)*

6. *Going to hell (Matthew 5:22)*

7. *The Greeks (1 Corinthians 1:23)*

8. *Rod (Proverbs 10:13)*

9. *Virgins (Matthew 25:1-13)*

10. *Aaron, his brother (Numbers 12:11)*

11. *Wise (Romans 1:22)*

12. *Isaiah (Isaiah 32:5)*

13. *Galatians (3:1)*

14. *Jesus (Luke 24:25)*

15. *Holiness (Isaiah 35:8)*

16. *Will (Ephesians 5:17)*

17. *Rod (Proverb 26:3)*

18. *Paul (1 Corinthians 1:20)*

19. *Anger (Ecclesiastes 7:9)*

20. *Iniquity (Isaiah 32:6)*

21. *Christ's (1 Corinthians 4:10)*

22. *Mischief (Proverbs 10:23)*

23. *Job (Job 2:10)*

 ## COMMON BONDS

If you see the names *Saul, David,* and *Solomon* and are asked, "What do these have in common?" you (of course) reply, "They're all kings of Israel." Test your knowledge of the common bonds in each of the following groups. And when you see the names, don't be content with "They're all bad guys." Get more specific—what else did they have in common?

1. Ahaz, Manasseh, Zedekiah
2. Eliphaz, Zophar, Bildad
3. Moab, Edom, Ammon
4. Stealing, murdering, coveting
5. Assyria, Babylonia, Persia
6. Molech, Baal, Ashtoreth
7. Nebuchadnezzar, Cyrus, Sargon
8. Frogs, hail, boils
9. Potiphar's wife, Tamar, Gomer
10. The evil one, the father of lies, the tempter
11. Delilah, Jezebel, Athaliah
12. Sargon, Sennacherib, Pul

13. Breaking the Sabbath, worshipping idols, swearing
14. Nebuchadnezzar, Evil-merodach, Belshazzar
15. Stoning, beheading, crucifixion
16. The Beast, the false prophet, the dragon
17. Annas, Caiaphas, Herod
18. Cain, Abimelech, Lamech
19. Abaddon, Apollyon, Legion
20. Dathan, Korah, Aaron
21. Philistines, Midianites, Ammonites
22. Herod, Caiaphas, Saul of Tarsus
23. Outer darkness, lake of fire, furnace of fire
24. Pharisees, Saduccees, Herodians
25. Lucifer, prince of this world, Beelzebub
26. Sodom, Babylon, Corinth
27. The witch of Endor, Simon the sorcerer, Elymas
28. Judas Iscariot, Saul, Ahitophel
29. Ahab, Jeroboam, Omri

COMMON BONDS (ANSWERS)

1. *Kings of Judah—to be specific, wicked kings of Judah*

2. *Job's three friends (who were also very poor comforters, because they were sure Job had brought his sufferings on himself)*

3. *Oppressive neighbor nations of Israel*

4. *Things forbidden by the Ten Commandments*

5. *Empires that controlled Israel at various times*

6. *Gods worshipped by Israel's neighbor nations (and sometimes by the Israelites as well)*

7. *Pagan emperors who played an important role in Israel's history*

8. *Three of the plagues God sent upon Egypt in Moses' time*

9. *Loose women*

10. *Alternate names of Satan*

11. *Wicked women of the Old Testament*

12. *Kings of Assyria*

13. *Things forbidden by the Ten Commandments*

14. *Kings of Babylon*

15. *Means of capital punishment*

16. *Evil figures from the book of Revelation*

17. *Men involved in Jesus' trial and execution*

18. *Murderers*

19. *Demons*

20. *People who rebelled against Moses in the wilderness*

21. *Neighbor nations that oppressed Israel*

22. *Persecutors of Christians. Saul, fortunately, made up for his bad beginnings by becoming the great apostle Paul.*

23. *Alternate names for hell*

24. *Three Jewish factions in New Testament times, all opposed to Jesus*

25. *Alternate names for Satan*

26. *Wicked cities*

27. *Sorcerers/magicians/mediums*

28. *Men who committed suicide*

29. *Three kings of Israel—specifically, wicked kings*

 ## WHAT'S IN A NAME?

In ancient times, names weren't chosen just because they "sounded nice." Most biblical names had specific meanings in their original languages (Hebrew and Greek). Below are the meanings of the names of several bad guys of the Bible, and to make your guessing a little easier, we've supplied the book (or books) of the Bible where you can find that character. Keep in mind, as elsewhere in this book, that the bad guys weren't bad *all the time*, so in this list you'll find some names of folks who were, on the whole, good people, but on some notable occasions wandered off the moral path.

1. Beloved (1 and 2 Samuel)
2. Red earth (Genesis)
3. Enlightened (Exodus—Numbers)
4. The Lord sustains (2 Kings)
5. Peace (1 Kings)
6. Rock (the Gospels)
7. Supplanter (Genesis)
8. Acquired (Genesis)

9. One who forgets (2 Kings)
10. Hot (Genesis)
11. Father's brother (1 Kings)
12. White (Genesis)
13. Watchful (Genesis)
14. Belonging to the goddess Demeter (Acts)
15. Praised (the Gospels)
16. Adversary (Job; most of the New Testament books)
17. Asked of God (1 Samuel)
18. Dainty one (Judges)
19. Slanderer (most of the New Testament)
20. The god Nebo protects the boundary (2 Kings; Daniel)
21. Hairy (Genesis)
22. Strong (Genesis)
23. Devouring (Numbers)
24. Violent (1 Samuel)
25. Devastator (Numbers)
26. May the god Bel protect (Daniel)
27. Man defender (2 Timothy)
28. Father is king (Judges)
29. The Lord is exalted (2 Kings)

WHAT'S IN A NAME? (ANSWERS)

1. David
2. Adam
3. Aaron
4. Ahaz
5. Solomon
6. Peter
7. Jacob
8. Cain
9. Manasseh
10. Ham
11. Ahab
12. Laban
13. Er
14. Demetrius

15. *Judas*

16. *Satan*

17. *Saul*

18. *Delilah*

19. *The devil*

20. *Nebuchadnezzar*

21. *Esau*

22. *Onan*

23. *Balaam*

24. *Agag*

25. *Balak*

26. *Belshazzar*

27. *Alexander*

28. *Abimelech*

29. *Athaliah*

 FAKIN' IT: THE IMPERSONATORS

Masquerades and costume parties may be a lot of fun, but in general, impersonating someone else is done by a wicked person for wicked reasons. (Maybe the obvious example of this is the all-too-common modern crime of identity theft.) In the few occasions in the Bible where a person pretended to be someone else, it was almost always done with a wicked intent.

1. Which king disguised himself in order to consult with a medium?
2. Who fooled Jacob by posing as her sister?
3. Who pretended to be a madman in order to escape from King Achish?
4. Who disguised himself while going to battle against the forces of Pharaohnechoh of Egypt?
5. Who posed as her husband's sister while in Egypt?
6. Which king's wife disguised herself in order to consult the prophet Ahijah?
7. What smooth-skinned man disguised himself so well that he passed himself off as his hairy brother?

8. Who persuaded the clever woman of Tekoah to pretend to be a widow in order to play on David's sympathy?
9. Who posed as Isaac's sister?
10. Who fooled Joshua by pretending to be ambassadors from a distant country?
11. What evil king of Israel disguised himself while going against the armies of Syria?
12. Who sent spies to act as followers of Jesus and to try to trap him?
13. Which king was confronted by a prophet posing as a wounded soldier?
14. According to Paul, who masquerades as an angel of light?

FAKIN' IT: THE IMPERSONATORS (ANSWERS)

1. Saul (1 Samuel 28:8)

2. Leah (Genesis 29:20-25)

3. David (1 Samuel 21:12–22:1)

4. King Josiah (2 Chronicles 35:20-24)

5. Sarai, wife of Abram (Genesis 12:10-20)

6. Jeroboam's (1 Kings 14:1-6)

7. Jacob (Genesis 27:1-29)

8. Joab (2 Samuel 14:1-24)

9. His wife, Rebekah (Genesis 26:6-11)

10. The Gibeonites (Joshua 9:3-16)

11. Ahab (1 Kings 22:30-40)

12. The chief priests and scribes (Luke 20:19-20)

13. Ahab (1 Kings 20:35-43)

14. Satan (2 Corinthians 11:14)